Praise for *The Mandala of Being*

"*The Mandala of Being* reminds us that inherent in being human are the forces that distract who we really are from the calm of who we can be. Richard Moss's formula for coming back to the present is a process we can all achieve."

— Anthony Robbins

"This is an important, deeply powerful, and simply magnificent book. What can be awakened, seen, and experienced here can save your true life and the life of our planetary family. I highly recommend reading it, now."

— Brooke Medicine Eagle, author of
Buffalo Woman Come Singing and *The Last Ghost Dance*

"So often we come home from a workshop or conference feeling at one with ourselves and the universe only to have it dissipate as soon as we have to decide who takes out the garbage. Moss gives us a way out. He's looked deeply into how we can maintain 'radical aliveness' in daily life. You will find many practical insights and innovative suggestions to help you. We highly recommend this book."

— Justine and Michael Toms, cofounders of New Dimensions
Media and New Dimensions Radio and authors of
True Work: Doing What You Love and Loving What You Do

"Once again, Richard Moss has written a groundbreaking work of inspiration and depth. Having used Richard's teachings and books in my classes for many years, I know of the power of his wise insights into the essential nature of being. As one of the leading spiritual teachers combining spirituality and psychology, Richard has brought forth a deep teaching of the process of self-inquiry into the ever-present Now where 'I am sufficient as I am.' His book *The Mandala of Being* is truly an essential contribution to the important work of living a life in spiritual fullness."

— Ray Greenleaf, MA, chair of counseling psychology, School of Holistic Studies, John F. Kennedy University

THE MANDALA OF BEING

ALSO BY RICHARD MOSS

THE MANDALA OF BEING

Discovering the Power of Awareness

RICHARD MOSS, MD

New World Library
Novato, California

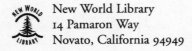 New World Library
14 Pamaron Way
Novato, California 94949

Text design and typography by Tona Pearce Myers

Library of Congress Cataloging-in-Publication Data is available upon request.

First printing, February 2007
ISBN-10: 1-57731-572-3
ISBN-13: 978-1-57731-572-8
Printed in Canada

g New World Library is a proud member of the Green Press Initiative.

Distributed by Publishers Group West

10 9 8

Who loves, loves love,
and loving love
forms a circle so complete,
there is no end to love.

— SAINT BERNARD

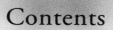

Contents

PART TWO

Utilizing the Power of Awareness:
WELCOMING OURSELVES HOME

Figures

Introduction

This book has been a true labor of love for me. It is the culmi-
nation and distillation of what I have learned in thirty years of
teaching, around the world, about being fully alive no matter
what the circumstances. It is an invitation to self-mastery, less
in the sense of attaining a state of enlightenment, and more in
the sense of living as a genuinely self-determining individual
free from the dominion of fear. Real mastery is the ability to
stay fully present for whatever life brings because we trust who
we are.

Joseph Campbell, the famous mythologist, observed that all
of us are seeking in myriad ways meaning and purpose in our
lives, but that what we really want is the experience of feeling totally alive and completely free. This yearning wells up from deep
within, and we know it to be essential and real. Responding to
it has been one of the principal impulses of human endeavor; it

is the true heart of spiritual life. To touch it is to awaken from sleep to such a sense of fullness that, for the first time, we recognize a certain emptiness that has always been a part of our lives. Suddenly, without thought, we know the answers to our deepest questions, such as why we are here.

Early on in my career as a consciousness teacher, I learned that it was relatively easy to bring people to a state of what I call "radical aliveness," where the mind is silent, the body is filled with presence, and a new enthusiasm for living is born. The secret, I realized, lay not in deliberately invoking a particular state of consciousness but in creating activities that require the body and the mind to be in the same place — in the Now.

Some of us spontaneously experience moments of this aliveness in meditation or in making love. Others have tasted it in the flow of artistic creativity or in the exhilaration of athletic pursuits. But when we leave the focus of these contexts and return to the routine and challenges of daily living, few of us know how to sustain a sense of centeredness and joy. I have written extensively about reaching these states of aliveness in my previous books, especially *The Black Butterfly* and *The Second Miracle*.

In *The Mandala of Being*, I offer a simple practice that meets the challenge of maintaining this aliveness in daily life without requiring the presence of a teacher, a special sacred environment, or the heightened energy of a group of people exploring consciousness together.

I long ago recognized that it was always easier to remain spacious and present while I was teaching than when I was at home and involved with the demands of daily living. So I set about trying to understand what my mind was doing differently, both for my own sake and the sake of those whom I counseled. I already knew it was not a question of holding onto the same expansive state that we attained in our work together, that it was instead about reclaiming an equivalent quality of relationship to ourselves in the midst of ordinary life.

I realized that we needed to balance the experiential activities that invite presence, such as meditation, movement, and breath work, with a specific form of self-inquiry that helps us understand how our minds leave the Now. Obviously our bodies are always in the Now. As I began to carefully observe what the mind is actually doing when it moves away from the present, I saw that there are only four places that it ever goes. This added an essential element to my work.

The word *mandala* comes from ancient Sanskrit and means "circle." In Eastern spiritual traditions, a mandala is a form of sacred art that depicts the totality of the Self. Mandalas appear to be universal symbols and have been found throughout many different periods and cultures.

In their simplest forms mandalas are circles with four primary directions oriented around a strong central focus. The circle represents the intrinsic wholeness of the Self, which naturally sustains within itself the fundamental tensions of opposing forces, such as chaos and order, masculinity and femininity.

One day while addressing a group and trying to share my insight about where the mind goes when it leaves the present, I found myself walking around to indicate a large circle on the floor and then tracing a smaller circle in the center of the larger one. I wrote the word *Now* on a piece of paper and set it on the small central circle. On the perimeter at the top of the large circle, I placed the word *Future*, and at the bottom the word *Past*. I then placed the word *Subject* on the left perimeter and the word *Object* on the right. *Subject-object* is the psychological term for the inherently dualist nature of our ordinary consciousness, in which, as soon as we become aware of ourselves as the "subject," *me*, we simultaneously become aware of the "object," *you*. *Me* isn't who we really are, but is the collection of thoughts we have about ourselves. Likewise, *you* is the collection of thoughts we have about others. With this simple mandala, I could show the four directions that the mind escapes to when it flees from the Now, usually because of an uncomfortable or threatening feeling.

I spontaneously named this model the Mandala of Being, and it has proven to be, both for me and those I have taught it to, a highly effective tool for deconstructing and understanding the mechanisms of our repeated patterns of emotional struggle and suffering. Using the Mandala model, we can see that our recurrent reactivity and defensiveness results from our being unaccustomed to living in the present. Moreover, the specific nature of this suffering is a consequence of which of the four directions our minds predominantly move in when we leave the Now. By recognizing that there truly are only four places to go when we step out of the Now, we can always find our way back home. Living in the Now becomes our starting point, not our goal.

The power to return our minds to the Now allows us to communicate more of our inborn authentic and spontaneous natures. The present moment becomes our ground of being, because that's where we'll find the juice of life and the truth of who we are and why we are here.

In working with this model, we start to understand the relationship between thinking and emotion. We learn how to recognize the particular thoughts, beliefs, and stories we tell ourselves as our minds move in each of the four directions in turn, and how each story contracts or agitates our bodily sensation in specific ways. When the mind is in the future, the body experiences worry or hope; when it is in the past, the body registers guilt, nostalgia, or regret.

An essential component of the Mandala of Being is that it will guide us to a new relationship with our bodies, where real understanding must occur before we truly know something. By elucidating how we "leave ourselves" in daily life situations, this work opens the pathway of awareness that consistently returns us to the Now. By feeling the shift in sensation as we return ourselves to the Now, our bodies begin to recognize presence. As we begin to understand the power of our own awareness to help us live in the present, we shift our emotional reality from what we typically call negative emotions to the sense of joyfulness and freedom that is our essential natures.

In learning to live more consistently in the Now, we increase the energy of our consciousness. In the sense that I am using it here, this "energy" is our capacity to be present and is what emanates from us through this actual act of being present. It takes heightened energy to give ourselves the spiritual muscle needed to embrace feelings that have for so long closed our hearts and dimmed our lights, instead of collapsing into them. This energy brings our awareness to the Now and allows us to see what *is*, not merely what our usual desires or fears might predispose us to see.

When our awareness is rooted in the present, we access our higher emotional potential — empathy, compassion, and forgiveness. We experience greater oneness with a vast field of awareness that far transcends our limited personal realities. We begin to touch the Source, to drink from a fountain of aliveness and intelligence in which we perceive each moment's innate wholeness and to which our natural response is a sense of gratitude, wonderment, and implicit trust in life's goodness.

As our minds move further from the Now, we begin to function from a lower emotional register. Lower energy represents a shrinking of consciousness, so we feel smaller and isolated. We become dogmatic, inflexible, and self-protective. Then we become the victims of fear, anger, distrust, neediness, and other potentially destructive emotions. The profound depths of our larger consciousness become less available to us, and even threatening. We lose our innate sense of delight in life. Instead of feeling connected to ourselves and embracing life with the fullness of our beings, we live more and more from a false and contracted sense of self designed to keep us safe from whatever we don't want to feel.

In this sheltered but simultaneously limited state of mind, we become spectators — and too often even critics — who believe that we are, and that the world is, what we *think*. When we are unconsciously in this Self-avoiding mode, *thinking* about ourselves, others, and the world at large is our favorite pastime because we do not know what it is to *feel* our own depths in the present moment and taste life directly. Eventually, our minds become addicted to states of ever-greater distancing from the "now-ness" of our beings. This is the fundamental reason we experience so much dissatisfaction with ourselves, and why we often lack empathy for others.

The first teacher of the unawakened mind is fear. As children we are always in the Now, transparent to love but also vulnerable to every traumatic moment. To survive emotionally we learn to project the mind away from overwhelming sensations like loneliness and shame. We withdraw our awareness from the present, where all sensations are the most alive and are potentially too intense. Gradually we become conditioned to avoid the Now and, as a result, intimacy with ourselves and with life diminishes.

In my years as a teacher, I have seen that what inevitably halts our spiritual maturity and compromises our capacity to love is believing that we must protect ourselves from difficult feelings, such as abandonment and despair. But the only reason we cannot face them is that we have not developed the energy to stay present with them as they arise. However, until we stop fleeing whatever feelings we believe can annihilate us, we cannot mature fully or love without restraint. Sooner or later we must embrace these dark parts of life. We must trust the soul's profound capacity to meet and be in relationship with whatever we experience, without having to defend ourselves or even react.

There is an enormous difference between how the *self* meets experience — how it judges and reacts to a feeling — and how the *soul* meets the same experience or feeling. The self's relationship to any aspect of life is always strategic: it seeks to increase its pleasure, security, or power, and it reflexively defends against any feeling or situation that threatens it. In contrast, the soul does not see a feeling as an extension of itself or a threat to itself. The soul appreciates any feeling for what it is, and in this nonreactive, nonstrategic relationship we learn to make room for our feelings instead of closing down or fleeing from them. The way the soul meets each moment transforms our sense of self.

Few of us are aware of the power of this inner relationship and how it can transform the way we experience ourselves and everything else. Instead we reflexively use our minds to defend against difficult feelings or challenging situations, not realizing that when we do this we are never in the Now. As a result, consciously or subconsciously, we frequently feel as if our lives are built on quicksand. We feel as if we are in danger of being engulfed by any sensation, thought, or event that threatens the tenuous foundation of self on which we are poised.

But when we become conscious of the subtle power of awareness and increase our ability to remain present, we begin to see that the reality of our experience, and what we are further capable of experiencing, is determined ultimately by the quality of our relationship to ourselves during every moment. We need not be determined by our defensive thoughts or by our reactions to what comes to us from outside. As our ability to stay present increases, we at last discover real freedom from fear and other difficult emotions that have ruled us. We realize our essential wholeness and gain the ability to enjoy relationships that spontaneously invite love, respect, forgiveness, and empathy. We claim the power to exercise our awareness in ways that liberate our minds and our hearts.

This book is a handbook for reclaiming the wisdom of your true self. It is an initiation of conscious intimacy with yourself, with all of who you are — even the darkest aspects. We can never feel whole by trying to eliminate any part·of our experience. As we begin to consistently trust this truth, we recover the aliveness we have yearned for.

In our hearts, all of us know that the human spirit is so much more than a "me" that recurrently feels threatened and dissatisfied, that endlessly seeks to find happiness while feeling that somehow, something is wrong with us. We intuit that we have the capacity to reconnect to the source of our own beings.

Soul, for me, is our capacity for self-awareness. It is the ability to ask "Who am I?" in a way that silences the thinking mind and opens us to immediacy. The soul imbues all that we are and, at the same time, can lead us beyond where we are, even to oneness with the source of our beings. For the soul, each moment is a new starting point from which it can take the next step to greater awareness.

Who we really are, always begins Now. None of us will become our true selves at some fortuitous moment in the future. Our real identities never originate from the remembered glory or traumas of our pasts. It begins anew with the attention we offer to ourselves and to life in each moment. The Now is not an ultimate state to be realized but rather a continuum to be lived. We can hide in the shallows or risk diving deeply.

At this evolutionary moment, humankind is wavering between fear and love, focusing on survival and yet beginning to touch the infinite potential of being. In brief moments we know the undeniable rightness of all things; we come home to ourselves and understand that we are already that which we have been seeking. Yet at the slightest threat, we revert to distrust and control, once again losing confidence in who we are. Simultaneously, we unconsciously externalize this inner breach of faith and perceive a threatening world. Instantly we are back with both feet in the dominion of fear.

With both feet firmly on the terrain of love, we find that life is not about survival, it is about thriving. It is about consciously embracing each moment, aware of our parts in a great wholeness. In the ecology of love, all things have their rightful place and purpose, including our most difficult feelings. In the wisdom of love, we gain the energy to encompass what we formerly fled.

What is needed now, what evolution itself is demanding, is that we experience the self-transcending power of the soul. We do not have to change the world. We need only reclaim the fullness of our beings that is ever present and always seeking to awaken in us. In so doing, we become transmitters of a profound faith in life, and the world begins to change.

What you will find in these pages can be tested in your own experience and will support your own emerging wisdom. When we live with true intelligence, we build our worlds moment by moment from a sense of our own wholeness and thereby always invite wholeness. There is nothing more important, now or ever. Wholeness is where our hearts want to go and where our souls are leading us.

Join me now, and let's dive deeply together.

PART ONE

Fundamental Principles
of Awareness

THE JOURNEY FROM SELF TO SELF

CHAPTER ONE

Our Earliest Relationship *to* Ourselves

In the broadest sense, everything in life is always in relationship: nothing exists that is not defined by, and that does not gain its meaning through, relationship to something else. Atoms, viruses, and galaxies all dance in highly complex and miraculous relationships.

This is no less true of human beings. Nobody exists in isolation. Right from infancy, and indeed from earliest conception, who we are, how we are, and, to a significant degree, who we will become all depend a great deal on how we are nurtured and the environment in which we develop. Everyone and every situation help create who we are, molding us and inevitably bringing out some unique nuance of our beings. Unfortunately, our relationships and circumstances can also inhibit or even totally suppress other qualities of our inborn essential natures. This is why our relationships are the primary means throughout our lives by which we develop our understanding of ourselves.

None of us, though, have the power or authority to control what others may bring to us by means of their attitudes, words, or actions. Our only real power lies in what we bring to our relationships with others, and what we bring depends entirely on where we start from. For example, if we start from a sense of insecurity, we are likely to be distrusting and needy. If we start from a sense of fullness, we are likely to be generous and forgiving. This is obvious and so may seem simplistic, but the emotional tone of all relationships we have in life are invariably determined by the quality of the relationship we have with ourselves in that moment.

We human beings have always strived to find a guiding principle by which to conduct ourselves in relationships. Perhaps nothing sums up this effort better than the Golden Rule, which asks us to treat others as we would have them treat us. The problem is that too often we treat ourselves terribly: We have impossible expectations for ourselves; we look in the mirror every day and tell ourselves we are too fat or otherwise not attractive enough. We work far past the point of exhaustion, pushing ourselves when our bodies are crying for rest. We chastise ourselves for every missed opportunity, oversight, or mistake. How then are we likely to behave toward others, and how can we expect them to behave toward us? Some people have been raised in environments so full of conflict, violence, and cruelty that they later look for love, or some semblance of it, in relationships in which they unconsciously expect, and perhaps even want, to be treated the same way. It is a fact of our psychology that we continue to seek out relationships that mimic the emotional environment of our early lives.[1] Even when we are raised in a much happier environment, we develop our earliest sense of self unconsciously and inevitably in response not only to the positive reinforcement of our parents but also to their often confused needs and fears. We can do unto others as we would have them do unto us, but who we really are and what we really need may be unclear to us, so that, while we are attempting to create love, we often end up creating suffering in our relationships with others.

It is often a truth of human relationships that our early psychology betrays us: we engage in relationships in ways that only partially express our true selves. As a result, the relationships we create tend to be manifestations of where we have lost contact with ourselves. A relationship is an energetic alchemy that two or more people create together which has the potential to accentuate the closeness or distance of each from his or her true self. How close to, or how far from, our true selves we live determines the quality of the relationships we create.

Each of us can start from an inner sense of security or insecurity, trust or distrust, enthusiasm or cynicism. Usually we don't really know where we are starting from until, eventually, what is created in the relationship itself shows us. For example, an insecure man who, like most of us, does not admit to himself that he is insecure may approach a woman while subconsciously believing that she will eventually reject him. But before he understands this, he is likely to idealize her, to make her his Beatrice, his soul mate — someone too perfect to ever reject him. Initially what he brings to her is so flattering and so healing to her insecurities that she may reciprocate with equal admiration, and the relationship may flourish. They will believe they are deeply in love. In this situation of reciprocal narcissism, the best way to feel safe and not be rejected is to be mutually adoring. However, the underlying psychology of insecurity has been only temporarily circumvented.

Over time, as this man's insecurity inevitably asserts itself, he may start to become possessive and controlling or cold and withdrawn. He may create conflicts, unconsciously testing to see if she admires him the way he wants to be admired and whether she is truly loyal. If she cannot understand that this is coming from his insecurity and cannot accept this part of him, she may become critical, reactive, and angry. As a result, both remain in a fearful place and the relationship deteriorates into accusations, judgments, blame, anger, and hurt that impoverishes both of them far more than their own personal psychology would cause them to experience outside the relationship. They may choose to separate, as many couples do, or decide to work on their relationship and perhaps learn to help heal these unconscious wounds in each other.

We each see through the lens of our sense of self, and the degree of our Self-realization determines what we bring to others, how we perceive them, and how we interpret their words and actions. So, the Golden Rule must be accompanied by the ancient wisdom "Know thyself."

When we bring to another person something innately authentic and whole within us — no matter how vulnerable we may feel — we create a space of relationship that is more than simply being "in love." This relationship becomes transformational and even sacred. It enhances our knowledge of ourselves in ways that help us to heal our old wounds because it also blesses us with greater recognition of who we really are.

If as children we are nurtured sufficiently to make us feel safe, approved of, and understood, and we are allowed to express our authentic feelings and inclinations, the person each of us becomes can manifest more of our true selves. In the mirror of an environment that consciously supports and respects our uniqueness, we learn to trust ourselves and unfold into life while essentially feeling good about ourselves.

If, on the other hand, we grow up with parents and educators who have their own agendas for us, their own ideas about who we should be and how we can best achieve success or simply survive, the mirror they hold up to us is so biased and distorted we do not learn to trust our true selves. We begin to develop a false self that is thereafter vigilant for impending criticism, a self whose core feeling is that we are not sufficient as we are.

This sense of insufficiency, this vague feeling that something is not quite right about us, becomes the ground state for our identities that then impairs the ability to relate clearly to our own sensations, feelings, and thoughts that constantly arise. Simultaneously this sense of insufficiency distorts how we perceive the external environment, so we distrust the world as well.

To understand how this happens, imagine that consciousness is like a sphere of fine clear crystal. When we stand at the center of the sphere — which is analogous to our true selves — in every direction we look the light (our consciousness) is bent in precisely the same way (or really not bent at all) so that nothing is distorted. We see clearly in all directions from a single, consistent point of view. We are living in our own spontaneous and authentic essence and appreciating reality as it is.

If we begin to move away from the center toward the perimeter, however, what we perceive from this off-center position becomes refracted and distorted by the differing thicknesses of our crystal in every direction around us. It is like being in a house of mirrors where each mirror is bent differently: in one we appear tall and thin, in another squat and wide, and so on. But we cannot know that we are off-center in ourselves and that our view of ourselves and of life in general is distorted. This feeling about ourselves, and attitude toward life, becomes who we are. And until we return to our true centers, we can never gain true perceptions.

As children we begin our lives right in the center of our sphere of being, spontaneously expressing our authentic nature; we know nothing else. However, it is not long before this begins to change, as we are partially or wrongly reflected back to ourselves by the relationships that surround us. Eventually, to a greater or lesser degree, each of us loses contact with our spontaneous essence and begins to live more or less off-center. This is a period in life — for all of us — in which soul awareness is dormant and we become identified with a false sense of self.

HOW WE BECOME WHO WE ARE NOT

We are not born, in essence, American, French, Japanese, Christian, Muslim, or Jew. These labels are attached to us according to where on the planet our births happen to take place, or these labels are imposed upon us because they indicate our families' belief systems.

We are not born with an innate sense of distrust of others. We do not enter life with the belief that God is external to us, watching us, judging us, loving us, or simply being indifferent to our plight. We do not suckle at the breast with shame about our bodies or with racial prejudice already brewing in our hearts. We do not emerge from our mothers' wombs believing that competition and domination are essential to survival. Nor are we born believing that somehow we must validate whatever our parents consider to be right and true.

How do children come to believe that they are indispensable to their parents' well-being, and that they therefore must become the champions of their parents' unfulfilled dreams, fulfilling them by becoming the good daughter or the responsible son? How many people revolt against their parents' relationships by condemning themselves to lives of cynicism about the possibility for real love? In how many ways will members of one generation after another efface their own true natures in order to be loved, successful, approved of, powerful, and safe, not because of who they are in essence, but because they have adapted themselves to others? And how many will become part of the detritus of the cultural norm, living in poverty, disenfranchisement, or alienation?

We are not born anxious for our survival. How is it, then, that pure ambition and the accumulation of wealth and power are ideals in our culture, when to live for them is all too often a soulless pursuit that condemns one to a path of unending stress, which fails to address or heal the core, unconscious feeling of insufficiency?

All such internalized attitudes and belief systems have been cultivated in us. Others have modeled them for us and trained us in them. This indoctrination takes place both directly and indirectly. In our homes, schools, and religious institutions, we are explicitly told who we are, what life is about, and how we should perform. Indirect indoctrination occurs as we absorb subconsciously whatever is consistently emphasized or demonstrated by our parents and other caregivers when we are very young.

As children we are like fine crystal glasses that vibrate to a singer's voice. We resonate with the emotional energy that surrounds us, unable to be sure what part is us — our own true feelings and likes or dislikes — and what part is others. We are keen observers of our parents' and other adults' behavior toward us and toward each other. We experience how they communicate through their facial expressions, body language, tone of voice, actions, and so on, and we can recognize — though not consciously when we are young — when their expressions and their feelings are congruent or not. We are immediate barometers for emotional hypocrisy. When our parents are saying or doing one thing, but we perceive that they mean something else, it confuses and distresses us. Over time these emotional "disconnects" continue to threaten our developing sense of self, and we begin to devise our own strategies for psychological security in attempts to protect ourselves.

None of this is accompanied by our conscious understanding of what we are doing, but we quickly deduce what our parents value and what evokes their approval or disapproval. We readily learn which of our own behaviors they respond to in ways that make us feel loved or unloved, worthy or unworthy. We begin to adapt ourselves by acquiescence, rebellion, or withdrawal.

As children we do not initially approach our worlds with our parents' biases and prejudices about what is good or bad. We express our true selves spontaneously and naturally. But early on, this expression begins to collide with what our parents encourage or discourage in our self-expression. All of us become conscious of our earliest sense of self in the context of their fears, hopes, wounds, beliefs, resentments, and control issues and of their ways of nurturing, whether loving, suffocating, or neglecting. This mostly unconscious socializing process is as old as human history. When we are children and out parents view us through the lens of their own adaptations to life, we as unique individuals remain more or less invisible to them. We learn to become whatever helps make us visible to them, to be whatever brings us the most comfort and least discomfort. We adapt and survive as best we can in this emotional climate.

Our strategic response results in the formation of a survival personality that does not express much of our individual essence.

We falsify who we are in order to maintain some level of connection to those whom we require in order to meet our needs for attention, nurturance, approval, and security.

Children are marvels of adaptation. They quickly learn that, if acquiescence produces the best response, then being supportive and agreeable provides the best chance for emotional survival. They grow up to be pleasers, excellent providers for the needs of others, and they see their loyalty as a virtue more important than their own needs. If rebellion seems to be the best path to diminishing discomfort while also gaining attention, then they become combative and build their identities by pushing their parents away. Their fight for autonomy may later make them nonconformists unable to accept the authority of others, or they may require conflict in order to feel alive. If withdrawal works best, then children become more introverted and escape into imaginary worlds. Later in life, this survival adaptation may cause them to live so deeply in their own beliefs that they are unable to make space for others to know them or to emotionally touch them.

Because survival is at the root of the false self, fear is its true god. And because in the Now we cannot be in control of our situations, only in relationship with it, the survival personality is poorly suited to the Now. It tries to create the life it believes it should be living and, in so doing, does not fully experience the life it *is* living. Our survival personalities have identities to maintain that are rooted in the early childhood escape from threat. This threat comes from the disjunction between how we experience ourselves as children and what we learn to be, in response to our parents' mirroring and expectations.

Infancy and early childhood are governed by two primary drives: The first is the necessity to bond with our mothers or other important caregivers. The second is the drive to explore, to learn about and discover our worlds.

The physical and emotional bond between mother and baby is necessary not only for the child's survival but also because the mother is the first cultivator of the baby's sense of self. She cultivates it by how she holds and caresses her baby; by her tone of voice, her gaze, and her anxiety or calmness; and by how she reinforces or squelches her child's spontaneity. When the overall quality of her attention is loving, calm, supportive, and respectful, the baby knows that it is safe and all right in itself. As the child gets older, more of his or her true self emerges as the mother continues to express approval and set necessary boundaries without shaming or threatening the child. In this way her positive mirroring cultivates the child's essence and helps her child to trust itself.

In contrast, when a mother is frequently impatient, hurried, distracted, or even resentful of her child, the bonding process is more tentative and the child feels unsafe. When a mother's tone of voice is cold or harsh, her touch brusque, insensitive, or uncertain; when she is unresponsive to her child's needs or cries or cannot set aside her own psychology to make enough space for the child's unique personality, this is interpreted by the child as meaning that something must be wrong with him or her. Even when neglect is unintentional, as when a mother's own exhaustion prevents her from nurturing as well as she would like to, this unfortunate situation can still cause a child to feel unloved. As a result of any of these actions, children can begin to internalize a sense of their own insufficiency.

Until recently, when many women have become working mothers, fathers have tended to transmit to us our sense of the world beyond the home.[2] We wondered where Daddy was all day. We noticed whether he returned home tired, angry, and depressed or satisfied and enthusiastic. We absorbed his tone of voice as he spoke about his day; we *felt* the outside world through his energy, his complaints, worries, anger, or enthusiasm. Slowly we internalized his spoken or other representations of the world into which he so frequently disappeared, and all too often this world appeared to be threatening, unfair, "a jungle." If this impression of potential danger from the outside world combines with an emerging sense of being wrong and insufficient, then the child's core identity — his or her earliest relationship to the self — becomes one of fearfulness and distrust. As gender roles are changing, both men and working mothers perform aspects of the fathering function for their children, and some men perform aspects of mothering. We could say that in a psychological sense mothering cultivates our earliest sense of self, and how we mother ourselves throughout life strongly influences how we hold ourselves when faced with emotional pain. Fathering, on the other hand, has to do with our vision of the world and how empowered we believe ourselves to be as we implement our own personal visions in the world.

Day by day throughout childhood, we explore our worlds. As we move out into our environment, our parents' capacity to support our process of discovery and to mirror our attempts in ways that are neither overprotective nor neglectful depends on their own consciousness. Are they proud of us as we are? Or do they reserve their pride for the things we do that fit their image for us or that make them look like good parents? Do they encourage our own assertiveness, or interpret it as disobedience and quell it? When a parent delivers reprimands in a way that shames the child — as so many generations of generally male authorities have recommended doing — a confused and disturbed inner reality is generated in that child. No child can separate the frightful bodily intensity of shame from his or her own sense of self. So the child feels wrong, unlovable, or deficient. Even when parents have the best intentions, they frequently meet their child's tentative steps into the world with responses that seem anxious, critical, or punitive. More important, those responses are often perceived by the child as implicitly distrustful of who he or she is.

As children we cannot differentiate our parents' psychological limitations from the effects they cause in us. We cannot protect ourselves by means of self-reflection so that we can arrive at compassion and understanding for them and ourselves, because we do not yet have the awareness to do so. We cannot know that our frustration, insecurity, anger, shame, neediness, and fear are just feelings, not the totality of our beings. Feelings seem simply good or bad to us, and we want more of the former and less of the latter. So gradually, within the context of our early environment, we wake up to our first conscious sense of self as if materializing out of a void, and without understanding the origins of our own confusion and insecurity about ourselves.

Each of us, in a certain sense, develops our earliest understanding of who we are within the emotional and psychological "fields" of our parents, much as iron filings on a sheet of paper become aligned in a pattern determined by a magnet underneath it. Some of our essence remains intact, but much of it has to be forfeited in order to ensure that, as we express ourselves and venture out to discover our worlds, we don't antagonize our parents and risk the loss of essential bonding. Our childhoods are like the proverbial Procrustean bed.[3] We "lie down" in our parents' sense of reality, and if we are too "short" — that is, too fearful, too needy, too weak, not smart enough, and so on, by their standards — they "stretch" us. It can happen in a hundred ways. They might order us to stop crying or shame us by telling us to grow up. Alternatively, they might try to encourage us to stop crying by telling us everything is all right and how wonderful we are, which still indirectly suggests that how we are feeling is wrong. Of course, we also "stretch" ourselves — by trying to meet their standards in order to maintain their love and approval. If, on the other hand, we are too "tall" — that is, too assertive, too involved in our own interests, too curious, too boisterous, and so on — they "shorten" us, using much the same tactics: criticism, scolding, shame, or warnings about problems we will have later in life. Even in the most loving families, in which parents have only the best intentions, a child may lose a significant measure of his or her innate spontaneous and authentic nature without either the parent or the child realizing what has happened.

As a result of these circumstances, an environment of angst is unconsciously born within us, and, at the same time, we begin a lifetime of ambivalence about intimacy with others. This ambivalence is an internalized insecurity that can leave us forever dreading both the loss of intimacy that we fear would surely occur if we somehow dared to be authentic, and the suffocating sense of being dispossessed of our innate character and natural self-expression if we were to allow intimacy.

As children we begin to create a submerged reservoir of unacknowledged, nonintegrated feelings that pollute our earliest sense of who we are, feelings like being insufficient, unlovable, or unworthy. To compensate for these, we build up a coping strategy called, in psychoanalytic theory, the idealized self. It is the self we imagine we should be or can be. We soon start to believe we are this *idealized self,* and we compulsively continue to attempt to be it, while avoiding anything that brings us face to face with the distressing feelings we have buried.

Sooner or later, however, these buried and rejected feelings resurface, usually in the relationships that seem to promise the intimacy we so desperately crave. But while these close relationships initially offer great promise, eventually they also expose our insecurities and fears. Since we all carry the imprint of childhood wounding to some degree, and therefore bring a false, idealized self into the space of our relationships, we are not starting from our true selves. Inevitably, any close relationship we create will begin to unearth and amplify the very feelings that we, as children, managed to bury and temporarily escape.

Our parents' ability to support and encourage the expression of our true selves depends on how much of their attention comes to us from a place of authentic presence. When parents unconsciously live from their false and idealized senses of self, they cannot recognize that they are projecting their unexamined expectations for themselves onto their children. As a result, they cannot appreciate the spontaneous and authentic nature of a young child and allow it to remain intact. When parents inevitably become uncomfortable with their children because of the parents' own limitations, they attempt to change their children instead of themselves. Without recognizing what is happening, they provide a reality for their children that is hospitable to the children's essence only to the extent that the parents have been able to discover a home in themselves for their own essence.

All of the above may help to explain why so many marriages fail and why much that is written about relationships in popular culture is idealized. As long as we protect our idealized selves, we are going to have to keep imagining ideal relationships. I doubt they exist. But what does exist is the possibility to start from whom we really are and to invite mature connections that bring us closer to psychological healing and true wholeness.

EDUCATION AND RELIGION: THE DIRECT FORCES OF CULTURAL INDOCTRINATION

When children have trouble learning, it is rarely because they are intellectually incapable. Instead, it is often because a one-size-fits-all educational process does not support their unique ways of learning. A system that requires them to fit a culturally expected norm, and often defeats them when they do not fit, delivers another blow to their faith in themselves. I suspect that many children who excel and are rewarded with good grades and special honors do so more as a survival reflex than because they experience a real joy in learning or because their souls are rejoicing at finding the support they need to express their innate genius. In any case, children subconsciously learn that they are valued for what they achieve and how they perform, not for whom they are. Once again the message, at least subconsciously, is "You are not sufficient as you are."

I have observed in my own children and their friends just how demoralizing the contemporary educational process can sometimes be. So many students come away feeling lost and alienated. The system has oversaturated them with information, yet it has not placed this information in a context that makes it meaningful in their lives or that helps them to learn about themselves — the most essential responsibility of an intelligent educational process.

The god of fear has its hands in every part of our contemporary culture, taking even our innate passion for exploration and discovery and distorting it until it becomes almost exclusively funneled into the survival quest. To paraphrase the author Joseph Chilton Pearce, too often the goal of education is to prepare the child to be "a dollar commodity" in the marketplace.[4] Education becomes part of the Procrustean drama drastically shaping us to fit its proportions.

There are those who have written scathing polemics on the subject of religion, and mainstream religion in particular, in terms of how it limits the full expression of the soul. It is certainly not my intention to do so. But it is important to realize that from early in life our sense of self is powerfully influenced by religious ideologies that often have little relationship to whom we really are.

The notion that all individuals can, if encouraged to know themselves, become the authors of their own sense of spirituality, is heresy for most religions. From the start, religion tells us who to be and how to be "before God," just as it told our parents and their parents before them, without respect for whom any of us actually are. Religion can place us on another Procrustean bed from conception on, through its pervasive influence on our parents and everyone else we come in contact with.

Most children naturally have a rich sense of spirituality. They have an inborn sense of compassion and fairness, and many have their own innate understanding of a higher love. In their innocence, they are often highly receptive to and deeply moved by their early experiences with religion. But along with teachings about original sin and images of a judging or punishing father God, they soon absorb the implicit message of most theistic religions: "There is something wrong with you that needs to be fixed."

Playing upon the fears they instill in us, these theistic religions go on to tell us, "Here is what you must believe and do to be worthy of God's love and to achieve salvation." Progressive churches attempt, on the other hand, to give us back the power to connect to the spirit and thereby reverse millennia of spiritual and psychological disempowerment. But, whereas traditional churches try to "shorten" us with admonishments that we are sinners, progressive churches attempt to "stretch" us with their insistence on upbeat positiveness. Positive affirmations and visualizations of our spiritual wholeness and beauty are powerful tools that can temporarily elevate our mood, but these still encourage us to avoid or disown our darker feelings. Repeating affirmations becomes in effect like talking to ourselves the way our parents did when they exhorted us to "cheer up," instead of really listening to and empathizing with how we felt. The message once again is "You are not sufficient as you are" — unless, in this case, you always feel positive, enthusiastic, and loving.

All the great world religions have at their origin and scattered within their lineage some individuals who have had profound mystical experiences resulting in a fundamental transformation of their consciousness. Thus there is a mystical core in all religions that supports our potential to realize our true natures. But most religions do not understand or acknowledge this mystical core, this experience of realization that is potential in everyone. Instead they deify and elevate only their spiritual icons, such as Jesus and Muhammad.

By accident or design, these religions reinforce and then exploit our early developmental tendency to project our souls' innate self-transcending intelligence outside of ourselves and onto others. Instead of guiding us to recognize our own personal relationship to spirit, they claim the spiritual authority we give away. They tell us who is holy and whose spiritual authority must by obeyed.

In accepting what we are told, we become disempowered. As the innate qualities of our souls are discouraged, denied, or rejected, we unconsciously become angry and brittle. This revenge of the unconscious that results from the denial and suppression of our real selves shows up outwardly as emotional and psychological inflexibility. We advocate a categorical morality, rather than a deep moral sense, and we become controlling, self-righteous, judgmental, and intolerant. The world beyond our own spiritual tribe becomes heathen, including sometimes our own children, and must be set straight or converted. To see ourselves in our original, innate wholeness and to appreciate it in others becomes nearly impossible. The Procrustean way of religion mutilates our inborn spirituality and substitutes a "mind-made" faith. We become proponents of a culture of fear, insufficiency, and survival without even realizing what has happened to us.

But whether or not we are under the sway of mainstream religion, we cannot adequately address the psychology of insufficiency and survival by efforts to make our selves feel better that involve acquiring more wealth, security, power, love, or even spiritual experiences. To stop our emotional suffering, or any unnecessary suffering, we must recognize the power of our awareness to create a new conscious relationship to any feeling and to all our limiting beliefs. We can learn to be present with our threatening sensations and difficult feelings in such a way that we create a new inner relationship to ourselves and, in so doing, actually awaken to the true self. It is in *this* relationship that we can begin to, in effect, "re-parent" and "respiritualize" ourselves and move closer to an authentic expression of our essential selves.

One of the remarkable qualities of our living universe is that it is self-reflexive. Whatever we project onto it is what it shows us. Science has taught us this. Whatever hypothesis we begin with, we always discover evidence to support this hypothesis. This doesn't mean that the hypothesis is necessarily true, only that we will find evidence that makes us believe it is true, at least for a while. One famous example is the hypothesis that the sun and stars circle the Earth.

This is why it is crucial that when we form beliefs and assumptions about ourselves, we begin in the right place. If we begin with an underlying sense that we are insufficient or damaged, or if we begin with an idealized view of ourselves that disguises and protects us from that feeling, then any discouraging experience will confirm our subconscious belief that there is something wrong with us. As we try even harder to "fix" ourselves, to shore up our self-image and make ourselves feel better, the very fact that we have to do this seems to supply further proof that something is essentially wrong with us. Unless we actually penetrate to the core feeling of insufficiency and learn to be present with it without reaction and defense, we will try again and again to reinforce our false selves, until eventually we are sucked down into the quicksand of endless, self-created neurotic suffering and stress.

There is no way to escape this cycle from within it. We have to step outside the whole structure and change our original hypothesis from a subconscious premise of insufficiency to a conscious premise that our souls have an unlimited capacity for awareness — which is our innate ability to be in relationship *to* and not identified *with* whatever we are feeling. We cannot simply choose a new assumption about ourselves by, for instance, verbally affirming "I am whole" or "I am perfect right now." We have to actually *realize* this. The thinking mind cannot effectively affirm its own wholeness, because even the intent to do so is already a reaction to a sense of being less than whole.

But if we begin to take the perspective that our souls have the capacity for awareness, then we realize that, when we are aware of unhappiness, the aspect of us that is *aware* is not itself unhappy. When we are aware of fear, that *awareness* is not itself afraid. By learning to exercise the power of awareness in a different way, one that is not taught to us in school or by conventional religion, we change our original hypothesis that we are defined by our threatening feelings or endless desires and instead become defined by the quality of our relationship with them. That we have the capacity for awareness is the spiritual essence of what it means to be a human being. This unlimited, unconditional awareness is the true self from which we can always begin.

CHAPTER TWO

Who Are We Really?

The Beginning of Deep Self-Inquiry

Like a fish that does not realize it lives in water because water is the only medium it has ever known, some things are so obvious that they escape our understanding. For human beings, awareness is the "water" in which we always live, yet few of us are taught to recognize and understand our own experience of being aware. Our individual consciousness determines what we are able to perceive, how we interpret our perceptions, what we value and make meaningful, and ultimately how we act. Yet we take the miracle of consciousness so completely for granted that we never really consider the nature and power of awareness itself.

Before we can go deeper in this discussion, it is essential that we reach an agreement about the mystery and subtlety of our own nature as conscious beings. Then we can question some of our implicit assumptions about who we believe ourselves to be and, as a result, arrive at a more intelligent understanding of who we really are.

To start this inquiry, let's try a simple exercise: As you read these words, become aware of your breathing. Follow the movement of inhalation as it peaks, and the collapse of your chest and softening of your belly during exhalation. Feel the sensation of the air moving through your nostrils or mouth. The sensation of breathing is a familiar one that has accompanied each of us since birth. Before that, in the womb, we are continuously serenaded by the sound of our mothers' breathing. Yet until I suggested that you pay attention to your breathing, your mind was engaged elsewhere and you were probably unaware of it. What we are aware of depends on where we place our attention.

Now consider what we mean when we use the word *attention*. Did you actually sense what moved or shifted so that you became aware of your breathing? It is facile to say "My attention shifted." What I invite you to attempt to isolate is your actual experience of this thing we call "attention." Rather than answer with your intellect, try to become aware: observe what it *is* that we mean when we say *attention*. Stay with this contemplation for a little while and see what happens.

A metaphor can help us take this inquiry a step further: Imagine that your breathing is like a big kite flying in the sky of your mind. You didn't notice the kite (your breathing) until I asked you to become aware of it. What keeps the kite flying is a string we can call "attention." (If we let go of the string — release the attention — the breathing drops out of awareness, just as a real kite would fall.) So once more, pay attention to your breathing and try to be aware of attention itself.

Now turn your attention around, away from your breathing, and point it back down the "string" toward whatever is holding the string. What do you experience? Who or what is holding the string of attention? Who or what is the kite flyer?

When I conduct this exercise in person with groups, most people tell me that "there is just a space" or "there is nothing." Some describe it as a "cloud." Some say, "It is Now." Others visualize the string as beginning in their heads or chests or bellies. When they say this, I ask them to imagine that these visualizations themselves are also kites, and then to reverse their attention and follow it back down the string toward where it seems to originate. Eventually, if people repeat this exercise a few times, they become speechless, unable to describe what they are experiencing, and they may say, "I don't know." I then suggest that they stay with their sense of not knowing, no-thing, or now-ness for a few moments.

I invite you to do the same: Pause momentarily in your reading and follow the string of attention back to where your awareness begins right now. As you do so, stay with your actual experience, rather than trying to conceptualize it or become abstract about it.

We can pursue this exploration a little further: Can you remember what you did first, or what you were thinking about, when you got up this morning? The moment such a question is posed, some memory immediately becomes accessible. Imagine that this memory is a kite. Focus on the memory now flying in the sky of your mind for a moment, and then on the string of attention. Now, as before, turn your attention back down the string and look for who or what is holding it. Where does your attention to this (or any) memory begin in you? Can you find the origin? Stay with this quality of curious receptivity for a moment. Is this place, or space, that is occupied by the kite flyer empty? Is it full? Most important, look to see if this place, or space, is, itself, in the past. Is it?

Now one last experiment: Imagine what you will be doing tomorrow. With whom will you be? Where will you be?

As soon as I suggest this, your mind automatically envisions the future and creates some story — an expectation "kite" appears suddenly in your imaginary mental sky. Carefully examine this future story. Try to see it with clear detail. Probe into your attention as you look up at the kite that carries your story about tomorrow, and then gently reverse the direction of your attention, away from the imagined future and toward the place where your attention emanates from.

As before, you will most likely experience a sense of a space, a sense of no-thing-ness. Observe softly but carefully: is this space, which is connected to an expectation about the future, itself located in the future? If we extrapolate a little from this inquiry, it is possible to realize that all the things that come and go and appear to "fly" around in our awareness — every sensation, emotion, memory, and thought, and all our fantasies, worries, and plans for the future — are kites of various sizes and colors. But the moment we turn our attention to whom or what holds the strings, we come back to something that is ineffable, that does not live in the past or the future, even though it encompasses both.

This places us at the threshold of a crucial and central insight. The most natural and spontaneous response to questions like "Who is aware of breathing?" "Who is remembering dinner last night?" "Who is anticipating tomorrow's business meeting?" is to say, "*Me. I* am doing these things." In other words, we automatically presume that *I* am the one holding the kite strings. This should naturally lead us to try to learn as much as we can about what we mean when we say or think the word *I* or *me*. To do so, let's return to the same line of inquiry we have been pursuing, and imagine that our sense of self-existence — which we implicitly refer to when we say *I* or *me* — is a kite flying in the vastness of the sky.

Think about how often in a day you say *me*, or how much everything you do presumes that you exist as some kind of separate, psychic entity that you — and all of us — take for granted as *I*. Now let your mind become open, receptive, and quiet, and say to yourself, "Me." With this word inviting your attention, follow your awareness toward whatever is evoked as you contemplate your own "me-ness." Stay with this contemplation for a few moments and observe your experience.

At this point, again repeat the experiment of turning your attention back to whom or what is aware of whatever you are imagining or sensing to be yourself. What do you find? Isn't *this* experience, once again, a space of no-thing-ness? Are you beginning to realize that this ineffable "space" is what always remains whenever you turn your attention back to find the origin of your experience of self? Because this no-thing-ness is what always remains, even though you cannot really name it or truly describe it, isn't this more truly your *me* than anything you can imagine about yourself? It's a remarkable revelation: Who we ultimately are, in our essence, is a potential for awareness, but the experience of awareness itself is never reducible to a thing.

For most of us, reversing our attention and trying to isolate the actual experience or existence of our me-ness is not easy, which is perhaps why we rarely do it. Whereas it is immediately obvious how to notice our breathing, recall a memory, or imagine a future scenario, we are so close to and seemingly embedded within whatever we mean when we say the word *I* or *me* that we seldom, if ever, think to turn our attention toward it, to try to become aware of it. Yet if we have not actually attempted to find who we really are, we have not taken even the first step toward wisdom.

We have many abstract ideas about what we mean by *me*: for example, we equate *me* with ideas like *soul* and *self*. We have concrete descriptions of our sensations and how we feel, and about things that we have been told define us: "I am handsome; I am smart." We have labels of near-infinite diversity: "I am a scientist, a Christian, a Jew, a Republican," and so on. The qualifiers for *I* are virtually limitless. But the actual thing itself, our direct experience of our own me-ness, prior to all these partial descriptions, labels, and abstractions, is much more mysterious. Like mercury under our fingers, our real me-ness, which is often termed *I-Am*, forever eludes our grasp. We all simply assume that *me* is a tangible thing, and we generally live unquestioningly under the illusion of our separate self-existence. But when we try to make ourselves the objects — kites — of our own awareness, we cannot. To do so stops our minds.

We come to a crucial insight: What we call *I* or *me* is a kind of default mental construction that our minds automatically return to unconsciously. We assume our own existence as concrete and objective, yet this assumption remains valid only as long as we do not directly look for our *I*. The moment we do, it is gone.

So what do we really mean when we say *me* or *I*? Am I my experiences? Am I the thoughts or feelings that I have about me? Am I my body? Who am I really?

None of us is innately a Catholic, an American, a mother, or a pilot, yet any one of these is who we might, without the slightest hesitation, claim to "be." In so doing we misconstrue the cultural and social labels imposed on us as who we are, or we mistake the roles we train for or grow into as who we are. Most of us actually believe these identities to be our true selves. If these identities become threatened, we feel that we, in our essential selves, are being threatened. For example, a self-important cele-brity might shout, "Don't you know who I am?" when she is unhappy with the service at a hotel. Or an ambitious politician might feel that he is a "nobody" and become depressed if he is voted out of office. The kites of self-identification become more real than who or what holds the strings. This is the beginning of unending misery in the human realm.

As children we grow into our sense of self without consciously understanding how we do so, and without recognizing the forces that cause us to constantly adapt ourselves to them, contributing to our original internalized feeling about ourselves. It is little wonder that, as a result, we confuse our essence with our sensations, feelings, thoughts, and roles. We have no way to distinguish between being aware and what we are aware of.

As adults, however, to identify ourselves as one of, or the sum of, our feelings, beliefs, and roles is to live in ignorance of our true natures as aware beings. If I choose to follow a path of wisdom, I have to first penetrate the nature of this illusion — as we are doing now. This gives me the opportunity to deconstruct these false identities and learn to abide in my essential self.

In my teaching, I introduce this further inquiry with a simple exercise based on the work of the consciousness teacher Douglas Harding. Imagine your finger is the direction of your attention, and point it toward any object you can see. Usually each of us tacitly assumes the point of view that *I* am *here* and everything else is *elsewhere*: the window is elsewhere, this book is elsewhere, and so on. There is usually no confusion about elsewhere: if it is outside of us, it is elsewhere. But things become interesting when we turn our fingers around and point them back to ourselves, wherever we imagine the *here* of ourselves to be.

Because we have the sense that we are looking out at the world through our eyes, we point toward our own heads, basically toward our own bodies, which is where we typically believe our *here* is located. This identification with the body is the earliest basis of the sense of separateness. So let us continue this same process of inquiry with the body.

What do you find when you point your finger of awareness toward your body? You find your body, right? Tell your body to stand up and it stands up; so it is your body. But if you close your eyes and look into this body, what do you actually experience? You experience a sense of space. It is not an empty space but is filled with sensation, with ever-changing feelings. If you continue to focus your attention on this space of sensation in order to find whether this space is who you really are, the final *here*, you intuit another space that is the viewer, or "awarer," of this dance of sensations. But, as happened earlier, you can't isolate or localize this awarer; it just is. We can say that a part of our sense of self is embedded within, or immanent in, our bodies, so we move and feel, but another part of us — that space of awareness itself — is not localizable in a part of the body, or in a sensation within it. In this sense we are — from the context of consciousness — also transcendent of our bodies.

Of course, our intellect has access to a lot of information about the body. I used to practice medicine, so I am aware of just how much information there is and how fast it is increasing. Within a particular context such as medicine, information about the body can have great validity and value; after all, we want the surgeon who operates on us to be as knowledgeable as possible. But in this inquiry, we are not looking for what we know *about* ourselves as a physiological entities or even psychological beings; we are looking for the immediate experience *of* ourselves. Where do we actually find this thing we refer to when we say *me*? Do we experience *me* as synonymous with the body? Our fingers of attention, when pointed to all that we experience as our bodies, bring us to something that is aware of what we are aware of. It is that space of no-thing-ness once again.

Yet we get confused; we believe we are our bodies. We look in the mirror and believe we are our appearance. We can be unhappy with our aging, our weight, or our muscle tone. The moment we are in default mode and believe in *me* as a concrete self-existence, we simultaneously identify who we are in our essence with our bodies. When our sense of self is based on what we see in the mirror, we are unconscious that there is a *more fundamental* part of ourselves aware of our self-observations and our self-judgments. We can spend our whole lives chasing after some ideal or improved image, never satisfied with how we look, without realizing that in doing so we move our minds elsewhere. We are not really home where our true selves reside.

If we are sick or dying, we may struggle with the sense that it is ourselves that are sick, ourselves that die. But these are thoughts built on our identification with *me* — a *me* we cannot actually find. Having these thoughts creates our suffering. But if we can find the state where we remain present, without any thought, then the turbulent, frightening sensations subside and the space becomes peaceful once again. The part that has been aware all along accompanies us, unchanged, as always.

Just as *that* which is aware of a memory, or an expectation, is not itself in the past or in the future, our aware selves can experience sickness and dying without themselves being either sick or dying. We can even be grateful.

The same awareness is present whether we look at the kites

of fear and despair or the kites of acceptance and peace. The awareness remains present and unchanged even when our health deteriorates. This is why the sage is not troubled by death and can remain openhearted even during illness.

Having seen that, when we believe we are our bodies, we are still *elsewhere* — not *here* in the Now where our awareness begins — let us look at the thoughts we have about ourselves, or at any other thoughts. Unlike what we perceive through our senses that we might generally agree is outside of us, or elsewhere, we usually think of our thoughts as being inside us: really here, really me. Let's see if this is actually the case. Point your finger of attention toward any thought. What do you find?

Generally when I ask people to do this simple exercise of looking to find where their sense of self begins, it causes a great deal of confusion. If we seriously try to follow our own fingers of attention back to where ourselves actually begin, we always arrive at emptiness, or space. But before we even allow ourselves to experience this space, our thinking kicks in: "Okay, I've found this empty space, so now what do I do with it?" This very question is a reflexive attempt to protect our default sense of an objective and concrete *me*, since it presumes that there is an *I* that should now be doing something with this otherwise potentially self-dislocating revelation. We are *elsewhere* once again.

But what about thoughts themselves? Can they lead us to our I-Am? Can they tell us who we really are? We are thinking all the time, aren't we? We are constantly using thoughts to tell us about the world, about who we are, and about others.

Turn your attention to any one of those thoughts: Have you arrived at where you begin? Doesn't this still raise a deeper question: if your thoughts, any thoughts, are your true self, then who or what is aware of them? Imagine that you are the greatest genius with the most knowledge about everything. Can you find a thought that is finally the absolute *here* of yourself? Perhaps you imagine you can. But whatever decisive thought you might come up with, wouldn't there still be a part of you that was aware of this thought? Point your finger toward this awarer. What do you find? There's that space again. And if you don't fight it, it will stop your mind *cold*.

Consider all the things we have been told about who we are, all the ideas, labels, criticism, and praise. Perhaps we have read in spiritual literature that each of us is "a child of God." Conceptually, this may be a perfect description, but it is still an idea; it remains just a kite in your mind. Does it have the power of real knowledge, the certainty and authority of Being that establishes you fully in your essential self, right now?

Take a moment. Try on various ideas or beliefs about who you are. You can see that each one may convey some specific quality or feeling, but does it change the awarer? Is not *that* which is aware always prior to any thought? Thus we must conclude that, try as we may, we cannot actually arrive at our true selves through thought. There will always be some part of us that our finger is pointing to, but which we cannot think about, cannot objectify.

And sometimes this can really dismay us. When our minds stop, we may feel that we have lost ourselves. This might be restful for a few moments, but any longer can provoke a sense of panic. Have you ever become deeply relaxed and suddenly come back to yourself with a start, as if you had momentarily lost yourself? In an instant such as that, the mind recoils into thinking — even about the momentary shock or agitation itself — thus recreating the sense of *me* once again. Of course, it is only our thinking — our surface minds — that stop, not our essence. But we are so unfamiliar with it that it might as well be no-self. We may momentarily tremble, experiencing a feeling of nonbeing.

What about feeling? We can feel something without thinking. Just as a picture can speak a thousand words in an instant, feelings can convey whole universes of meaning. Is what we *feel* who we *are* at the place of original awareness?

Point your finger of attention toward any feeling that may be present in you. Can you locate fatigue or anxiety? Is there a sense of frustration or curiosity? Sometimes our feelings are so powerful, such as when we are engulfed by despair, that it can be very difficult not to become captured by the feeling and identify ourselves completely with it. Yet, if we point the finger of our attention toward even the most compelling feeling, is this feeling, finally and without question, the place where ourselves begin? No matter how intense and compelling a feeling can be, if we consciously point our attention toward it, something remains that is aware of the feeling. Anything we can see or name, we are already larger than.

Some part of awareness must be present in a feeling, or we could not feel it. But another part also remains prior to, and transcends, any feeling, or all we would be is a feeling. If that were the case, we would cease to be a human *being*. We would be a laugh that went on forever or a moan that never stopped. Thus we must conclude that our casual way of speaking — when, for example, we say, "I am angry" — is not really accurate. It would be far more precise to say something like "Anger is present in (my) field of awareness," or more simply, "Here am I, experiencing anger." Obviously, this disidentification with our feelings would be cumbersome as a form of communication, and we don't do it; indeed, we never even think to do so. But we pay for this linguistic imprecision by easily being captured and identified with our feelings. Language itself conspires to help us lose connection with the essential part of us that is aware. As the Tao Te Ching says, "The Tao that can be named is not the true Tao" — or in this case, the true self.[1]

Are you beginning to feel a little confused or disturbed? Are you wondering, "Then, who am I, really?" or "What am I?" If you are, then you are in good company. Human beings have contemplated these questions since the beginning. Can you let this inquiry begin to inject the creative energy of the statement "I don't know"? Can you begin to appreciate that allowing unknowing, in the face of your beliefs about yourself and the ways you identify yourself, can create fertile ground for discovering more of who you really are?

When we let our minds grow quiet and receptive, wherever we may look to discover ourselves, there is no-thing, just a space. Everything we are aware of implies the existence of something aware of this awareness, and if we try to name the awarer — *that* which is being aware — then there is still another awarer. This is like standing in a mirrored room and seeing your reflection repeating infinitely into the distance.

Similarly, one of the first teachings of Jesus, in the Gospel according to Thomas, begins with the injunction "Seek and never cease seeking until you find, and when you find you will be troubled."[2] The seeking that Thomas invites the reader to undertake is precisely what we are doing here. It entails using the innate power of awareness to turn our attention toward deep self-inquiry. Since our individual consciousness determines everything we do, it becomes absolutely essential to rest our sense of self on something that is real, not on something we have identified our consciousness with and have identified ourselves with.

The ineffable I-Am that is our true selves, is the *being* in "human being." It is the organizing field of intelligence at the center of our extraordinary capacity for awareness. It makes possible a ceaseless relationship to all and anything that we can ever know or name, yet we can never actually locate it in space or time. It does not exist in the domain of things or categories of experience. It is so obvious, yet so ineffable, that most of us spend our whole lives in "default" mode, presuming our self-existence through identification with our bodies, our thinking, and our feelings instead of realizing our true authority.

Yet that authority is undeniable. There is a dimension of each of us that is *always* prior to, and that transcends, whatsoever we are aware of. This is what makes it possible for us to consciously turn our attention toward any aspect of our experience in a fresh way at any given moment and in so doing, be capable of constantly renewing ourselves.

The experience of a forty-year-old man whom I counseled illustrates this point. He took his commitment to spiritual life seriously and, on one occasion, admitted to me that he felt ashamed of masturbating. He believed that he needed to achieve complete chastity in order to live a pure spiritual life. Because I could see that he had become overly identified with an idea about spirituality, I asked him to carefully try to find the person in him — the specific *me* — who wanted to live a pure spiritual life. Experienced in self-inquiry, he turned his attention inward and very quickly said, "Yes, I can sense that *me*." I asked him to simply observe the quality of feeling evoked by that particular *me*. He said it felt heavy and sad.

Then I guided him to turn his attention toward whatever in that moment was aware of that *me*. It took no more prompting. Suddenly I could see him relax. He then explained that understanding "spiritual purity" was a story he had been telling himself about how he should be, not his true self. He realized that striving for spiritual purity was an attempt to create a sense of power to compensate for his shyness and awkwardness that made intimate relationships difficult. I pointed out that, by becoming the "failed seeker," he had invited equivalent suffering in another form. Recognizing that his idealized self, not masturbation, was the real issue, he turned the energy he was using to create an image of spiritual purity to instead risking sensitive intimacy with others.

To recognize a false self, as this man did, to know that we are not it, means we are capable of continuous growth and change. Because we are always already more than whatever we are aware of, no matter how difficult something may be for us to face, we can outgrow it. This is why human beings are said to be created in the image of God; we too, in our essence as consciousness, have no beginning and no end and cannot be reduced to a thing. I doubt, though, that we are created in God's image; I believe God, as we imagine him, is more likely the externalization or projection of our own transcendent nature.

All of us at some level feel a call, a yearning toward something more. To be called to greater awareness is innate to the soul. We are designed to ceaselessly evolve in our consciousness. Yet while many are called, only a few choose to even inquire, "Who am I really?"

Many of us strive to improve or fix ourselves when we are unhappy. Understandably, we want to make ourselves feel better. But trying to fix something that is not real is a fruitless task. What we don't know how to do is turn our attention toward the very *me* who wants to fix itself in order to feel better. We don't know how to stay unconditionally present until we eventually discover that this *me* is just a sensation of our larger being, not who we really are.

This inquiry is troubling because the moment we turn our attention to finding the *here* of ourselves, we challenge the very basis of our identities. The inquiry undermines the basic sense of *me*.

Who are we without all the judgments we use to define ourselves? Who are we without our habit of making ourselves the victims of our feelings? What is life like? We discover that we have been living in a dream in which this false identification and the material, social, and cultural world it has constructed collude to keep us in that dream. We find we are not who we thought we were, and as we awaken from the odd dream, we find that we are strangers to ourselves.

But as vertiginous as this may be, it is a healthier state, because at least we know who we are *not*. Those who believe they do know who they are, when they have not yet even been called to true self-knowledge, pose the greatest threat to life on earth. When we do begin to live our lives as who we really are, we become transmitters of a new culture. Since it is not rooted in something that can be threatened, this culture is no longer based on fear for survival. Then the amazing creativity and capacity for love that comprise the true richness of being human finally have a chance to flourish.

CHAPTER THREE

The Power
of Awareness

Any story you tell yourself about who you are, any belief you have, any feeling you are aware of, is only an object of your larger consciousness. You, in your essence, are always something that experiences all these and remains more complete than any of them. When you realize that you are inherently larger than any feeling that enters your awareness, this very awareness will change the feeling, and it will release its grip on you.

Similarly, ideas that you have about yourself are relative, not absolute truths. If you simply look at them and do not let them lead you into further thinking, they will *give way* and leave your mind open and silent. There is always a relationship between who we believe or feel ourselves to be and something else, the Self that is our larger awareness.

In awakening to this Self-me relationship, we begin to be present with our experience in a new way. We learn to consciously hold our thoughts and feelings in our own larger fields of awareness. Then, even if we are troubled and confused, this nonreactive quality of presence to ourselves allows us to restore ourselves to a sense of wholeness. This is the power of awareness.

SENSATION AND PERCEPTION: OUR ORIGINAL CONSCIOUSNESS

The great Indian sage Ramana Maharshi said that if we want to know our true selves, we must "go back by the way that we have come." Our original state of consciousness in childhood is not one of being a separate entity with our own thoughts and sensations, but rather is a relatively undifferentiated domain of sensation and perception. Our parents, having already reached the developmental stage of separate-self consciousness, provide the model by which we begin to develop our own sense of the separate self.

But when we take the developmental step into the consciousness of the separate self and leave behind the universe of immediacy and undifferentiated sensations, as a consequence we also become identified with our sensations. Who is happy? *Me*. Who is angry, tired, frustrated...? *Me*. Our feelings acquire names, however, and at the same time, we are defined by those feelings.

The same is true with perception: we may not feel that the sunshine on the trees is *me*, but we cannot identify it without simultaneously existing as a separate *me*. In psychological and philosophical theory, this level of consciousness is called "subject-object." It is the level of ego awareness where most human development stops. We are aware as *me*, we react as *me*, we defend as *me*, we desire as *me*, but we are not aware of the true self. It is the true self that looks at all we think, do, and experience, including our sense of *me*. In this looking, a relationship is created that has the power to transform our experience of ourselves and our worlds.

Throughout our lives, the moment we bring our awareness fully into the Now, we enter the domain of the true self, and our immediate conscious reality is once again that of sensation and perception. As I sit in the park, the sunlight brightens the leaves and casts shadows on the ground. I have a feeling of contentment. And as long as "I" don't create stories about what I am seeing or about the fact that I am feeling content, which leads me away from my *immediate* experience, what I experience remains simply perception and sensation. The same is true for any feeling, any emotion. In the Now, it is just what it is. In the Now, I "go back" to my original awareness "by the way that [I] have come." When we directly perceive and experience whatever is present in our larger fields of awareness, it is possible to have a relationship with it without becoming lost in it or defined by it.

EXERCISING THE POWER OF AWARENESS

We exercise the power of awareness and strengthen our spiritual muscle by bringing ourselves, over and over again, into the immediate present. To do so, we must become present with what we are feeling and thinking. We can turn our attention directly toward what we are experiencing instead of staying enmeshed in a feeling or blindly accepting our beliefs about ourselves.

It makes all the difference in the world whether we are caught in a negative emotion and say, "I am sad, angry, lonely," and so on, or are able to recognize, at that moment, "Here am

I, all wound up in sensations of resentment. Here am I, fuming with anger." Awareness of our sensations is not the same as identifying with our thoughts or feelings. Every movement back to present-moment awareness grounds us in the body and opens the connection to our larger awareness.

Even the smallest movement toward exercising the power of awareness, instead of collapsing our larger awareness into our thoughts and feelings and thereby becoming identified with them, restores us to a more complete consciousness. It gives us the power to start from a fresh, open, less conditioned relationship to our experience. This doesn't necessarily mean that our problems disappear. But as we exercise the power of awareness, our reflexive reactivity diminishes. We respond from a state of greater presence. When we collapse into our feelings, we lose this capacity. We default into *me*, and this limited self seems like the whole of who we are. Then we have no choice but to react because we feel as if we must defend ourselves.

THE FUNDAMENTAL RELATIONSHIP

What are we actually doing when we bring our awareness fully into the present and realize "Here am I . . ."? We are moving into a more spacious awareness and thus creating conscious distance from what we are experiencing. At the same time, we are opening toward our immediate experience to see it as it is, to see it fully, to invite it to reveal itself more completely to us. We are seeing as objectively as we can, without reacting or judging. This lets us more completely realize what we are actually feeling or sensing; we do not merely remain in our heads, interpreting and analyzing.

It is important to point out that moving our awareness into

the Now and thereby gaining distance from our feelings and thoughts is not dissociation. A frequent mistake people make with Eastern meditation practices is to try to rise above and detach from an experience, especially whenever the experience is considered negative. To exercise the power of awareness, we are required to become more present in our experiences without losing our larger awareness. With this quality of attention, we gain true understanding. We naturally begin to respond to our experiences in the most appropriate and intelligent ways.

This intimate viewing of ourselves by our awareness is the most fundamental of all relationships. We create the possibility of a conscious, empathetic connection between *me* (or self) and our true selves, or what is alternatively referred to as the Self. The personal self that we experience as ourselves is held, seen, and felt deeply by *that*, which will never reject *me*, never turn away, never judge *me*. It can see us judging, attacking ourselves, creating our own misery; but it does not judge even this. It is simply present with *me*.

This presence need not be merely neutral or indifferent. We can let it be our trusted friend, like the Persian mystic poets Hafiz and Rumi did when they referred to it as the "Guest" or the "Beloved," to whom they offered themselves and who always received them.

The key to cultivating the healing potential of the self-Self relationship is the quality of our attention — the steadiness, gentleness, and acceptance of the "gaze" we turn toward ourselves. We must be truly willing to experience our feelings and clearly see our thoughts without reaction, allowing the moment to be exactly as it is without defending ourselves against these feelings and thoughts, without our minds moving away into further thought. Then *that* which transcends our capacity to name or categorize it in any way, is present to us and has the same accepting quality that we present to ourselves. This is also the essence of meditation and prayer. By keeping our attention in the present moment, we can become transparent to what is transcendent. It is the Self's profoundly empathetic acceptance of self that ultimately sustains us when we face our deepest fears, including even our egos' primal terror, nonbeing.

LEARNING THE INNER GAZE
OF NONREACTIVE ATTENTION

The power of awareness rests on the ability to be present with our experience in the way that a wise, experienced, and loving mother holds her baby. Whether the baby is calm or disturbed, the mother's attention is present. Her whole being is oriented toward the child. She speaks to him, touches him, and maintains a constant, steady presence. If the baby is upset, she herself does not become upset but, through her voice and eyes, conveys to the baby her awareness of his feeling. She conveys to her baby the knowledge that these feelings are part of the self, not something ultimately destructive to the self. And on the occasions when she is actually concerned for her baby, she knows that, by not losing touch with her deeper center, she transmits much less of her fear to the child.

How we hold any feeling, whether anger, anxiety, or despair, either intensifies our sense of *me* and leads us away from our transcendent presence, or it lets us relax and even dissolve that *me*. *Me*, in this sense, is analogous to a movie screen: if the screen is opaque we see (or in this case, live) the "movie." If the screen becomes transparent, the movie disappears.

A feeling that we make space for and do not react to, do not create thoughts to support, and do not invent "worry stories" about gradually ceases to have power over us precisely because there is less *me* reacting to the feeling. In this way we are learning to become more transparent. We begin to experience feelings in their purity. A pure feeling is one that exists as simple sensation. It does not become intensified by thoughts that judge it or become warped by the mind's efforts to analyze, change, prolong, or eliminate it. Then every feeling has the opportunity to help us arrive at a new depth of intimacy with ourselves naturally, without effort, without seeking for anything at all. At the same time, once the mind releases its grip on the feeling, the feeling automatically begins to change. Everything is impermanent when the mind isn't holding it fixed. Then we begin to enter deeper layers of our beings, where we are already intrinsically more whole.

It is our judgment of our feelings — and especially our desire for them to end if they are unpleasant, or to continue if they are good — that locks us into suffering. To reject a feeling is essentially to refuse the present: it is like deciding this Now has less God, less wholeness, than some other moment. Wanting a good feeling to continue is the same thing in reverse: it causes us to resist anything else life presents, and therefore we have less *presence*.

Each of these ways of reacting to our feelings represents a movement away from the immediacy of our experience and is thus actually a disengagement from reality. Just as we thrive when we feel we are seen, listened to, and met, so do we begin to thrive when, instead of reflexively reacting to our feelings, we consciously touch them with exquisite attention. A pure feeling is never a threat to us; only when we attempt to control or alter feelings do they become threats. Such control would be like a mother asking her child to stop crying before she will love her, instead of loving her just as she is. This is precisely what we do to so much of our own experience: we ask it to be different before we have even turned our attention toward it to experience it and accept it as it is.

This kind of direct and nonreactive relationship to our immediate experience breaks the choke hold of the inner critic. We all have internalized a disapproving voice that harshly judges us and, in so doing, keeps us trapped in a cycle of emotional contraction, defense, and self-rejection. We are particularly vulnerable to the power of the critic, because it confirms what we already deeply believe about ourselves: our early conditioned sense of insufficiency. But the moment we ask how we are aware of the critic and the negative state it causes, we return to simple awareness: "Here am I . . . judging myself. Here am I . . . aware of this harsh inner critic that is attacking me, calling me selfish."

The critic wants us to contract into a state of self-doubt or into a renewed cycle of self-improvement efforts. It keeps us self-involved. The critic says, "You would not be feeling this if . . . ," and the reasons it gives are legion. The critic is the defender of the original false hypothesis of insufficiency, even while purportedly offering us a way out. Paradoxically, listening to the critic, even though it makes us miserable, allows our egos to feel supported and safe, because the unconscious, familiar premise of insufficiency — upon which our egos rest — remains intact. But the moment we utilize the power of awareness to become directly present, without having any goal to change what we are feeling, this threatens the unconscious premise of insufficiency. Then the whole house of cards begins to tumble.

To sit and feel a difficult feeling *without identifying with it* may be unfamiliar and may make us feel vulnerable. We may feel as if we might cease to exist if we don't collapse into the familiar struggle with ourselves and our sense of insufficiency. But allowing ourselves to be vulnerable is the path that takes us to a fuller aliveness.

SPIRITUAL MUSCLE
AND THE MYSTERY OF FAITH

The ability to stay present requires muscular attention. The effort to develop this ability initially resembles willpower. It does take intention and determination, but an attitude of tender curiosity and attentiveness to whatever we are experiencing eventually takes the place of willpower. This attention does not intrude on the feeling, does not try to control it. Instead we give the feeling as much space as it requires by becoming soft and vast around it.

When we apply our will to arrive *at* wholeness instead of beginning *from* wholeness, we once again succumb to a distrust *of* our experience instead of experiencing a relationship *to* our experience.

Spiritual muscle is not something we can coerce in ourselves. Our initial reaction to negative feelings is to want to escape them. We may consciously direct our attention toward positive thoughts by means of intention and will — by so-called positive thinking and the use of positive affirmations. But in doing so, we are only reacting, and we remain caught in our fear or discomfort. We can instead use real spiritual muscle (and true positive thinking) and turn our nonreactive inner gaze toward whatever we are afraid of. We can use the power of awareness itself. The more we do so, instead of throwing our minds into some form of self-protection, the more we grow in the mysterious power that is faith.

Faith is perhaps the most profound and most mysterious experience of all, and it is inextricably related to our power of awareness. Faith grows as the self-Self relationship deepens and as we learn to remain present in difficult situations that, at an earlier stage of life, we would have completely identified with.

We associate faith with traditional religious belief systems and notions of God. True faith, however, cannot rest on beliefs or thoughts, or even on feelings, because we are always already *more* than these by virtue of our awareness of them. Beliefs, especially as they bring us meaning and purpose, can act as a transitional medium for faith. Consider how a teddy bear or soft blanket can act as a positive transitional object and temporarily replace the comforting presence of a mother for a child when she is not present. Similarly, to the extent that we cling to beliefs to define and defend who we are, we remain children as far as faith is concerned. Faith can never be proclaimed in words; it can only be radiated or transmitted through the quality of our presence, through an inner poise that is not shaken by outer circumstances. To proudly assert one's faith as unquestioning acceptance of a particular religious belief system is to declare one's lack of faith in oneself. It is a proclamation of ignorance of the nature of one's own consciousness.

One paradox of faith is that when we sense it in another, it gives us hope that we too can face our fears. Yet faith itself is the capacity to meet fear without hope. If we require hope, how can we say that we have faith? Faith is not a state of fearlessness, but rather an ability to hold fear with the power of our awareness and not lose touch with *that* in us which is more than whatever we are afraid of.

A second paradoxical aspect of faith is that we can neither see nor measure it. It is defined by the shape of our fears. For example, when we approach intimacy with another but become so afraid of rejection or abandonment or engulfment that we withdraw, these fears mark the limits of our faith. But if we choose to remain in the pure feeling of these fears and not withdraw from a relationship, we empower ourselves and grow in faith, which makes us capable of greater intimacy.

Many people discover the limits of their faith when they are afraid of not having enough money. Too many of us let money fears — basic survival consciousness — keep us in jobs we don't enjoy or in relationships that are no longer healthy for us. When we do so, our faith is only as alive as the security we derive from having enough money. But if we can look at this fear and see that it is simply a sensation that can be accommodated and not reacted to, we increase our faith. We demystify the power we have given to money and can make wiser choices. Then money ceases to be such a defining force in our lives.

In any aspect of life, whenever we dare not step forward because of fear, whatever form it may take, we have reached the limits of our faith. What we must do then is exercise the power of awareness to remain present with our fears until nothing is moving inside of us. In this stillness, there is no longer such a strong sense of *me* — the *me* that can be threatened — and so the fear loses its power. As we become transparent, the energy in fear is freed up and just becomes more energy to feed and increase our power of awareness. In this way the power of awareness transforms fear to faith.

One of my favorite stories about developing muscular attention comes from the martial arts tradition of aikido. Master Morihei Ueshiba, the founder of aikido, challenged his senior students to rouse themselves from sleep every night and follow him with their eyes as he walked across the dormitory to the bathroom. At this point he was an old man and had to urinate several times a night. If after a while a student had not learned to wake up and become present, that student was deemed unfit and asked to leave. The master was trying to cultivate in these advanced students an exceptional capacity for attention that extended even into their sleep. Willpower alone would not have been successful. If these men had willed themselves to stay awake, they would have become exhausted. What they had to learn was to empower their attention with intent, as well as to let go and enter a higher level of relaxed alertness.

We can bring this warrior quality of relaxed alertness to our awareness of ourselves. We can *wake up* the moment we see our minds fashioning stories that lead us away from the immediacy of the present, and turn our nonreactive eye-of-attention toward who we are right now.

If a particular feeling is painful, we can surrender to it while simultaneously refusing to allow that feeling to drive us into self-judgment or an escape strategy. In this profound intimacy with our pain, which I call conscious suffering, a transformation begins to occur. As we grow more muscle and can stay fully present, whatever events we can allow without reaction — without collapsing into them and losing ourselves — gradually release their power over our reality. Then we begin to rest in a natural state of presence — the luminosity of our faith. We can live from our deepest selves. Even at the darkest times, when we finally stop resisting, what one moment seems like hell can suddenly become peace and stillness, and we can regain a fundamental sense of wholeness and gratitude.

Gradually, as our capacity for conscious suffering grows, so does our faith. It is not that we no longer feel fear, but that we discover we have much more freedom even in the face of what used to be our greatest fears. It takes consistent intention to learn to live in the present and meet our suffering consciously. But fundamental change occurs not because we find inventive ways to avoid suffering; it emerges organically out of the depth of our awareness in such suffering. The power of awareness itself can set us free.

Even if our survival patterns have dominated us all our lives, one day we will become aware that we are giving in to fear, and we will turn consciously toward awareness of the fear instead of going where it is trying to point us. In that moment we will have transcended, by some small degree, our ego's continuous self-protection, what I call the survival project. New possibilities for our lives are born in such moments.

THE SURVIVAL PERSONALITY
AND THE IDEALIZED SELF

The adaptations we have unconsciously made during preverbal and later stages of childhood to escape from feelings of abandonment, engulfment, or annihilation powerfully influence the way we present ourselves to the world as adults. These frightening feelings are repressed, buried in a subconscious stratum of our beings, and we are no longer aware of them under most circumstances. A part of early ego development is the adoption of strategies for maintaining this repression by constructing a false self that becomes the essence of the *survival personality*, a term I borrow from psychosynthesis theory.

The survival personality is the one we present to the world — and more important, to ourselves. This generally positive personality disguises our inner sense that something is wrong with us. The task of the survival personality is to keep us from facing this feeling by imagining, and ultimately becoming fully identified with and believing in, a special or idealized self, as mentioned in chapter 1.

The concept of the idealized self explains how most of us manage to solve the problem of our core anxiety by endowing ourselves with special capacities and gifts.[1] We ameliorate the wounds of childhood by fabricating a set of beliefs about ourselves in which ordinary qualities become glorified and our weaknesses are envisioned as virtues. If we have loving feelings for a parent, a child, or a partner, this love becomes evidence of our saintly devotion. If we are angry and aggressive, we imagine ourselves as strong and heroic. When we are compliant, we believe we are acting selflessly. There is a compulsive quality to our need to glorify ourselves and thereby distance ourselves from the core feeling of not being good enough as we are. Consequently, there is also a compulsive quality to how we later defend our idealized selves.

The idealized self grows out of our personal lives and how we have unconsciously adapted to the psychological environment of our early lives. If we have acquiesced to our mothers' psychology, rather than seeing ourselves as submissive and weak, we may create an ideal of loyalty to her feelings and needs. Later in life this causes us to feel indispensable not only to her but also to anyone to whom we have transferred our allegiance.

If instead we rebel, we see our own combative and reactive defenses as heroic intolerance for injustice. We might be cynical about authority and haughtily believe we have a superior understanding of the world and what it needs. But we never really know what our own feelings or needs are, because they are derived from what we reject and judge, rather than from what actually lives within us.

Those of us whose defensive adaptation is to withdraw have a tendency to retreat into an imaginary world and spend long hours alone. Later in life we might hide in the world of books or computers, eventually becoming more intimate with our area of expertise than with the people in our lives. We may even become aloof and disdainful of others, seeing them as unworthy of our serious involvement.

If we never free ourselves from our survival personalities, we can never simply be ourselves, can never really accept ourselves as we are. We cannot be ordinary in the true sense of objectively appreciating our bodies, our appearance, or our intellectual or athletic abilities without feelings of superiority or inferiority. We cannot just be who we are with our own feelings and our own natural strengths and weaknesses. In a word, we cannot be humble.

And since our survival personalities are never who we really are, but an ideal — which by the very definition of the word is not real — we constantly fall short of their expectations. No matter how we strive, we never can be attractive enough, loving enough, secure enough, powerful enough, honest enough, smart enough, and so on, because even when we are, we do not believe it. We have to keep striving to fulfill the ideal, which is like trying to reach the constantly receding horizon. The resulting self-judgments arising from our inevitable failures to fulfill the demands of our ideal selves lead us into neurotic suffering. And this suffering creates an environment of self-involvement that blinds us to the existence of our true selves. From the point of view of our true selves, the whole survival project is entirely unreal, even less than irrelevant. But from the point of view of the survival personality, the effort to begin to open to our true selves seems utterly futile and carries the threat of annihilation.

In my own observations of thousands of people, the existence of underlying and extremely threatening feelings, even in individuals considered to be highly functioning, is unquestionable. We can function very well, believing not only that we are satisfied with our own lives but also that we are exceptional. Yet eventually the illusion of our idealized selves begins to disintegrate. Often this happens when there is illness, loss of a loved one, or sudden financial ruin. For many people, the demise of the idealized self begins when they have gone through the misery of divorce, often multiple times, and begin to suspect that the problem doesn't just lie in their partners. Or it shows up when we actually begin to experience some of the success that our idealized selves would lead us to expect is our due, but which we deep down don't believe we deserve and, eventually, subconsciously sabotage.

There is a yearning for authenticity and real freedom in all of us, though, and so our souls cannot permit us to live indefinitely in denial and self-deceit. When we finally decide to follow that yearning, we find we must recognize and outgrow our idealized selves. In this process of growth, we find ourselves facing what I call "untamed" emotions, such as a sense of utter despair and dread (see chapter 5). It is these feelings that limit our faith, and no further fundamental growth in consciousness is possible until they can be met and embraced in a nonreactive way.

Beneath our survival personalities lie something we are trying to protect ourselves from feeling. And sooner or later it inevitably surfaces. This may happen with the breakup of a relationship, the loss of a job, or some other traumatic event. It may happen simply because our failure to fulfill the impossible expectations of our idealized selves leads us to finally collapse in exhaustion. At times like these, we can plunge into such despair or irrational rage and self-hate that we feel as though we are being *undone*, that we will go mad. We might even contemplate suicide.

At this point we have finally reached the inner Armageddon, the battle for supremacy between our false selves and our true selves. When this happens, we must, above all, learn to exercise the power of awareness with unresisting attention and unlimited compassion for our own suffering. Because we have for so long mistaken our survival personalities as ourselves, we can experience the deconstruction as loss of self. This is a crisis in the journey of awakening to fuller consciousness, akin to the dark night of the soul that Saint John of the Cross wrote about.

Ironically, we are then in an innate healing and self-transcending process, yet it feels like it can, and eventually will, lead us to a fundamental crisis of identity.

Meeting and freeing ourselves from many of our fears ultimately brings us to the deepest fear of all: the ego's primal fear of nonbeing. This is why genuine transformation requires our most sincere commitment. I believe this deepest fear ultimately rules not only our individual survival personalities but also, through it, our collective human survival project. Modern society, and the culture it has constructed, is a collective idealized self, a collective survival personality, and is founded just as much upon the feelings we do not know how to meet and hold as upon any higher vision we have for life. Until we individually, one at a time, face this in ourselves, we will continue to unconsciously live under the aegis of the god of fear. The resulting quest for survival, unconsciously externalized in so much of our way of life, will continue to pose a terrible threat to our futures. In our reflexive universe, fear, even if unconscious, only gives birth to more fear.

How the Survival Personality Survives Self-Realization

Even though I had a realization that profoundly transformed my sense of being and awakened me to a new level of consciousness — what some might call Self-realization — in which I understood the unity of all things and that love is the heart of our universe, and even though I experienced then, and many times since, the most profound sense of wholeness and well-being, I have had to accept the humiliating truth that my own survival personality continues to operate. If my attention isn't fully in the present, I can still lapse into distrust concerning the future, or I can communicate indirectly to protect myself or to avoid hurting or disappointing others. If my wife or children are critical or flare at me in anger, I can still, at times, close down and become defensive or judgmental. And does one ever finally defeat the beasts of self-involvement and self-importance that so easily insinuate themselves into our behavior and thinking? I haven't.

Just as we wake up each morning having forgotten ourselves each night, our survival personalities wake up with us and in so many subtle and not so subtle ways assert themselves into our lives. I believe that all people, no matter what degree of Self-realization they may have achieved, experience the ongoing influence of the survival personality. Appreciating this is important because it explains why some spiritual and religious leaders who are, in many ways, exceptional, nonetheless act immorally. Alternatively, they might create communities that become elitist and insular, often limiting the essential individuation of those who devote their lives to these communities. Especially when we are in a position of authority, we must watch vigilantly for the survival personality's potential influence. If not, it will pervert even the best intentions and make even the most brilliant teachings or leadership into instruments for its own ends. The moment we believe ourselves superior because we think our understanding is greater than others', and that this gives us special rights with respect to our students, employees, congregation, or fellow citizens, the survival personality has us firmly in its grasp. Only by continuously exercising the power of awareness can we begin to free ourselves.

AWARENESS VERSUS SELF-IMPROVEMENT

Once we understand that the power of awareness leads us to essential humility and ordinariness, then we can grant ourselves permission to inquire deeply into all aspects of ourselves that constitute our identities. Often we are afraid to do this, imagining that if we were to look at the darker parts of ourselves and discover something particularly unpleasant or disillusioning, we would not be able to face it. But I am not talking about dwelling obsessively on the negative. As soon as we turn our full, nonreactive gaze on a difficult feeling, we are, by the very nature of awareness, already more than it is. Our identification with that feeling weakens. It is not what we feel or experience that we need fear; it is what remains unconscious that poses the real threat. Parts of our survival psychologies, such as an unconscious need to feel loved and secure by helping others, eventually betray us. They will always affect our motives and inevitably distort our behavior, undermining even our best intentions.

This is why in my work, as I guide people to ever-deeper self-inquiry, I frequently ask them, "Are you undertaking this work because something is innately wrong with you? Do you believe you need to be fixed?" The true answer is "No!" This work is not about self-improvement. It is only and simply about developing a fuller awareness. We do this work not because it can relieve suffering but because, when we are suffering, this suffering, in whatever form it takes, is the truth of this particular moment. We must turn toward it as if it were a child who needs the full and loving attention of its mother. Remember: Anything we can become aware of, we are already greater than. Any attempt to change ourselves or improve ourselves as a means of avoiding a feeling only leads to ceaseless self-manipulation or the manipulation of others, and it does not change the underlying sense of insufficiency from which we unconsciously continue to run. To turn toward what is, in the here and now, and to meet it with the full power of awareness, is to arrive all at once at the wholeness that *is*, and always has been, our essential selves.

Transforming ourselves by means of this path requires us to become more aware in our suffering. Simply by being present, without blinking — which means keeping the mind completely still as it gazes at the specific feeling — we cease to create the *me* that is the home of that suffering. The image of not blinking comes from my childhood enjoyment of Western movies, where, when two gunfighters faced each other, whoever blinked first was shot. At a deeper level, masters of martial arts know that the contestant who moves from thought, which is much slower than moving from presence or being, generally loses the match. There are legends in the world of martial arts that tell of victory being awarded in competitions even before any physical contact has taken place. Some judges are so attuned that they sense the movement in the minds of the competitors and call the match in favor of the one with the deepest stillness.

In my work, to blink means that in the face of a difficult feeling, we let our minds move away from the feeling into thoughts about the past or the future, or into stories about ourselves or about the feeling itself. In so doing we leave the original feeling and become involved instead with these thoughts and the secondary feelings they engender. This propels us away from the Now, and this movement sustains and intensifies the *me* that is resisting the original feeling. We wind up suffering even more, but in a way that feels familiar because it preserves our usual sense of *me*. If we don't blink, *me* recedes. As we come into direct relationship with the original feeling, we evolve and our interior becomes more spacious. What began as fear of a feeling transforms into energy and presence. Then we can make our choices, such as leaving a job or a relationship, in response to a sense of openness and possibility rather than as a means to avoid a feeling.

THE GOD OF FEAR AND THE GOD OF LOVE

Fear is the principal force that divides our hearts. It will continue to do so unless we increase the muscle of our attention and faith that lets us remain present for more and more of reality. When we consciously meet our fear, our faith grows. In the deepest solitude of ourselves, when fear has brought us to our knees and there is nothing left to do but surrender to it, we discover what has all along been supporting us.

Fear is a great god, one that we can never defeat if we resist or react to it in any way. Learning to grow faith is an incremental process. I know of no one who has fully conquered fear. I certainly haven't. But I know that if, at the end of a lifetime, our faith has grown a measure no bigger than just the space between two hairs on our heads, we will have to a degree transformed the very fabric of reality for ourselves and everyone else.

As this power to resist fear grows within us, we begin to realize a greater god: the god of love. I am using the term *god* here to refer to the dominant unconscious force that influences us at a given stage in our lives. We could say that, at this point in history, in the majority of us, the soul lives under the sway of fear. Yet there is a growing minority whose souls obey the god of love, and the primary evidence of this is that our lives are dominated by the yearning to know who we really are. Love is not mere consolation for our otherwise troubled lives. Nor is it the sentimental, but pleasurable, "mush" it has been reduced to in popular culture. Love, as Walt Whitman wrote, is "the kelson of the creation."[2] The *kelson* is the keel, or backbone, of a sailing ship that unites all the ribs to form the hull.

Love is the backbone of reality: it is the unbroken connectedness of all things, everything in relationship to everything else. Nothing is ever in exile from it; there is nothing in life that does not belong here, in reality. Even fear.

When love is our god, we have permission to be in relationship to everything, even the darkest places of dread and terror. When love is our god, we can enter into conscious relationship to any aspect of our experience and consciously suffer it until we realize that the very fabric of reality is love. There is always *that* within each of us that is greater than fear in all its forms.

The god of fear offers hope but demands obedience: do this, obtain this, follow these rules and you will be safe, you will be happy. But the price we pay for the illusion that we can attain happiness and security this way is an eternal battle for survival, one that always starts from a sense of insufficiency. The god of fear was our first teacher of survival. No doubt, without fear we could not have survived. But now our mindless obedience to this god threatens us with disruption at every level of society and, perhaps, may even lead us to extinction. Our obsession with survival and security always ultimately leads us back to fear and all its minions — power, control, righteousness, jealousy, neediness, greed, blame, hate, and revenge. We live in endless hope for imagined security, for freedom from an endless legion of external threats, but in that very hope hides the root fear, that which we have not yet turned to meet and hold. Hope can never break us out of the cycle of survival.

While fear thrives on obedience, the god of love asks only for conscious relationship, and not to an abstract idea of God, but to the immediacy of every moment. When fear is overlord of a particular moment, filling our minds with endless worries and demanding all kinds of actions in the service of a hoped-for outcome or reward, love will hold and support our aware selves as we turn trembling to stand and face fear itself, straight on, whatever its guise. In facing fear, we gradually become free of the cycle of fear and hope and begin to fulfill the higher purpose of our human existence: to reveal and express the fullness of our beings.

But what of those of us who derive our faith from belief in God or Jesus or any other symbol that represents to us a reality greater than ourselves? Experiencing faith in this way entails projecting our own self-transcending capacity onto a symbol of salvation and then deriving feelings of inspiration and sustenance from those symbols. But even though in our survival-oriented culture this passes for true faith, it is really just borrowed faith: we borrow it from something external to us, something we can think or imagine, without realizing that *that* which resided in Jesus and all the great souls resides as well in ourselves. This fundamental consciousness, which everyone has the potential to realize, is clearly what Jesus was referring to when he said, "Before Abraham was, I Am" (John 8:58).

Depending on borrowed faith when we do not ultimately have faith in ourselves, we remain prisoners of the god of fear, even as we worship the icons we have dedicated to the god of love. We claim to know what God wants, but we remain ignorant of our own essence. We continue to be rooted in a survival-based consciousness. There is a deeper faith that comes from exercising the power of awareness to find our own source, what existed prior to anything whatsoever that we have believed. If we inquire deeply enough to realize that our conditional faith comes at the price of giving away our own divinity, then we meet the true test of faith: we finally face our egos' primal fear of being utterly and hopelessly extinguished. When we face this fear, we ultimately come to realize the true source of our beings.

THE PROBLEM WITH GOD

The problem with God is that "God," as we think of God, is a creation of our own minds. If in a given moment our god-idea helps us to enter more fully into the present and into the wholeness of our being, then this god-idea is alive in that moment, part of the vital transformative conversation between self and Self. But when our god-ideas become more real to us than the awareness that allows us to contemplate them, these ideas begin to imprison our souls.

It is always a mistake to separate our own consciousness from our god-ideas. Jesus himself said, "Whoever knows the All but fails to know himself lacks everything."[3] Whatever we believe about God, we are knowingly or unknowingly speaking about ourselves, and frequently it is our survival personalities that influence what we say. If we want a god to support us in battle or our nationhood or our religious supremacy, we invent a god who legitimates our cause. If we want a god who exonerates us and forgives us, we open our hearts to a god who does that. If we want a god who is pro-life or pro-choice, we create this god in our minds. And once we have created this god, we always construe evidence or scripture to support our belief.

But it is not really a question of what God does or doesn't want. For the religious person, God excites the mind; for the mystic, God stops it. When we speak of God from a spiritual perspective, we refer to *that* which, when we turn our attention completely toward it, ends all thought and instead reflects us back to the ineffable source of our consciousness, the true beginning of ourselves. God in this sense is the ultimate mirror: whatever we see in it is God. We must embrace every aspect of ourselves until, ultimately, we each know that *I* and God are one.

AWARENESS IS THE PATH

If we begin unconsciously from the premise that we are insufficient, we end up caught in the endless cycle of reacting to our insufficiency and trying to fill ourselves. The only way to get off this misery-go-round is to begin by being aware that we are whole. Consciousness itself is that wholeness. It is like water: it can assume any shape into which it is poured, yet it never loses its own essence. Through the power of awareness, we can enter into relationship to anything whatsoever that we are experiencing and still remain, in our essence, whole and full. We can be aware of the most devastating feelings of insufficiency, and yet, the moment we say, "Here am I," and turn toward what we are experiencing, the part of us that makes this awareness possible eternally receives us. Our experience may not change immediately, the pain may remain terrible for a while, but we know, even if only to the tiniest degree, that we are more than this pain. The essential part of ourselves is never broken, is never in itself corrupted in any way. The true self is not a thing we can know; it is an inexhaustible power that can carry us deeper and deeper into ourselves and into reality.

How much more complete our knowledge of ourselves can become depends on how deeply we yearn to know ourselves and how much reality we can bear before fear chases us into a dream of our own fabrication. The limit to Self-realization is set the moment we reach a fear, such as the fear of abandonment, that we experience as too great to face, or an idea so compelling that we identify ourselves with it, like the idea of communism or the idea that there is only one Son of God. At such a moment, we lose connection to the beingness of *human being* and become only human.

Like the aikido students learning to wake up when the master walks by, we have to wake up. We have to wake up out of the dream created when our awareness buries itself in our stories or roles, and particularly the dream created when we flee difficult feelings. The path to awakening consciousness is a path of conscious relationship to everything we experience and feel. It is ceaseless self-inquiry and necessary, conscious suffering, which must continue until more and more easefully we can rest in the fullness of being.

CHAPTER FOUR

Who We Aren't Really

Understanding the Process of Identification and Differentiation

At the level of thought, the human mind is endlessly complex. Yet if we approach it through awareness itself, for us to begin to master the intricacies and waywardness of the mind is not that difficult. Consciousness is far more than intellect: it gives us a capacity for relationship, a potential for a direct and profound intimacy with life. But before we understand the power of awareness as an instrument of conscious relationship, we become identified with and imagine ourselves to be what we are aware of. We unconsciously become the kites, not the kite flyers.

The process of self-identification starts with our sensations, until eventually we crystallize into the false belief that we are our bodies. It goes further as we confuse our feelings and emotions with our essence. Then almost any emotion can become the basis of who we believe ourselves to be and a distorting lens through which we see the world around us. We also become identified with patterns of thought, emotion, and action and believe that our primary identity is as a Christian, American, lawyer, soldier, or poor or wealthy person: the possibilities are endless. The mind can carry us anywhere, into anything, and when we believe we *are* that, we cannot grasp our true power as aware beings. We become lost in a dream, and we do not even know it, while virtually everyone and everything in our lives help to keep us in this ignorance.

All teachings designed to develop wisdom acknowledge that until the mind and the body are in the same place in the Now, we cannot truly experience a sense of our own wholeness. We hear crucial injunctions such as "Be here now" and "Seek the Self" — that which is changeless in the midst of constant change — and we are told, as I emphasize in this book, that identification with our beliefs and emotions is the root of unnecessary suffering. This is wise counsel, but if you have been on a path of self-knowledge, you have probably noticed that living in the Now and realizing the Self is not easy. This is why in my work I feel it is helpful to investigate the process of self-identification. If we can understand who we aren't, and how "who we aren't" has become who we believe ourselves to be, it is far easier to stand back from our thoughts and emotions and create, at least initially, a capacity for *unknowing*. Unknowing is not the same as not knowing, where we feel uninformed and perhaps helpless. It is a state of receptivity that doesn't immediately label and define what we are experiencing. In the space that unknowing opens us to, we can know ourselves and claim ourselves much more authentically.

One way to unravel the process of self-identification is to start by simplifying the nature of our human experience into three categories of consciousness: thinking, feeling, and action.

Thinking includes anything that we formulate conceptually: ideas, memories, fantasies, speculations, and so on. Feeling is a way of knowing that involves sensing with our whole being, with mind and body. Feeling can be specific or nebulous, but feelings always flow, so it is hard to tell where one feeling ends and another begins. Emotions are a subcategory of feeling: they are feeling states that have crystallized and thus have ceased to flow in a continuous process of sensing. When we experience anger, for example, we "know" only one thing: anger. It becomes very difficult to sense or know anything else. The third category, action, contains all forms of doing and volition, all of our behaviors.

To these three we must, however, add a fourth category of consciousness: awareness. Independent of and immanent in the first three categories of consciousness is *that* which, in each of us, is aware. All these functions are inextricably interconnected, but what becomes crucial to the way we ultimately live and act is *how* they are related to each other — what happens when we become identified with our thoughts, actions, or feelings and lose connection with our I-Amness, our root awareness.

In our most integrated and balanced states of consciousness, we are aware of our thoughts, feelings, and behaviors, yet we remain at a certain distance from them. This distance, the ineffable "space" (see chapter 2), allows us to remain poised in the present. We are aware of our thoughts, but we are also more than our thoughts; we are aware of our feelings, but we are also more than our feelings; and we are aware of our behaviors, so that we remain independent of them and can readily change them when necessary. We can regard this as a well-differentiated state of consciousness. We are connected to the present moment and thus grounded in ourselves as conscious beings. We are not completely identified in any specific or limiting concept, quality of feeling, or behavior. When we are well differentiated, we have more room to appreciate both the merits and limitations of many points of view, and thus we are innately more inclusive and tolerant. To be well differentiated is synonymous with having a higher level of consciousness.

Things change, though, the moment the distance collapses between our awareness and any of the other functions. If we become caught up in and ultimately identified with a thought, our awareness identifies with this thought because it is no longer separate or differentiated from it. Then our thinking immediately recruits our emotions. A thought by itself has little power, but a thought supported by anger, fear, trust, or inspiration is powerful indeed. Of course, the instant our thinking is reinforced (and generally intensified) by any emotion, their union automatically recruits and powerfully determines our actions. For example, ideological thinking tends to recruit feelings of righteousness and superiority, as well as negative judgments about those who do not adhere to the same beliefs, and this frequently results in actions that are divisive, as is the case with partisan politics. When we start from a thought but end up amalgamating the four functions of consciousness, we create an identity in which what we *think* becomes the core of who we are.

The same process can just as readily occur if we identify first with our feelings, so that instead of remaining in a state of flowing awareness we are captured by an emotion. Then the emotion — such as feeling shy at a party — will recruit our thinking, and we might tell ourselves a story to rationalize our feeling: "I don't like these people." This emotion-thought amalgam will in turn determine our behavior, and we may decide to leave or act haughty and unapproachable. In this instance what we *feel* becomes the basis of who we are.

Finally, if our awareness becomes identified with repetitive patterns of activity at work or our athletic pursuits, this too will persuade us to tell ourselves stories about who we are and what life is about, which in turn will enlist the emotions that give these stories greater intensity. In this way, what we *do* becomes who we *are*, and once again we give ourselves identities unrelated to the true I-Am. This process of identification is one of Self-forgetting because we forget (or never learn to recognize) our true selves.

As I am using the term here, an *identity* is a constellation of thoughts, feelings, emotions, and behaviors that is so consistent and predictable that we assume this to be who we are. Through this identity, we engage the world, and we interpret and react to what life presents to us. Instead of awareness and presence being the essence of who we are, we lose ourselves into creations of our own minds. We become a slave to our beliefs, our feelings, and our roles, lacking the conscious distance necessary to question their veracity and legitimacy or to consider their consequences.

Once our I-Am — the root of awareness — has been supplanted by a specific identity, we use a lesser awareness, including intellect, strategically, as an instrument for the defense of the needs and goals of this identity. Let us imagine that, for example, we are an adolescent. We glance in the mirror and see recent surgery scars and think, "These are so ugly," and become ashamed of how we look. Our own thinking — a judgment of our body — has recruited and indeed created the emotion of shame. If we cannot face this shame consciously and become anxious about how other people will see us, we might decide to never wear a bathing suit or go to the beach, or we might become timid about having sex. After a while this negative identification with our bodies can become so familiar that we might adapt by centering our lives around intellectual pursuits, and in this way develop an "intellectual" persona that appears successful but has at its root our own self-judgments and unmet feelings of shame.

If I overly identify with my ideas, I might believe that when anyone criticizes these ideas they are discounting or belittling me. In a split second I can feel unseen, perhaps reexperiencing childhood moments when I was poorly mirrored. Then, before I realize it, I am fleeing from the pain of feeling unseen and I begin grandiosely arguing some intellectual issue, maybe even becoming condescending. Without understanding what has happened, I become a victim of my unconscious identification with "my" ideas. Within an instant of having them challenged, I enlist the emotion of insecurity, which I quickly compensate for with grandiosity and verbal deftness. Thus my identity might appear to be exceptionally capable — I might look like a winner — but underlying that idealized image are feelings about myself that I have not met.

Our identities are actually beliefs about ourselves, or ways of defining ourselves through judgments about ourselves, about others, or about "reality" or "truth." We continually repeat these stories so that they either ceaselessly rationalize what we are feeling or evoke emotions that legitimate whatever we are thinking. When we think *me*, we are really referring to whichever identity is dominating our sense of self at that moment, not our true selves.

As long as we are inhabiting an identity, we do not consciously have the capacity to engage each moment afresh. We are capable only of interpreting each moment in terms of whether it supports or threatens our identities. Thoughts and feelings seem to engulf us faster than we can observe them arising within us. Thus we tend to live our lives in a state of nearly perpetual reaction and self-protection. This is what happens to every one of us, everywhere in the world, under every variety of circumstance, as soon as we lose contact with the awareness center of our beings.

The feeling of insufficiency that we carry from early childhood is embedded in the idealized self through which we represent ourselves as confident, independent, heroic, loyal, and so on. The idealized self, in turn, is embedded within the army of lesser identities that arise from our religions, nationalities, roles, and careers. But underlying all levels of identification is the threatening possibility that we ourselves can be exposed as faulty and even unreal, and that we potentially face feelings of nonbeing, the deepest of our fears. This is why so many of us live out our lives engaged in dynamics that produce a more or less perpetual level of familiar struggle and unhappiness. Even though our identities inevitably place us in conflict with others or cause us to withdraw or withhold ourselves, we accept this unhappiness because we cannot imagine who we would be without our familiar suffering, and we are too afraid to risk finding out.

It is important to understand the difference between *identities* and the many *roles* life requires of us. A role is a set of thoughts, understandings, and behaviors necessary to perform a specific function like that of parent or doctor or teacher. We train for roles or have them modeled for us by others, and we learn to emulate them. They are forms of conscious differentiation of mental and behavioral skills appropriate to the nature of the role itself. Roles are intelligent: they permit the highest level of functioning in their particular arena. In contrast, identities are generally not conscious and can inhabit our roles in ways that diminish our effectiveness or outright sabotage us. Identities function to protect the ego from threat, and we slip in and out of various identities according to the situation.

The boundary between roles and identities can easily become

blurred when our role becomes our identity. For example, if we overidentify with making money and with the value of money, we may look at every situation in terms of how it furthers the growth of our own wealth. Virtually all our thinking, actions, and self-esteem become defined by increasing our net worth. As a result, relationships too may have meaning to us only insofar as they strengthen or weaken our ability to make more money. Moreover, a loss of money can be experienced as a devastating loss of self.

If we subjugate the sense of self to our roles as husbands or wives, we become emotionally or psychologically dependent on our spouses and too easily defer to their needs and values. Because our security and identities invariably revolve around addressing our spouses' behaviors and moods, our own authentic selves remain undeveloped. Similarly, when we do not understand that a time comes when we must, as mothers and fathers, step out of the parenting role, we can stifle our own fuller potential as well as the potential of our children.

So is there really a *me*? Of course there is, in one sense. We are each unique. The Richard Moss who is typing at this computer right now does not exist in any other person who has ever existed or ever will exist. But to the extent that my I-Am inhabits a limited identity or subpersonality — that is, is self-important, a teacher, a wise man — *that* Richard can, at best, be considered only partially conscious. Yet our power of awareness always contains the potential for us to enter into an inquiry concerning any of our identities. If *I* can become aware of them, *I* have the capacity, as we all do, to *transcend* them. But this self-transcending aspect, the soul, is not who we are or what we feel or what we do, ever. Literally. If we can give a name to ourselves, or tell ourselves a story about who we are, it can only be a rationalization of our current state or a habitual way of referring to ourselves; it can never be who we really are.

One of the central understandings in the work to reach awareness is: Anything you can verbalize, imagine, or name about yourself is not who you really are. And this means that, if you find yourself telling yourself a story about who you are, it is time to stop and become conscious of what you are doing. Chances are you are trying to avoid something and would be better served by giving it your full attention. This is also true in our relations with others: We tend to limit others by how we think of them. Acknowledging that we may not know who we or others are is crucial to restoring us to a much higher level of functioning, which has to do with more than productivity or efficiency and is about openness, presence, compassion, forgiveness, and love.

OUR FIRST LANGUAGE

When we are children, sensation is our first language, our first universe — the language of our bodies in the Now. Even for adults, in the Now the immediate experience of *me* is sensation and perception. If we can be aware of these sensations without reacting to them, without moving toward or away from them, then we will not identify with the sensations: they will subside and we will remain free in our deeper nature. But the moment we lose our open attention to our sensations and perceptions, we begin to think *at* ourselves: instead of remaining fully present, we may endlessly interpret, analyze, and evaluate what we are experiencing, or we may try to direct our behavior according to how we believe we should be. The reaction to, desire for, or avoidance of any specific sensation — by thinking *at* it — is the root of our sense of *me* and of all our various identities. We could say that the ego-I is not a thing: it is an activity that generates the sense of *me*.

One way to understand identification is as a result of the need to maintain continuity in our thinking and actions in order to sustain and protect a familiar level of sensation we have made the basis of our identities. But even when we assume an identity based on our work, money, parenting, and so on, beneath it still lurks the core identities, the underlying understanding that "I am not sufficient as I am," which has come with us from childhood. No matter which role we may be operating from, this underlying feeling, *if not consciously recognized and allowed without reaction to it*, predisposes us to assume a basic survival mentality, at least to some extent. If we do react to it and try to defend ourselves against it, we will overvalue whatever we have identified with and undervalue everything else to some degree.

THE NEED TO DIFFERENTIATE
OUR CONSCIOUSNESS

What plagues humanity is that, though we all have minds, very few of us understand our own minds. Said in another way, we are poorly differentiated. One consequence of poor differentiation can be seen in our political debate. What is discussed in the media as a polarization of moral or cultural points of view is more accurately the division between individuals who disagree primarily because of their degree of differentiation of consciousness. Well-differentiated people tend to see more points of view and have less need to limit or dismiss those of others; they are inherently more inclusive, more individual, and better able to tolerate moral ambiguity — without being immoral. They are less threatened by not-knowing and more capable of intuiting what feels right, because they have glimpsed more of the mystery of their own depths. Poorly differentiated people are less able to accept differing points of view and must defend their sense of self through strong identification with a group image and consensus values. These individuals are much more likely to feel threatened by any position that approaches un-knowing, and they cannot trust their own deeper instincts be-cause they borrow their identity from outside themselves rather than listening within. This tends to make them highly dog-matic, categorical (especially in their morality), and easily influ-enced by the opinions of those whom they elevate to positions of higher moral or spiritual authority. Their beliefs and values are elevated to unchallengeable "Divine" truths, because in this way they make their identities secure.

To differentiate ourselves is to keep stepping back from any strongly held opinion or self-definition. It is to be able to exer-cise the power of awareness and gradually challenge our own limited, secondary, and less-conscious ways of self-identification. We realize our essential selves precisely because we become aware of and thus *less* identified with who we are *not*. Exercis-ing the power of awareness leads naturally to differentiating who we really are, as aware beings, from what we feel or think or believe. If you can name it, describe it, or even fantasize it, you — as aware beings — are already more than it. In this way we have the power to evolve through ceaseless differentiation.

It is not our I-Am that differentiates. This essential aspect of who we are remains ever the same, ineffable and prior to all forms. What does become more differentiated in us is the ego. The ego is the vehicle of our personal awareness, and it is not destroyed or transcended in order to attain Self-realization, as is so often suggested. This is a common misunderstanding. If the ego were destroyed, we would lose the vehicle for expressing ourselves personally. And if it were transcended, we probably would have skipped past the crucial work of dealing with our survival personalities and their shadows. Rather, as we grow in awareness, our egos become ever more differentiated, accessing our higher functions without grandiosity or inflation, and descending into our shadow areas and slowly elevating these to where they are no longer functioning destructively in our lives.

From a psychological perspective, as we become better differentiated we bring more of our personal unconscious into conscious awareness and become capable of choosing new behaviors that are less defensive or neurotic than those of our survival personalities. We also begin to recognize the influence of the deeper archetypal forces upon us — what Carl Jung has called the shadow, the anima, and the animus — as well as those that can be thought of, in mythological terms, as the gods and goddesses within. Then we can begin to work with these archetypes to increase their positive influence, and diminish their negative influence, in the expression of our humanity. The effect is that as our sense of self begins to reside more and more in *that* which is unchanging, we gain a broader perspective and have less attachment to how we express our beliefs and respond to our feelings. This invites us to be our most effective, spontaneous, authentic, and humble selves.

A good example of a well-differentiated person is the current Dalai Lama, the fourteenth in his lineage. He is the spiritual leader of Tibetan Buddhists, and in this context he is worshipped as a living Buddha by millions of people. He is a fine teacher of Buddhist philosophy, yet I have never heard him advocate his religion over any other. Instead he actively works to bring the fruits of the long and rich tradition of Buddhist meditation practices — freed from their ritual and orthodoxy — to Western psychologists and neuroscientists to help support a renaissance of consciousness, especially in the West. He is a successful author and a humanitarian involved with many projects. As the exiled leader of Tibet, he is a renowned political figure who frequently confers with world leaders. Yet he knows himself to be a simple monk. He can be self-effacing, and he radiates good humor. I believe his ability to move so gracefully between his different roles and remain healthy and good-natured depends on knowing himself to be none of them, even while inhabiting each of them as completely as the occasion requires.

Poorly differentiated persons cannot do this. Sooner or later they identify with the power, the self-importance, or the burden and become victims of that self-delusion.

Most of us are frightened at the idea of assuming our true destinies as conscious beings, of being our own contexts and living from the inside out. It can be daunting to realize that we are each here to pioneer a new possibility, to let our souls sing forth their own unique life songs, and not to simply become what family or culture tells us we should be. When we grasp this purpose, we realize that there is no final identity for a human being, no place to lay our heads and to rest, as Jesus says in the Gospel according to Thomas. No matter what level of understanding we reach, we can turn our attention toward ourselves and open the door of awareness to further understanding. Our potential to keep differentiating ourselves is unlimited.

When we look at progress — for example, in the area of human rights — we see the evolutionary force of differentiation in action. Gradually we human beings are grasping the fact that race and gender are not immutable forms of division between us. Yet still, too many of us, out of our own unmet feelings of insecurity, tend to assume that those who are in some way different are dangerous to us. Until we face our own inner fears, we want our laws and other external constraints to protect us from change. We fail to see that even our deepest fears are just sensations to be met with tender attention, and that our most sacrosanct beliefs must be further examined when they lead us to categorize others in ways that generate fear and distrust.

When our thinking, our belief systems, or our feelings have captured us, genuine relationship between people is very difficult. Identities may be intrigued or infatuated with each other for a little while, but identities cannot love. Only when essence meets essence can love thrive. One of the most destructive forces in human affairs emerges when we become so identified with our own beliefs that they become absolutes. Arguments about who has the "real" truth have torn the world apart for millennia and are never resolved. In my observation, individuals who believe that literal truth can be found in the Bible, the Koran, and other sacred scriptures are also the ones who are poorly differentiated and least likely to be self-reflective. In believing in the literal truth of anything, we are not really interested in knowing truth; what we are doing is defending our own identities. So much misery has been perpetrated by people who believe they know God's will or what is best for others, when in fact they are afraid to know themselves beyond the proscriptions about themselves and life that they impute to God.

My pointing to the need to differentiate our essential consciousness from what we identify with through thought is not a blanket indictment of thinking. Thinking is one function of our consciousness; the capacity for consciousness makes thinking possible in the first place. Thinking is an essential and distinguishing aspect of what it means to be human. This very book is an exercise in thought: I am using a progression of thoughts to elucidate a path to a more complete understanding of our humanity. Through thinking we have the ability to enter into subtle relationships with our worlds and with our own minds, and through these relationships we come to appreciate ourselves more fully. The problem, however, is that we become overly identified with the various selves we construct from our thoughts, sensations, and actions. Rather than discovering ourselves more fully as we flow from one temporary identity to the next, we become crystallized in our identities and are soon slaves to them.

Instead of using our thinking as a means to appreciate the wholeness and interconnectedness of all things, we use it to protect a false or limited self. In this fear-based psychology, thought is primarily an instrument for survival rather than a vehicle for intimacy with existence.

Intimacy is the experience of being brought close, whether to a flower or a lover. In this rich connectedness we know this other, and ourselves, in ever more complete and fulfilling ways. Thought depends on using words to identify things, and the process of naming which makes something conscious also creates psychological distance from whatever has been named. I had this experience to an almost overwhelming degree while studying medicine. The information I needed to learn gave me a profound glimpse into the subtlety and wonder of the living body, but the mechanistic application of this information tended to obscure the miracle of the body's innate wholeness that persisted despite degeneration or disease. Ironically, the very reductionist nature of survival-based thinking actually traps us in a profound unconsciousness, though we imagine ourselves to be highly conscious, especially if our intellects are well developed.

Overidentification is a bane to human relationships, but some degree of self-identification is unavoidable and even necessary from a functional and developmental standpoint. Each identity becomes a position, a stance in life, through which we learn the consequences of that identity as we relate to others and to our worlds. The successes and failures of our relationships — the suffering or love they create — reflect both the value and the limitations of how we have identified ourselves.

As we advance through life, we try on identities like clothing. I once listened to author Neale Donald Walsch give a humorous talk about stages of identification. As a teenager, he said, "I was my hair," and then a few years later, "I was my car," and a few years after that, "I was my women," he drolly admitted. This is what happens to all of us in our own way, and while none of these stages of self-identification reveal who we truly are as aware beings, we learn a lot about ourselves from each stage once we grow beyond it.

Realizing that virtually all forms of self-identification are a kind of ignorance does not mean that we should, or even can, avoid engaging them at the stage of life when they tend to hold sway. To reject, refuse to fully embody, or try to transcend more ordinary levels of life in our spiritual quest is itself another form of identification and does not ensure a more complete expression of our essence or our humanity. That said, we should remain cognizant that people are capable of comprehending their lives only in accordance with their depth of self-knowledge.

I believe that, at different stages of our souls' process of awakening, we wisely choose a particular religious, philosophical, or political orientation, or a role that we fully embody, or work that we invest ourselves in, that is appropriate and useful for helping us differentiate ourselves more completely. For instance, choosing to become Buddhist — or rather, becoming identified with Buddhist culture and philosophy — can help some of us to discover ourselves more effectively than we would if we stayed exclusively with our religion of origin. Similarly, practicing law for a few years could be exactly what prepares some of us to choose to become schoolteachers, a career that can provide a means to give life to a new part of ourselves.

I doubt that any of us could learn to be our own context and create our lives from essence outward until we have discovered ourselves against many other more external contexts. Consciousness thrives on contrast. Thus as we evolve, we seem to need to periodically generate a new sense of ourselves through association with a different religious tradition or political affiliation, or career, or social activity, which becomes a new foundation for our evolution. But our essence is always more than these, and we begin to intuit that underneath all these possible identities is, like a snake shedding its old skin, something else that is all and none of them. We learn to differentiate: in becoming for a while who we are *not*, we may begin to realize who we *are*. To become a spiritually mature human beings, eventually we have to stop imagining who we are and borrowing our language, metaphors, emotional orientation, and social demeanor from outside ourselves. As if we are learning to ride our own bicycles, we must remove the training wheels and see if we can find our balance as psychologically and spiritually self-determining individuals who need not borrow identity and authority from *anything* external to our own I-Am. As an old Sufi adage says, "We are in the world, but not of it." Then we can choose any wardrobe of identity, but we possess something and transmit something that is greater than any of them.

THE DISTANCE FROM ANOTHER IS THE DISTANCE FROM OURSELVES

Once we have touched something of our own essence and deepened our sense of self, we are less likely to be threatened by other people, because our own sense of identity rests on something substantial within us. The challenge to find common ground between people does not require that we always agree with each other's ideas; rather it requires a deeper appreciation of ourselves. To be wisely human means we must strive to outgrow any of our positions or stances — really trances — when identification with them stops us from being able to meet each other in the nakedness of the present.

Deriving our identities from anything that is not our essence as aware beings leads to the illusion of immutable separateness and begets distrust that becomes the foundation of the culture of competition and survival. Yet if we finally ask why we cannot find common ground with another, we will eventually see that the only actual distance between people is the distance each of us stands from our essential selves. You are as far from me, and I from you, as each of us is from our I-Am. This self-created and self-perpetuated distance is not caused by the other, but by our being caught in our own identity and in exile from our true selves. The only way to remedy this is to return our attention to the Now and to exercise the power of awareness. In such a moment we have the ability to step out of old patterns and choose to act in a different way that renews the possibility of mutual respect, cooperation, and even love that always awaits us. This love that is innate to who we are in our I-Amness is the deeper potential that can always unite us, even when our religions, nationalities, races, or genders seem to perpetually divide us.

LEARNING TO INTERRUPT
THE PROCESS OF IDENTIFICATION

We can begin to educate ourselves to interrupt the process of identification by learning to focus on our felt sense of awareness. By *felt sense* I mean the way that our bodies register how we are in our ourselves right now. Our bodies are always in the present, so when we sense what we are experiencing in our bodies, we anchor our attention in the present. The felt sense is not necessarily a specific feeling or emotion that we can readily identify. It is more a gestalt of our sense of being that tends to rest close to the domain of sensation. Being attuned to our felt sense creates an intimacy with ourselves that does not entail thinking *at* ourselves, explaining, interpreting, or analyzing what we are sensing. It is a form of inner listening in which we let our minds sink into our bodies rather than continue to let our awareness be deflected away from the Now through thinking.

The first step toward inner listening, and one of the best ways to shift to maintaining open and present awareness, is to connect our awareness to our breathing. I call this creating the "friendship" of breath awareness. Our breathing has been a friend that has accompanied us through every moment of life; it has never deserted us no matter how terrible we have felt. Friendship in itself connotes a quality of feeling that has elements of warmth, trust, and welcome. Our hearts always relax when we greet a friend. To add this felt sense of friendship to the awareness of breathing invites a quality of attention that carries a positive feeling. We all live in the Now and we all breathe. Why not let our breath awareness join us to the present with a feeling of belonging and trust? This by itself releases us from so much of our reflexive self-protection and restores us to a simple state of openness.

Our beings are always registering enormous amounts of information, both from within us and outside us, a lot of which must be filtered out or they would overwhelm our conscious selves. How much we filter depends largely on where our attention is focused and, most important, how we are identified in our selves. We might filter out the sound of the wind and the color and fragrance of flowers when we are angry or jealous. We might also filter out memories of being loved and feeling happy because they are incompatible with such an emotional contraction. This filtering and skewing of our perception and memory is essential to sustaining any process of identification. But it is hard to remain captured in a victim identity, or in jealousy or anger, if we are simultaneously able to appreciate the sound and caress of a refreshing breeze or feel the gentle rise and fall of our own breathing. To return to our breathing is to bring our attention back to the present.

Restoring ourselves to a more open field of attention, one that filters out fewer immediate perceptions, automatically weakens the power of any identity. All movement of our minds away from the present narrows our awareness and ultimately limits our intelligence. Whatever brings us back to the present enhances our awareness and restores us to a more holistic or heartful intelligence. Narrowing our awareness amounts to living in our heads and not in our bodies, not in our whole beings. While it is necessary to be able to focus the conscious mind and intentionally become absorbed in a specific project, such as writing or painting, the moment this specific concentration of our attention is relaxed we can return to a fuller awareness. But if our minds are perennially identified with, say, our work, then no matter what we are doing we will continue to unconsciously limit all our perceptions and the ways we respond to our experience. Thus we are never really present.

STREAM-OF-CONSCIOUSNESS WRITING:
AN EXERCISE IN STAYING IN THE PRESENT

A powerful way to learn to interrupt the process of unconscious identification is a particular exercise of stream-of-consciousness writing. You simply sit down with a pen and paper and begin to write, as immediately as you can, whatever you are sensing in the present moment. Try to stay closely and constantly connected to the stream of sensations in the body and to the perceptions arriving through the senses. For instance, right now I am aware of my fingers on the keyboard, the heaviness of my feet, the waterfall noise outside, my dry lips, and so on. In writing your observations, you can abbreviate whatever you perceive so that you can write fast and remain as close to the present as possible in your reporting. If I were doing the exercise myself, then instead of what I have written above, I would simply write: "fingers, water, lips." Since sensation and sense perception are always in the present, you can restore your present-moment awareness by returning to these streams of consciousness.

Write whatever feelings you may notice. Record being tired, irritated, sad, and so on, but don't dwell on any particular one. If you can't quite name the feeling, simply write *F* (an abbreviation for *feeling*), then return to the immediate present and capture the current streams of sensation and perception in words jotted down as fast as possible. While feelings come and go, the streams of sensation and perception are perpetual, therefore there is never any lack of things to report.

The last and most important guideline is this: Make a very strong effort *not to follow* any thought. The moment you realize you are thinking, simply write down the letter *T* (for *thinking*) and return once again to the immediate present and the streams of sensation and perception.

One of the most valuable things we can learn is to be able to voluntarily interrupt sequential thought and especially to be able to simply stop the inner dialogue at least briefly. The process of identification rests on our tendency to continually identify ourselves with various stories; these stories are always constructed by our thinking. The moment we collapse our awareness into these stories, we recruit various emotions. Then, before we know it, we are lost in these stories and they become the basis of our sense of identity. Whatever identity we construct or otherwise inhabit then continues to influence how we are feeling, which in turn engenders more thinking, and this can spiral on ceaselessly. Since we can never actually "think the present," whenever we are truly present our minds are inherently silent. Learning to interrupt thinking is a prerequisite to creating a felt sense of being in the Now.

I recommend that you try stream-of-consciousness writing for fifteen minutes initially, and then relax and sit quietly for a while or go for a slow walk. Eventually, you might want to explore it for longer periods. It will help you strengthen the power of your attention so that you become aware much sooner whenever you have collapsed into your thinking or emotions. Since it holds your attention as close to the present as possible, you can also use it to help free yourself from any emotional state.

DIFFERENTIATING "THIS ISN'T IT": THE UBIQUITOUS DISSATISFACTION

As our capacity for self-awareness deepens, we may begin to observe a subtle, almost omnipresent sense of stress. We may notice that our minds keep moving restlessly from one thought to another, that we often feel somewhat pressured or hurried or a little tense without any apparent reason. We have all felt at times an obnoxious or extreme sense of agitation, but what I am describing here is a much more insidious and subtle felt sense, and unless we are quietly attuned, we may not be receptive enough to notice it.

If while gazing out over the ocean you have suddenly noticed a group of small fish leaping out of the water into the air and scattering in all directions, it is clear — even though you don't see what has excited them — that they are trying to escape something, likely a predator. Often the agitations of our restless mind and more recurrent emotions are like little fish surfacing into our consciousness because there is a dangerous "predator" just below the surface of our awareness.

If we allow our minds to become still and to sink down into its depths, we may begin to get a glimpse of this predator. Because all of us have internalized and buried feelings of insufficiency, we are subconsciously always teetering at the edge of some kind of survival anxiety. One of the most inchoate feelings, although we are loath to admit it, is a vague yet pervasive disturbance that we might describe as "I'm not good enough." If we don't realize that this feeling begins in our sense of self, it tends to be continually projected outward — attributed to someone, something, or some lack in our external lives. Then we tell ourselves, "This lover isn't the right one," "This job isn't good enough," or "This house doesn't feel right." In short: "This isn't *it*."

Most of us, if we look carefully, will see that we are haunted by a perpetual sense of dissatisfaction, a subtle, unfocused state that invests us with restless urgency and tension. It generates a tendency to be increasingly vigilant and driven, and we attribute the feeling to something external, rather than recognizing that it is generated from within us. Until we can turn our nonreactive attention directly toward this feeling and be softly present with it, we continue to identify with the sense that "this isn't *it*."

Then, of course, we begin to seek whatever we imagine will be better, the ultimate "this *is it*." We enter into an addictive cycle of dissatisfaction, perpetually seeking satisfaction. Even when we believe "this is *it*," when we have fulfilled a desire, like finally buying the car we have always longed for, or meeting someone we think is Mr. or Ms. Right, the underlying predator of dissatisfaction persists, because it emanates from our own unconscious feeling of insufficiency. Therefore, the cycle repeats itself anew.

There is also within each of us what we might call an evolutionary or transformational impulse, a kind of dissatisfaction that is the soul's innate yearning to know itself more completely. This yearning is our intuition that greater wholeness is possible, prodding us along on our journey of awakening. But an addictive cycle of dissatisfaction that chooses only temporary remedies is a destructive form of unconsciousness. Until we can begin to isolate the specific addictive sense of "this isn't *it*" within us and become capable of allowing it without reacting to it, we remain victims of this cycle.

THE ESSENCE OF WISDOM

We have seen that, when our sense of self inhabits our identities, we inevitably narrow our fields of awareness. When this narrowing is conscious and intentional, it concentrates our mental, emotional, and behavioral forces in service of a specific task. But when we finish with that activity, we must be able to fluidly return to a much more open state of awareness and rest more fully into the present.

Intelligence is not a fixed attribute in a human being; it is a potential constantly in flux that depends on how closely we are to living to the present. When we are present, our intelligence tends to be holistic, related more to our hearts than our heads. Because in the present we are closer to our essential being, we are also closer to the world we perceive. This gives us an inherent sense of connection and belonging, of the interrelatedness of all things. Even in the midst of apparently conflicting aspects of life, we can appreciate the intrinsic harmony that pervades all of existence. Finding harmony in the midst of life situations that seemingly conflict is the essence of intelligence. It can also be called wisdom.

Wisdom is distinct from intellect. Intellect is specific to the particular *me* with which we identify, and to the particular focus of activity to which that *me* is primarily dedicated. We can have exceptional intellect yet still be unable to intuit wholeness. With such intelligence, we are capable of being present only to a limited extent; we still perceive the present solely through the lens of our specific agenda.

COLLECTIVE FIELDS OF AWARENESS INFLUENCE OUR IDENTITIES

The concentration of the mind on a specific arena of activity, or a dominant attitude, creates an awareness field. An awareness field can be thought of as a presence that subconsciously influences our consciousness. It is a field of information generated by a specific and repeated activity or conscious focus that then begins to operate autonomously to both support and regenerate that activity or focus. At the individual level, when a man has collapsed into anger he begins to generate a field of awareness that causes him to perceive the world itself as angry. Unless he consciously interrupts the energy of the anger, he will continue to create ways to sustain it, rationalize it, defend it, and express it. But awareness fields are not limited to individuals; the fields become stronger as more people are caught up in them. (See appendix 1 for a short discussion of the evidence supporting the hypothesis that these awareness fields become autonomous once they are constituted.)

If you are not deeply centered in your true self, these collective energy fields can overwhelm personal consciousness in potentially positive or negative ways. On the postive side, a group of people in meditation deepen an awareness field of stillness and peace and maintain their individuality. A negative collective awareness field, for example, was generated by Hitler's exhorting of the masses at the Nuremberg rallies and happens in religions where people subscribe to collectively held dogmatic beliefs and lose their ability to reason individually.

Any form of focused collective activity will generate an awareness field, whether in sports, business, a church group, or the military. When we enter this field, it begins to exert an autonomous influence over us. If we are not firmly rooted in our true selves, we may easily succumb to a form of group mind. When this happens, the essential creative process does not emerge from each person as an individual. Instead the group awareness field becomes the dominant creative force, and it induces members of the group to fulfill its nature. Before we know it, sustaining that field can become the basis of our identities.

I believe we are always — generally unknowingly — being captured by collective awareness fields, so that much of what we do in life is only partially conscious. When any one of us enters any kind of organization or institution, very quickly our consciousness begins to express the group mind that underlies and sustains that entity. Whether we've become part of Microsoft or the Marine Corps, from that point onward we will derive our identity from the overall consciousness of that field of activity, including our values and what we deem to be most intelligent. In this way the field of the group mind is sustained and regenerated. Some of these arenas of activity may enlist the best and the brightest, but once we begin to function inside the group mind we perceive and interpret all information within the awareness field in ways obedient to that field. We become, to varying degrees, herd creatures. As individuals we become blinded, because how we invest our energy, how we choose to live, how much time we spend at work — virtually everything we are aware of — is processed through the specific awareness field.

We think we are operating as a conscious individual, but our consciousness is co-opted. Unbeknownst to us, it narrows our ability to direct ourselves. It is as if we have been paddling along a river in our own canoes, unaware of a powerful current carrying us wherever it wants to take us.

Because we are already captured in these collective awareness fields without knowing it, it is very hard to differentiate ourselves from them, to see their relativity. They become part of our identities, our truths. When we achieve success within such an institution or system, our very sense of survival can depend on maintaining a relationship to it. To wake up to our souls' deeper potential inevitably puts us in conflict with the consciousness fostered by these awareness fields and stirs up our survival fears. It takes immense courage to trust the call of our deeper beings and, if need be, choose a new life path that supports a more complete understanding of our humanity.

The problem of identification rests with the psychological foundation upon which so much of our engagement with the world is undertaken. In every area of life, we see that there are so many layers of self-identification, which are like the layers of an onion. But if at the core there lies a feeling that we are, to some degree, not good enough, then every new layer wrapped around this core is inevitably distorted by it.

This is our predicament: We are conscious beings, yet unless we start from our essence and exercise the power of awareness to resolve our deepest fears, then with each successive layer of self-identification we become further imprisoned in a restricted sense of self. This inevitably perpetuates our suffering and the suffering of others. Clearly we must learn how to claim ourselves from deep inside. The Now is our source that forever enlivens us independent of any identity. When we realize this and learn to become more present in the Now, we spontaneously begin to express our own wholeness and emanate a presence in which everyone has greater freedom from fear.

CHAPTER FIVE

Tamed *and* Untamed Emotions

We are enlightened only to the degree that we are able to fully experience, and not become identified with and captured by, our emotions. The great challenge to letting our consciousness evolve is facing our terrifying feelings and difficult emotions, like shame and despair. On any given day, we might imagine ourselves as truly progressing on the path of enlightenment, and yet, as soon as we feel threatened in some way, we may discover just how easily we can lose our center and become defensive, reactive, or aggressive.

We evolve in consciousness by turning toward our immediate experience and learning to be present yet nonreactive. However, not all emotions offer the same challenge or the same degree of transformative potential. Some of them I think of as "tamed," and others as "untamed." A tamed emotion is one that does not disrupt the continuity in our ego-I (me-consciousness). Who is angry? *I* am. Who is jealous? *I* am. Who is happy? *I* am.

Who is going to get even? *Me.* When we are captured by anger, emotional injury, anxiety, or jealousy, the only thing actually threatened is our self-image: the way we want to feel, would like to be seen, or prefer to imagine ourselves. Our basic sense of identity — *me* — remains unchallenged and intact. Almost any emotion that we can readily identify or name tends to fall into the category of "tamed." With a tamed emotion, we readily recognize what we are feeling and usually believe that we know why we are feeling it.

An untamed emotion so embeds us in the feeling that we cannot readily separate ourselves from it, even to name exactly what we are feeling. We can have a sense of drowning, of dissolution, and of devastation. It is like an abyss, a black hole that seems to suck us into oblivion. We may use words such as *dread, unnameable terror, annihilation,* and *suffocation* to describe what we feel. We may panic, thinking that we are losing our minds, are possessed, or are dying of some hideous force we cannot understand. In the depths of the untamed emotions, we are caught in the darkest of dark feeling states. The untamed emotions amalgamate time and identity, creating a sense that they will go on forever, that this is all of who we are. Everything collapses into this kind of feeling state so that all other ways of knowing ourselves become submerged.

We might imagine that most people, when faced with these annihilating feelings, would go into shock and shut down or fall into panic. But very few of us ever reach shock or panic. Instead, at the first sign of an untamed emotion, we activate our survival personalities and divert ourselves into a tamed emotion, like anger or anxiety, and assume the identity that it simultaneously generates. It is far easier — and from the ego's point of view, far safer — to feel anger or hate, hurt or guilt, hope or fear, than nonbeing.

It may seem incredible that anger and hate are "tamed," given how destructive these emotions can be. But in distinguishing between tamed and untamed, we are not gauging the suffering we may experience or cause with these emotions. All tamed emotions can be destructive when we identify our sense of self with them and, in so doing, submerge our power of awareness. Then we may act in violent ways that harm ourselves and others. But we are still not in danger of losing our sense of self. In fact, this way of being is the essence of our survival personalities: we accept a bearable level of ongoing suffering if that is what it takes to protect our identity and maintain our sense of self. But it is not actually a question of acceptance, because this implies a degree of conscious choice. It is an unconscious adaptation developed early in our lives, a way of creating a persistent familiar emotional environment. To *not* feel these emotions is far more disturbing.

I believe that the tamed emotions are almost invariably the ego's survival adaptations, and that they stem from avoiding, at all costs, the untamed emotional states that threaten the ego's integrity. This suggests that some of the untamed emotions originate in, or at least mimic, early childhood threats to our emerging and still mostly undifferentiated sense of self.

When we are adults, these untamed emotions are often triggered by a disruption of a primary relationship, such as a divorce, indicating their similarity to the kind of terror we might feel if we were abandoned or treated violently as young children and experienced the perceived loss of bonding with our mothers. If our primary caregivers severely mistreat us when we are very young, the thread of innate faith that connects us to ourselves and the world is easily torn. When this occurs in very young children, they don't experience themselves as being *in* pain; rather, all of reality will *be* pain. Young children protect themselves by withdrawing from this pain (and thus from reality itself) in any way they can, usually through unconscious defense mechanisms like repression and dissociation. Older children in such circumstances often create fantasy worlds into which they can withdraw. But later in life, situations that represent a similar kind of threat have the potential to rekindle these buried feelings and can throw us into total emotional pain and chaos in which we experience a loss of self: the ego's primal fear of nonbeing. If our survival personality cannot protect us by helping us present a positive demeanor, its next strategy will be to immerse us in the familiar morass of tamed emotions — anger, rage, grandiosity, depression, or guilt — and their accompanying behaviors: withholding, being the victim, blaming, or engaging in numbing busyness. If this doesn't work to maintain our sense of self, then there is only the raw untamed pain, which will rule us until we can gather enough power in our awareness to turn toward it. Once we do, we set ourselves free.

The second potential cause for the activation of untamed feelings is inherent in the process of self-transcendence, in the evolutionary potential of human consciousness itself. Me-consciousness is the basic or ground level of consciousness presently attained by the vast majority of people, and the spectrum of how it is lived is very broad. It can extend from crude self-interest and total identification in the most primitive self-protective social dynamics, such as aggressive ambition, racism, or religious fundamentalism, to rich creative expression, principled living, and self-discipline that is truly admirable. But there are higher levels, variously described as cosmic consciousness, universal consciousness, Christ consciousness, satori, and Self-realization. Historical figures who may have attained this higher consciousness are spiritual icons such as Buddha, Krishna, Socrates, Jesus, Mary Magdalene, and Muhammad.[1]

The evolutionary process that brings about this level of trans-formation is not as rare as we might imagine. Almost everyone has brief moments of brushing the edges of this higher poten-tial. These are moments of profound peace, of feeling asolutely safe, held, and connected to existence, moments of clarity of mind and understanding that transcend anything we have known before. Usually these peak events are brief and only minimally integrated into our usual way of living; they are not fundamen-tally transformative. But to whatever degree we glimpse such states of wholeness, our basic orientation toward the god of fear becomes weakened and we turn, however incrementally, toward the god of love and the beginning of a new potential for con-scious relationship.

More rare, but affecting more and more people all the time, are events that are profoundly transformative: deep realizations of new levels of consciousness and states of fundamental whole-ness. This evolutionary movement is a real force in our world today, though poorly understood and not acknowledged by mainstream culture. But as exalted as Self-realization or Christ consciousness can sound, it is actually no picnic to make this evolutionary shift. In the movement from me-consciousness to higher levels of consciousness, we glimpse the vastness of the psyche, which in spiritual terminology is typically referred to as the Divine, and in Jungian psychological parlance as the collec-tive unconscious. As long as our minds are in a unitive state — deeply rooted in the Now — such openings, or realizations, are profoundly enlightening and evolutionary. But the moment we return to ego-level awareness, where we generally live and where we can now contemplate our "experience" and speak about it, the ego can become overwhelmed by the energy and content now available to it. Just as with the reactivation of buried childhood psychological trauma — although for a very different reason — we may experience at the level of our me-consciousness the sudden feeling that we're about to be annihilated: the untamed emotions once again.

Experiencing fundamental evolutionary transformation can be profoundly threatening to our basic sense of self. We can readily illustrate this process through the simple analogy of a sugar cube dropped into a glass of water. In this metaphor the sugar cube is our me-consciousness and the water is pure consciousness itself: the Self, or our Divine nature. Imagine that when first immersed, the sugar cube, not appreciating the nature of what is about to occur, relaxes into this new environment. It experiences itself participating in a new reality that may seem glorious. Just as we tend to think of ourselves as beginning and ending at the boundaries of our skin, and therefore we thoroughly identify with our bodies, the sugar cube is also identified with its form — its edges and sharp corners and the sense of its own solidity. Dropped into cold water, Mr. Sugar Cube will undergo a transformation so gradual that he may be able to integrate it without trauma, though also with little consciousness of the change that is happening. But if he finds himself in hot water instead — that is, where the evolutionary impulse toward self-transcendence accelerates — he can suddenly become overwhelmed and terrified as his edges begin to soften and blunt, his sense of solidity crumbles, and he melts completely. What started as a great expansion becomes an equally great disruption of his identity. His former identity as Mr. Sugar Cube, which constitutes his familiar referent for self-existence, can no longer isolate him from a much vaster level of awareness, and his me-consciousness interprets this dissolution and simultaneous expansion as annihilation or loss of self. He is becoming *one with*, immanent in, the water — a larger sphere of being — but can no longer "locate" the self he has known himself to be.

Something similar can happen to us. Despite the fact that what we experience is a soul-driven evolutionary movement of consciousness, and it rarely occurs until we are, in a deeper sense, ready, we still begin at a stage wherein ego-identification dominates us. Even if we were brought up in a loving household, not mistreated, and our essence was generally well-mirrored — and thus we have a genuinely healthy core of self — we nonetheless have an unconscious identification with our bodies, with a familiar range of sensations, and with our basic sense of being a separate self. Suddenly that self is thrown into a process of spiritual emergence and is threatened, because initially there is no way for us to know what is happening, just as there is no way for Mr. Sugar Cube to know, at first, that soon his separate self will actually *merge* — become one with — all the water: a new, expanded state of consciousness.

Generally, the process of spiritual opening is initially profoundly uplifting and expansive. But soon afterward the shadow (in Jungian nomenclature) arises. This is the disowned sensations and the states of being that are buried in the unconscious, the dark, unloved (and in our collective consciousness as yet unmet) images of ourselves that are terrifying to behold. To the extent that our me-consciousness becomes inflated and identified with the positive sense of "enlightenment," the descent into darkness is all the worse. If we could accept this dark passageway in the same way that we received the expansive phase, and not resist it, we would complete the integration of the new consciousness and awaken to a new level of freedom and potential as conscious individuals. But most often, after the grandeur of the initial expansion, comes the experience of untamed sensation and emotion, the overwhelming feeling of melting into oblivion, into nonbeing. We get the sense that "I am losing my mind" or "I am going to die" or "I am being attacked by demons," and this is where the real work of integration has to be done.

The untamed emotions — whether implanted in response to poor early nurturing or arising because we are in a process of spiritual emergence — stand at the threshold of our wholeness. They are the Now we don't know how to meet, don't know how to accept and surrender to. The untamed emotions are the Now we are continually, unconsciously trying to avoid. When we can turn toward these feelings and learn to hold them in the present without reacting by protecting ourselves against them, when we can stop refusing these feelings because of our own negative labeling and beliefs about them, we will have obtained our freedom. No longer will we be the followers of the god of fear. The untamed emotions are like guardians at the gateway, the ultimate fears that we must face in order to begin to develop a strong sense of self. And when we have claimed that stronger sense of self, they become the guardians at the gate of self-transcendence, the awakening into a higher level of ourselves.

As adults, when something first triggers a threat to our sense of self, we go into a self-preserving mode of inferior or lower functioning. We leap away from the Now, where these feelings are most intense, and duck into our survival personalities and behaviors. These are marked by the tamed emotions and lived out in endless repetitions of the same basic identities, rather than lived in our essence as conscious beings. Alternatively, we construct elaborate occult or spiritualistic belief systems and "exorcise" these purportedly evil forces. While this can help us control disturbing feelings, it does not set us free or advance our consciousness, because we have not faced the darkness and found a greater wholeness. What we do not face, we project onto the world.

The untamed feelings in our personal unconscious and in the collective unconscious are at the root of the perpetual sense of insufficiency and insecurity that drives our unrelenting quest for survival, long after our basic survival needs have been assured and far exceeded. This perpetual shrinking away from the feelings that threaten our sense of self stops the moment we take a stand to face these fears with our full attention in the Now. It is always Now where the ultimate battle is fought, just as it is always Now where the fullest revelation of love is bestowed.

CHAPTER SIX

The Four Holding Environments

In the course of our lives, all of us are subjected to a progression of influential physical, psychological, social, and cultural contexts within which we develop and continually re-create our interior sense of who we are. Having some understanding of this process gives us a greater appreciation for the suffering we all experience and makes our fears and self-concerns a little less personal.

D. W. Winnicott, a British pediatrician and psychoanalyst, asserted that what we call a *human being* emerges out of an interpersonal context.[1] In other words, a baby doesn't exist in isolation but arises from a matrix of protective care beginning in the womb and extending to the nurturance it receives from its mother. From there it develops a relationship with the world at large. How the baby is cared for determines the internal environment conditioned within that baby: its sense of self. If the care is poor, the individual may never actually achieve a sustaining sense of self and thus even in adulthood will always be searching for itself as a reflection of others and through external circumstances in general. If the care is good, the individual's sense of self will be predicated less on externals and more on what lies within, which gives the individual a greater capacity for authenticity and autonomy.

In separating the developmental progression of our lives into four distinct "holding environments" — a concept that comes from the work of Dr. Winnicott — I am synthesizing what is really a vast terrain in the story of the human soul. The progression I outline here is designed to explain the psychological and ontological stages we go through, by which we develop and sustain our sense of self. Perhaps with this understanding, if we can bring ourselves more fully into the Now, we will progressively — or even, as it is said in Isaiah, "in a moment, in the twinkling of an eye" — outgrow, and no longer be so determined by, our early psychological and cultural conditioning.

THE FIRST HOLDING ENVIRONMENT

The first of these environments is the womb. From the moment of conception to the implantation of the developing embryo in the wall of the uterus, and continuing throughout the nine-month journey to birth, a profound cocreative process occurs between mother and fetus. Although we cannot say that the fetus is consciously participating in this collaboration, the genetically guided development of each fetus is now understood to be mutable, responding in complex ways to the biological, chemical, emotional, and behavioral environment provided by its mother.

It is common knowledge that during pregnancy a mother's illness, nutritional deficiency, or injury can have a deleterious effect on her baby, and there has also been conjecture that her mental state can affect the developing fetus. Now we have evidence that the mother's emotional state does play a powerful part in the fetus's neurological development. According to research reported by author Joseph Chilton Pearce, women who feel anxious and unsafe during pregnancy tend to give birth to larger babies, in which the most primitive, so-called reptilian, brain is more fully developed, while the brain newest in evolutionary terms, the prefrontal lobes, is less developed. Women who feel loved, secure, and happy while pregnant tend to give birth to somewhat smaller babies in which the reptilian brain is not overly developed, and in which the prefrontal lobes are more mature.[2]

The reptilian brain is intricately involved with survival. It regulates heartbeat, digestion, and other basic life functions. It is implicated in the speed of our reflexes, basic mating drive, and territorial defense, and it does not support any form of rational thinking or any emotion except fear. The prefrontal lobes are implicated in a variety of "higher" cognitive functions, such as language, abstract reasoning, critical self-reflection, problem solving, planning, social interactions, and moral understanding.[3] In other words, the prefrontal lobes allow us to express the self-transcending nature of the soul.

Pearce concludes that when pregnancy is overshadowed by fear, the developing fetus tends to adapt and emerges predisposed to being a warrior survivor. When the first holding environment is predominantly one of love, nature tends to create babies better prepared for self-transcendence. These infants, at least neurologically, will tend to grow up to be more capable of emotional and spiritual intelligence.[4]

It is important to understand that even as early as the womb, our emotional reality is influenced in significant ways, predisposing us to a life in which fear will play a greater or lesser role. (For additional discussion of developmental dynamics that occur in the womb, see appendix 2.) The earlier the inclination to be fearful is imprinted, the more difficult it is generally to change the person's survival psychology. But on the positive side, the human nervous system constantly evolves throughout life. It can, in a sense, be rewired. Therefore even the neural pathways laid down in the womb that incline us toward survival or transcendence can be reversed or augmented, both positively and negatively, later in life.

THE SECOND HOLDING ENVIRONMENT

This environment begins after birth and is shaped primarily by the quality of nurturance provided by our parents and other caregivers, as well as by forces applied by the total cultural milieu that influence how we are raised. The first five to six years are the most crucial, because during this time we internalize a sustaining sense of self. But this holding environment exists throughout our lives. Events such as disease, accidents, war, and changes of fortune have a strong impact on our sense of self, as do new beliefs, images, values, and worldviews that we continually encounter.

Unlike other mammals, human babies are born neurologically incomplete. (By one year of age, our brains nearly triple in weight. If birth were to be delayed much beyond nine months, the baby's head would be too large for either mother or baby to survive the birthing process.) In the first days, weeks, and months after birth, the care our mothers give us is therefore essential not only for our survival but also for our continued neurological and emotional development. And as was the case in the womb, brain growth is not just a matter of genetic patterning and physiological unfolding but is directly influenced by one's emotional milieu. For example, at birth our visual cortex has not yet been activated, since we have not yet used our eyes. For proper sight to develop, a human baby requires gazing into a human face (preferably its mother's) from an ideal distance of about one to two feet, beginning immediately at birth and for many months after. But more than just recognizing a human face is important: the emotional atmosphere in which this takes place also determines healthy development of the visual cortex. We don't just see objects impersonally; the visual cortex and the limbic system are linked, so we perceive objects and simultaneously register a feeling quality. This feeling quality is engendered by our primary caregivers and the field of emotional resonance in which they nurture us. Their emotional state provides the atmosphere that embeds visual perception in a larger psychological framework: the sense that what we see has emotional meaning. This may well be the root of our later ability for ethical consciousness. Negative emotional states or the absence of a positive "felt relationship" can cause severe psychological disturbances later in life.[5]

In this and many other ways, physiological maturity is not just a mechanical capability but also a felt relationship. Connectedness and belonging are essential to proper expression of physiological potentials such as heart rhythm and immune functioning. (For further discussion of the correlation between emotional environment and physiological development, see appendix 3.) We need relationships that help model for us our separateness while at the same time providing an emotional environment of connectedness, and this need continues throughout life.

Genetic expression is a tendency, not an absolute, and the range and variability of that expression is intimately connected to the emotional quality in which we are nurtured. Physical and psychological development are the head and tail of the same coin; indeed, I believe they actually evolve simultaneously. What serves our bodies best early in the second holding environment also brings forth in us the greatest potential for psychological health, and this remains true as we mature. A happy body leads to positive feeling and a calm mind. This is why, in my seminars, I emphasize breathing dynamics, dancing, singing, voice play, relaxation, adequate rest, and solitude in natural settings to support the process of self-discovery. This cocreative relationship between our physical well-being and our emotional and spiritual intelligence exists throughout life.

The internalized self-sense that is consolidated by about age six becomes externalized as our way of viewing and responding to the world. If we internalize a basically positive sense of self, we tend to have a more trusting relationship to our worlds. If we internalize a sense of fear and distrust, then the world will always seem threatening or dangerous, requiring us to be in control and to emphasize self-protection.

The formation of our core identities beyond our earliest nurturance involves a continuous and highly complex relationship with our parents and others during the first years of life. These early relationships act as psychological mirrors in which we are constantly organizing our perceptions, sensations, and thoughts. *Mirroring* does not mean that our parents imitate our behaviors. Rather, it is the way in which they respond and relate to us, as well as how they care for themselves and each other, that provides the reflection by which we begin to make sense of our worlds and of who we are.

During our formative years, we unconsciously emulate, react

to, or defend ourselves against our parents' psychologies, which of course are capable of expressing multiple identities. One day we are with an expansive and forgiving father, the next day we find him morose and withdrawn. Our mothers might be tender and empathetic in one situation, but opinionated and competitive in another. Since we are constantly internalizing an ever-changing psychological panorama, our own core sense of self can become deeply confused and insecure.

If our care during the earliest years was inadequate, or the ongoing emotional environment was highly erratic or violent, we may not internalize any consistent felt sense of self, as is the case in the so-called borderline personality. People with this condition may spend their whole lives trying to find a sense of who they are by means of others. Any time they do not feel reflected by the external environment in a way that provides a familiar sense of intensity, it can instantly provoke overwhelming feelings of non-being. To avoid this, a borderline person might, for instance, unconsciously manipulate his or her relationships to endlessly generate unresolvable conflict. Children of very narcissistic mothers, even if they have not been abandoned or treated violently, do not ever have their own unique being mirrored back to them. Instead, they learn that they must, for their own emotional safety, hide their own feelings and needs and make themselves players in the mother's drama. Such children do not develop a strong sense of self. They may then spend the rest of their lives deferring to others and feeling unseen. They actually may feel threatened by anyone who does express a more determined sense of self, because they fear they will once again be discounted and expected to play a role in someone else's theater.

A baby is not a blank slate, and parents alone do not determine their child's sense of self. Children, even very young ones, have their own unique characters. Some are happy, others melancholic; some are outgoing, and others introverted. And just as a child adapts to the parents' psychologies, that child's temperament is also influenced by the quality of attention he or she attracts from parents and others. The second holding environment is, like the womb, a cocreative adventure.

Child rearing, even when done with a great deal of love, can never address all of a child's unique needs and always positively accommodate his or her essence. Ideally, children are treated in healthy and empowering ways the majority of the time, and never with violence and neglect. But no parent is fully conscious of her or his own psychology; each of us is the product of our own early nurturing, as well as of the culture in which we were raised. Therefore we cannot be fully conscious of what we inevitably pass on to our children. No matter what, each child is confronted by aspects of the second holding environment that frequently conflict with his or her internal state.

Because many of our cultural norms are actually forms of extreme ignorance expressed in gender and racial prejudices, political ideologies, religious belief systems, and through material and economic values, enculturation in the second holding environment often amounts to sanctioned indoctrination of a form of insanity. As children, we respond to this imbalance and insanity by unconsciously creating survival personalities that continue to bring us the necessary level of attention and relationship while, at the same time, diminishing our sense of confusion and threat. We disguise our deeper discomfort with ourselves within an idealized sense of self while subconsciously believing, "I am not good enough as I am." In our hearts it is difficult to reconcile our own innate essence with the psychological and cultural reality communicated to us by parents, schools, and religious institutions. This core feeling of being out of place or somehow "wrong" becomes an ever-recurring sensation that we implicitly accept, whether we realize it or not.

Among the thousands of people whom I have counseled, whenever we have inquired into places in their lives where they experience conflict or have reached a limit in their capacity for intimacy and love, we inevitably uncover their effort to defend some underlying feeling of insufficiency, deep anxiety, worthlessness, or unlovableness, especially in the context of their most important relationships. And if encouraged to stop defending against these feelings (because the defense only continues to substantiate the core identity), they often encounter the formidable sense of not existing at all. It is as though their original perception of their egos is a feeling of profound insufficiency, and if they are deprived of this, they are left with the terror of nonbeing. They have spent years keeping this terror walled off, and they avoid it at all costs. Often this means inventing a counterfeit sense of sufficiency while enduring the quiet desperation of actually feeling inadequate and unworthy of love.

Significantly, for most of us our innermost pain may never fully reach consciousness and so may remain literally a secret story, one we hide even from ourselves. But the unconscious mandate to defend against the surfacing of this story ends up calling the shots in every area of our lives. If I have internalized (created a core identity of) a strong sense of worthlessness, I may never let myself *feel* this. Instead, I might spend my whole life being a "pleaser," or I might do the opposite and spend it grandiosely and aggressively pushing for my agenda. Outwardly compensating for the core feeling can take so many forms, but what this really amounts to is a threshold beyond which we dare not meet life fully. Being a pleaser or an aggressive go-getter never, ultimately, provides a satisfying life. Living ever in fear of rejection or filled with scorn for others who don't get out of our way are equally unhappy forms of existence. But often it is a tolerable unhappiness, a taken-for-granted way of being that is far preferable to facing the core feelings.

We are able to continue our self-deception because we trick ourselves with *hope*. Living in hope, with its promise of something better to come, we conveniently sidestep into the future, where we imagine the grass is greener, rather than meet our core feelings directly. Hope traps us in a continuous, self-perpetuating loop. But because our core identity *needs* us to be limited and unhappy in some form, we always end up living in a way that never permits us to escape that loop, and we return inevitably to some kind of unhappiness.

This emotional matrix of self-sustaining stress and unhappiness, internalized in the second holding environment, is how we feel real, how we know in ourselves that we exist. It becomes its own holding environment: if we were not somehow unfulfilled, perpetuating a sense of struggle, believing that struggling is necessary in order to make our lives better, we might lose the only selves we know.

THE THIRD HOLDING ENVIRONMENT

In cartoonist Charles Schultz's *Peanuts* comic strip, Snoopy declares, "I have met the enemy and he is me." During our formative years, we innocently internalize an emotional and psychological reality very much like this. And our constant, unconscious recreation of it makes up the third holding environment.

Long after we have departed the homes of our families of origin, we hold ourselves in a self-generated and self-perpetuated psychological and emotional matrix that encloses us just as surely

as the womb did, and which tells us who we are just as continuously and erroneously as our family did. This third holding
environment is the way we re-create a familiar internal feeling
state. We develop it through the stories we tell ourselves about
who we are and through the feelings we create in ourselves as we
think about others. It is how we incessantly seek out others to
complete us; at the same time, it is what we use to sabotage
relationships in which our needs might be met. This holding
environment is what permits us to live everywhere but in the
Now of ourselves while we regenerate and preserve an emotional
quality similar to whatever we internalized earlier in our lives.

While we live psychically embedded in the third holding environment (though not knowing this is the case), our secret stories are cocreating our identities, predetermining our reactions
and our choices, moment by moment. If our core sense of self is
built around unconscious and unmet feelings of inadequacy, we
tend to look at the world as a series of challenges to be overcome.
But we will never be good enough no matter how hard we try,
or how well we succeed. There will always be something as yet
unattained before we can reach the sense that "this is it."

An unconscious core identity based on feelings of distrust
breeds a life in which nothing — neither love nor success nor
friendship — is ever truly trusted. There is always some danger,
some impending betrayal, some improvement that has to be
made in order to increase security, and on and on. Likewise, if
we have invested our identities in what we do,. we can make
ourselves into unconscious sacrifices to our titles and roles. We
may exceed all expectations others have of us in terms of worldly,
and even spiritual, success, yet within ourselves we can live a
ceaseless drama of striving without ever experiencing real satisfaction, no matter how admirable our achievements. Held firmly
in the grip of our own psychologies, we convert whatever we

perceive or achieve into something that continues to require still more of us, so that we can never really rest in the simple fullness of ourselves.

The irony is that whatever we do to free ourselves from this suffering, we invariably do it in ways that engender the suffering once again. The very nature of the third holding environment is that we re-create situations in our relationships and in our work, and even in our work toward personal growth, that perpetually return us to some form of familiar struggle. It is as though we do not know or trust that we *exist* if we are not hovering close to this kind of emotional tension.

I see examples of this all the time: there are people who begin feeling better about themselves as a result of doing inner work, and who, the moment they revisit a former unhappy feeling state, chastise themselves more than ever for not managing to maintain the good feeling. There are those who have courageously left marriages in which they were deeply unhappy, believing that they owed themselves and even their spouses something better, only to continue making themselves unhappy by stigmatizing themselves for being single. Or those who successfully find a new partner, but soon begin their familiar ordeal as issues similar to those in the earlier relationship arise once again.

We leave a job in which we are financially secure because our souls are "dying" and it is time to do something "more creative" or "more expressive of our real gifts" or "for the good of the world," only to find ourselves mired in the angst of financial stress or depressed that our gifts seem to go unrecognized. We work hard to get the promotion and recognition we have been coveting, but along with the increased prominence and salary come the increased responsibility and hours, so we begin to feel guilty because we have less time at home with our children. We trade one form of objection, complaint, demand, or need for another. We think we are making important choices and supporting valid changes, but while outer circumstances constantly change, the secret story that is the mainstay of the third holding environment remains unchallenged, unchanged, and ubiquitous: "This isn't it" and "I am not sufficient as I am."

This environment of emotional holding permits us, at least for a while, to live in something less disturbing than the core feelings we learned to bury early in life or the untamed emotions that we encounter when this identity (even if it is based in misery) is threatened. As a result, while we live physically in the Now, we are afraid to rest nakedly in it. We don't treat this present moment, in which we all actually abide, as our beloved, or as the "welcome guest" of the mystics. Instead, much too often, we live a drama of avoidance and struggle. Rather than coming to know and trust the fullness of ourselves that is our birthright, we console ourselves within a virtually ceaseless state of psychic unrest that varies only in degree.

In this third holding environment, we *imagine* that we are conscious because we perceive, interpret, reason, react, initiate actions, and reflect upon much of what we do. But this self-reflection rarely penetrates to our core identities; we remain unconscious of the underlying sense of ourselves that governs how we exercise our awareness.

President or pope, it is the same. We believe we are acting of our own volition and functioning as a conscious individual, but this is true only to the extent that our thinking and actions remain obedient to that which is *permitted* by our core identities. To *transcend* this identity we would have to consciously face our own unmet feelings and cease to empower our survival personalities. Since this is tantamount to loss of identity, we would have to face some degree of nonbeing. Until we are ready to do so, we continue as if we are looking through a lens that distorts everything in a predictable way, and are unaware of the existence of the lens itself. Is it any wonder then that our human affairs are so permeated with craziness?

We don't realize that this unconscious dynamic is how we re-create our own sense of existence as a separate self. We don't understand that we depend on some sense of conflict and distrust to maintain a *known continuity* of being. Out of this is born a relentless self-interest and a blinding self-involvement. Once this becomes unquestioned in us, our needs and our point of view become more important than anyone else's. Add a touch of fear to our self-interest, and then greed, competitiveness, prejudice, and all manner of social iniquity are never far behind. If we are really honest, we might see that even when we imagine we are selflessly devoting ourselves to others, often what we are actually doing is using them to make ourselves feel loving, purposeful, and good.

In the third holding environment, we are perpetually living the most basic law of consciousness: As you sow, so shall you reap. I refer to this ancient understanding as the Principle of Relationship. We can think of it this way: React aggressively to anything, and you frame the situation as either black or white. You become irritated, intolerant, angry, and will likely exhaust and ultimately hurt yourself. Approach the same issue *attuned* more gently, and you are more likely to experience something subtle, complex, and even intriguing. Refine your awareness still further, and this time approach the same thing with exquisite softness and receptivity, and you may experience something sublime, even joyous.

I invite you to prove this to yourself by a simple experiment: Sit on the floor, cross-legged if that is comfortable for you, and press the fingers of one hand quite forcefully against the floor.

Sustain this aggressive pressure, and just notice how you begin to feel in your whole being (not merely in your fingers and straining arm). What kind of mood begins to pervade you? Next, using your other hand, touch your fingers to the floor much more softly and receptively, and notice what quality of feeling or mood now begins to arise in you. Finally, change hands again and slowly rest your fingers with a truly exquisite attention — very, very receptive, barely touching the floor, as if a butterfly's wing could almost slip under your fingertips without disturbing the colored dust on it — and notice how this begins to make you feel in yourself. Pause and take in that moment.

It is not the thing itself that holds the power to hurt or save us, but the quality of awareness we bring to it. In the third holding environment, we often believe we are planting good seeds, but unconsciously, even as we sow, we continue to maintain our sense of insufficiency and our conditioned and enculturated survival psychologies. Again and again, we return to fear in one disguise or another.

Awareness is always a relationship. "Our" awareness "touches" or "holds" each moment in a way that depends on which identity is determining our state of mind. The crucial understanding is that how we hold each moment in our awareness is how we are simultaneously held by that moment. This is the reciprocal, cocreative nature of the reality in which we live. How we unconsciously or consciously engage each feeling, thought, or sensation, moment by moment, determines how we in turn are affected by that thought, that emotion, that sensation. If we reject a particular feeling — "I don't want to feel this" — automatically and simultaneously our sense of self will experience a sense of being threatened, because rejection is a form of violence against ourselves. If we reject the feeling of threat that our own rejection creates, we spiral down into more and more misery.

Within the third holding environment, we exercise our awareness in a limited, survival mode because we are unconsciously defending and re-creating our core survival identities. As a result, the reality we experience is always part of that struggle for survival. If we judge ourselves, the inherent violence and self-rejection simultaneously disrupts our feeling of connection to ourselves and to others. This spiral of rejection tends to become ever more violent. Hence the great wisdom in the injunction "Judge not, lest ye be judged," which speaks of the folly of self-judgment as much as the practice of judging others around us.

By blaming ourselves or others, we further our survival-oriented behaviors, which in turn perpetuate our suffering and struggle ad infinitum. In this holding environment, the cocreative nature of our consciousness permits us to drive ourselves to terrible mental misery. Yet at the same time, our me-consciousness is at a level where we can also begin to exercise the power of awareness. Our ability to undertake our own self-liberation paradoxically grows alongside our ability to incarcerate and torment our hearts. We must learn to exercise this power of self-liberation in such a way that we do not continue to re-create the same old negative holding environment over and over again. And if our suffering is great enough, or if perhaps we feel called by the presence of someone who is modeling the next possibility for our consciousness, our awakening will begin.

THE FOURTH HOLDING ENVIRONMENT

When we awaken to our capacity to exercise the power of awareness more completely, we can realize the fourth and final holding environment, that of the present moment itself. The Now is eternally holding us; it is where we have been living all along. Yet we are blind to it while we live inside the dream: our unchallenged identification with me-consciousness.

Years ago, I spontaneously entered a profound state of consciousness, one that I have great difficulty describing. In that state I hovered at the very edge of where consciousness expands beyond all ego references. But the quality of the experience was such that I termed it Existence Is the Mother. The essence of this experience was a sense of being *held* as though lying upon my mother's chest shortly after birth. "I" — my point of view, which was almost completely undifferentiated during this experience — could feel "her" breathing, could feel the rise and fall of "her" chest. Doubtless, what I was feeling was my own breath, but it seemed as though all of existence was breathing. "I" understood that "I" was identical to "my" perceptions at all levels, not separate. "I" was utterly continuous with "All That Is." And all of it sustained and held me like an endless cosmic "mother." Existence, at that (and any) moment, was a "womb" holding and sustaining "me," birthing "me" instant by instant, but it was also not other than "me."

I had this experience abruptly while deeply engaged in an inquiry exercise built around the question "Who am I?" Just before this realization, I was suddenly overcome with the most intense sense of terror I had ever known. I felt as though my veins ran with ice and that I was about to explode and be utterly annihilated. I wanted to flee, but instead I willed myself to just sit where I was, and I asked myself the question "Who am I?"

In the very instant of that inquiry, "I" dissolved. But instead of experiencing annihilation or nonexistence, "I" *was* Existence, and this Existence was as intimate with "me," and cared for "me," as if it were "Mother." It was a most paradoxical state of being: I was simultaneously infant and mother, the created and the creator, All That Is and the source of All That Is.

In retrospect, I understood that this experience was tied to one that had happened nine months earlier, and I believe I can now see a pattern. In both instances, intense fear preceded a fundamental shift in consciousness, and the shift did not take place until I faced directly into the fear and began a process of self-inquiry.

In the earlier event the sense of imminent annihilation had lasted for four days, not moments; but before this I had experienced months of almost unrelenting anxiety and despair.[6] I think perhaps the protracted duration of that suffering resulted because I could not help but *resist* despair, and perhaps the despair itself was some kind of readying process, like wheat being ground into flour in a mill. In any case, in trying to cope with the dread I finally began to carefully observe myself and actively label whatever I was aware of: "This is a thought." "This is a feeling." "This is a sensation." I was spontaneously turning toward my experience as I tried to address the continuous sense of impending doom. This contemplation gave me some minimal sense of control, and perhaps I intuitively knew that my true self was not to be found in the ordinary content of my mind.

Then suddenly, while I was sitting in the garden absorbed in that contemplation, a black butterfly landed in the middle of my forehead. Instantly my intense vulnerability evaporated, and I spontaneously entered a state of inexpressible peace.

I have come to appreciate that these two experiences — the four days of despair followed by the encounter with the black butterfly, and then the later experience, Existence Is the Mother — were seed events that changed me forever. Both were realizations that occurred as I was spontaneously released from the third holding environment and I entered the fourth holding environment, the eternal Now. Both brought me to the origin of my being, the beginning of myself, and gave me the deepest tastes of my innate wholeness and the wholeness of all of existence.

But the two experiences initiated different understandings. In the weeks and months following the black butterfly event, I could sense how the realization that had accompanied it seemed to be drawing me deeply into an impersonal realm. "I" had understood a sense of identity with All That Is, and simultaneously I had had a feeling of supernal peace. But this consciousness was somehow outside or above, and the new sense of unity was detached, indifferent. The second event had a sense of infinite intimacy, of uninterrupted connection, and the sense that, above all, existence, every moment of it, is a matrix of profound nurturance and tenderness.

Looking at these two openings I could say that everything we experience and perceive, moment by moment, is our "Mother" holding us, and how we offer our attention to "her" constitutes the other partner, much like a "Father," in the cocreative process. All of existence is the Mother who forever reflects us to ourselves in an infinite variety of ways. But the quality of our attention "fathers" what we see. It creates who we are and the meaning we attribute to each experience.

When we are in the Now, the fourth holding environment, me-consciousness recedes until just enough remains to allow a vestigial point of view while our being resides in the vastness of consciousness. Silence and presence are the language of this holding environment, and within it everything is relationship.

When we hold the present with the utmost tenderness, in this relationship we exist as beings of peace and love. When we hold the present without any judgment or reactivity, in this relationship we exist as timeless consciousness that neither is born nor dies. When we hold fear without reactivity, without distance, in this relationship fear transforms and is no longer fear: it becomes energy and spaciousness. Of course, if we react to fear, then in this relationship fear is fear once again.

The ultimate form of cocreation is how the Self holds the self

— the personal experience of our being. This is what determines what we experience and who and how we are as we live, breath by breath. This Self-me relationship is the fundamental relationship, because moment by moment it is the gaze we turn upon ourselves that creates our sense of self. This relationship is mediated not by thinking but by the quality of attention we bring in the Now to our me-ness: how we are present with our sensations, emotions, and thoughts. That which we touch with a nonreactive attention, even physical pain, loses its power to really hurt us. Instead, by this very quality of relationship, we are "accepted" by reality; we experience ourselves as belonging, as grateful, not as outside or exiled or struggling. Survival is no longer the issue.

When our attention originates within the love that is innate to us, and we reside at the beginning of ourselves, then the world is love. When we hold even the most painful places in ourselves with loving, open attention, we experience compassion. When we rest at the beginning in ourselves, no longer in conflict with what *is*, our pasts are the perfect prelude to the wholeness that we *are*. Forgiveness for ourselves and everyone and everything is innate at such moments. And with compassion and forgiveness, our whole world transforms.

I hear people again and again say that they are trying to "find themselves." What they are really saying is that they are continually rejecting what *is* in themselves or in their lives. We can't find ourselves, because we can't lose ourselves; every feeling, every thought, and the quality of life they bring *is* the Self. React, and suffering results. Receive with tender attention, and fullness results. Beauty is in the eye of the beholder, and likewise ugliness and limitation are also in the eye of the beholder. The word *be-hold* says it all: we are always *holding* ourselves each moment in our *beings*, and how we hold is how we experience being held. This *is* the reality of the Now.

CHAPTER SEVEN

The Beginning
of Ourselves

One of the most obvious and yet mysterious aspects of life is the elusive nature of the present moment. Consider how easy it is to speak about the past or the future. Observe yourself in your next conversation, even one taking place in your own mind, and you will see that invariably you are talking or thinking about something that you have already lived or that you anticipate living. We can think and talk about virtually anything from the past or future, but about the present moment itself, nothing can be said.

Approaching the Now by thinking about it is like following an asymptote in geometry: a line converges on another line but never quite reaches it. Our minds may become quieter and quieter, but we can never be fully in the Now and still maintain the ability to observe it or comment on it. In the depths of the present moment, ordinary mental activity stops.

Nonetheless, it is valuable to contemplate the Now not as

an absolute but as a continuum on which what we actually experience, at once, in any given moment, is varying depths of connection to ourselves, others, and the world in general. Take the example of a kiss: In such a moment of intimacy, we can feel profoundly tender and alive. There is no doubt that we are meeting our lover, and simultaneously we feel completely met. Yet if our minds are caught in the past, and we are comparing this present relationship to a former relationship or worrying about where this kiss might be leading, our lack of presence causes the kiss to lose its potential richness.

The simple fact is that whereas our bodies are always in the Now, our minds may not be. During most of ordinary life, we live shallowly in the present. Our survival psychology makes us afraid to risk opening fully and directly to our immediate experience for fear of being hurt or veering out of control. By judging what is appropriate or right, we restrict our capacity to perceive and accept our experience as it is. When our minds are not really in the present, we are more or less blind.

We encounter our most profound sense of the Now when there is no separation between the experience and the experiencer. The subject, or "I," and the so-called external, or objective, reality become a single state of being. This state of consciousness has been called unitive, cosmic, God-realization, and Self-realization. Such experiences of oneness are the essence of all mystical states, and the desire to enter these states directly is the root of spiritual practices of all kinds. Deep realization of unitive consciousness, the state in which we experience universal consciousness, is relatively rare. Those who have known it and have been able to integrate it find themselves profoundly transformed and usually leave a deep mark on the societies in which they have lived.

But profoundly deep and beautiful experiences of the Now are common to all of us to some extent. These are the times when suddenly, without understanding what has happened, we feel a deep peace and sense of gratitude. These moments show us that there is much more to life than we ever imagined, and they may awaken our slumbering yearning to know more of who we really are. Even when the experience is fleeting, it can initiate us on a lifelong path of spiritual searching. In daily spiritual practice, however, instead of seeking God or some form of Self-realization — which is the way much of spiritual practice is contextualized — we should focus on turning toward our immediate being in the Now.

We can think of God as a theological referent synonymous with the absolute Now, since we can realize God directly only when in a state approaching absolute unitive consciousness. Likewise, we can think of the Now, in the language of depth psychology, as the archetype of the Self. In this discipline, the Self is the source from which emerge all possible psychological dynamics and all levels of consciousness. To approach the Self is to be more authentic and spontaneous, more capable of integrating the dark and light of our nature, and better able to express our true essence. It is to be closer to the collective unconscious and, thus, capable of inspiration, vision, and intuitive abilities that are far beyond what is available to our ordinary personal consciousness. But when we demystify words like *God* and *Self*, what we are really talking about is the most profound depths we can reach when body and mind, flesh and soul, are united in the Now.

In counseling people who have chosen to pursue a spiritual path, I find it is most helpful to encourage less emphasis on attaining enlightenment and more emphasis on developing the practice of living closer and closer to the Now in daily life. To get a better sense of what it means to live in the Now, we can think of it as living from "the beginning of ourselves," the place where our experience of ourselves starts anew in each moment. Who we really are always begins right now, because our true selves are an ever-renewing continuum of immediacy and original presence.

In daily life, we may see ourselves as being affected by circumstances, such as someone else's moods or behaviors, or an unexpected change, such as the loss of a job. In this victim identity, with so many things influencing us, our reaction might be a sense of being overwhelmed and not knowing where to find solid footing from which to tackle the challenges life presents. But we can ask ourselves: "Where does my true story, my real self, start? Where do I have the power to determine what I want to live, and how? Do my problems really begin in the past? Does my present situation necessarily have to result in any of the future scenarios I have been imagining?"

We might see something that happened in the past as being responsible for our current concerns. Perhaps we believe we made a bad decision, married the wrong person, or had an unfortunate childhood. Or our disturbance could be as minor as resenting and blaming an unexpected visitor because the disruption throws our schedule off. But even if these explanations provide convincing rationalizations for our immediate unhappiness, the simple truth is that these are *thoughts* right now. Why should the past or the future be given more attention than the present? We can become the victims of these stories, or we can see that they are just stories and thereby withdraw some of the energy that makes them seem real. It's like watching a movie: We can remember that the villain or victim on the screen is just an actor playing a role and consciously suspend our disbelief in order to enjoy the story. Or we can entirely lose touch with the fact that we are watching a movie and get lost in seriously worrying about the characters and the dramatic situation they are caught up in. Our stories about the past or future are not *real* in the Now, but we treat them as if they are.

But what if we choose to accept that our true story always begins *now*, that this very moment is, for each of us, perpetually the beginning of ourselves? Immediately this places us in a position of authority, of being the authors of our own lives. Minute by minute and hour by hour, we can create ourselves anew by the way we are present to ourselves and our situation, independent of the past or the future. When we realize that, from the perspective of the soul, or true self, every single moment is wide open to us for a completely fresh start, we claim and inhabit our destinies as cocreators.

Then love spontaneously ignites in our hearts and claims us. Instead of trying to direct love, we can choose how to join with that love and express it. Likewise, as we begin our true stories anew, we can turn toward our fears and create a space of conscious presence in which to embrace them, rather than letting them dominate us. In the fullness of our beings, we can choose to forgive and, in so doing, let go of our suffering over the past. We can choose to put our trust in *trust* itself and stop worrying about the future. Our true story is that we are pregnant with possibility. We literally originate ourselves in every moment.

None of us would wish for yesterday's heartbeat or yesterday's breath — we would be dead. Wanting tomorrow's comfort or being the victim of tomorrow's anticipated unhappiness is just another form of death, because it steals vital energy from today. Our only true power resides in our conscious relationship to what is, at this moment.

When we habitually leave the present, we are postponing a direct relationship with reality. In so doing we distance ourselves from our true selves and lose awareness of the present. Our minds become weak and subject to our fears and hopes. The beginning of ourselves is where we can exert the most direct influence on our lives and gather the most energy to meet whatever is present.

The story of a woman named Michelle helps to illustrate what happens when we do not know how to live from our beginning. Her boyfriend, Eric, who was also her co-worker, told her that he didn't feel ready for commitment, and he ended their yearlong relationship. Michelle was devastated. Her mind ran wild with all sorts of angry thoughts and judgments about what was wrong with Eric. At first she contemplated looking for a new job so she wouldn't have to see him at work. But then she reconsidered. No, she wouldn't turn tail and run; she would focus on going for a promotion to prove she could thrive without him. She wasn't about to waste her life on a loser who didn't appreciate her.

This hopeful fantasy gave her a reprieve from her feelings of rejection and abandonment. But then she began to agonize over how her previous relationships also had not worked out, and she started to wonder what was wrong with her. Was she too strong, too controlling? Had she steamrolled Eric? Did she have to hide her strength to be lovable? "Why do men seem to be so easily threatened?" she asked. She began thinking about how her parents' marriage was never happy, and about the nastiness of their divorce when she was a teenager. She thought about her mother's life of isolation as an embittered elderly woman. "Is that what is going to happen to me?" she fretted. Looking back, she wondered if maybe she should have married her college boyfriend, John, instead of focusing on a career. By now she probably would have had a family of her own and a "real" life. Had she missed her last chance for a happy relationship? With these thoughts, the real despair set in.

I imagine most of us can identify with this kind of pain. And most of us, like Michelle, would find an explanation for it that began with someone else's actions, or at least with something that happened somewhere in the past. But when we do this, we place the power to determine our feelings elsewhere, not at the beginning of ourselves. In the same self-protective process, we might think ahead to the future and try to create hope by resolving to make a new start, or by planning to take a holiday and be good to ourselves. But when we create an imaginary problem-solving strategy for the future, in the hope of regaining love, attaining success, or re-creating a sense of comfort and security, we are usually skipping a crucial step. We are throwing our minds into the future to avoid what we feel in the present moment. In so doing we postpone the possibility of real intimacy and conscious relationship with ourselves until some uncertain future time. It is a time that never arrives. And the more we habituate this process of Self-avoidance, the less we are aware that we are not actually living our own lives. We are constantly fleeing into an imaginary life rather than living the exact moment — now — when life is juiciest and offers us the greatest opportunity to become more aware, to risk being authentic. By fleeing to the past or the future, we reject what *is* and unconsciously affirm the core feeling "I am not sufficient as I am."

Isn't this what Michelle did? She unconsciously — as a result of her core feeling of insufficiency — placed the power to make herself feel whole in Eric. (It could have been any man to whom she had become attached.) When he withdrew, it was as though he took a part of her with him. Of course she felt abandoned and hurt. But, unable to hold these feelings, she became angry and blamed Eric and, later, men in general. At the same time, she imagined how she could change her life and regain a sense of power and control.

But our fantasies about the future rarely have the power to overcome the immediacy of real wounding. Michelle couldn't escape so easily. As a result, she began blaming her parents' marriage, and then she resurrected regrets about not marrying John. She demoralized and diminished herself by telling herself that she came on too strong or had been too controlling or was incapable of being loved; but then she drove the last nail in the coffin by imagining that she would end up miserable and alone like her mother.

For Michelle, the cause of her pain and a way to rationalize and remedy it lay elsewhere: in her boyfriends, in the past, in the future, in her stories about herself. Because she felt threatened in her *being*, she activated her usual survival strategies: anger, blame, hope, regret, and self-negation. She stayed in the domain of tamed emotions, and her survival personality remained intact. Of course, none of this had anything to do with her true self; it was all a dream, the kind of dream any of us might spend our whole lives believing. For Michelle to awaken from her dream, she would have had to return to the immediacy of her direct sensations in the moment and allow herself to become intimate with the feeling of despair. By avoiding that risk, she continued to limit her capacity for intimacy with any man who might become her partner.

CONSCIOUS SUFFERING

Children need to feel safe, experience approval, and gain some sense of control over their world, otherwise they cannot thrive and may not survive. For an adult, these feelings are not essential to survival. We can develop the ability to remain present with certain sensations, such as vulnerability, disapproval, and even despair, because as adults we have the potential to recognize these as simply feelings arising in the space of our beings, not as ourselves. But if we cannot consciously face a feeling because we perceive it as a threat to our sense of self, we will flee from ourselves the way we did as children. If we are to live fully, then when we are suffering we must not run away. We must be willing to allow this suffering as a conscious process.

To be human is to feel, and the more conscious we are, the less restricted our repertoire of feeling. Concurrently, our capacity to be in a nonreactive relationship to any feeling becomes greater. It is not that we choose to be nonreactive; the result of such a willed stance would just be numbness, indifference, or cold detachment, not fullness of being. It would be only another strategy for avoiding difficult feelings. Nonreactive attention grows organically as a consequence of deepening consciousness. We turn our attention toward every moment and really *taste* it — as it is, sweet or bitter. To become more conscious is to experience the Now in ever-greater depth.

As long as we flee from the present moment into the past or future, as long as we allow unmet feelings to dictate story after story about who we are or what we should do, we are victims. But when we allow ourselves to experience all these feelings in their own right, we stop being victims and become conscious disciples, students of our own lives. This is the most extraordinary state of vulnerability, and *if we blink we lose*. Just that quickly, if we break our attention and lose sight of the immediacy of our experience, the feelings we then blind ourselves to pull us into time, into story. But if we refuse, if we stay present in the here and now, then the energy in those feelings loses the power to pull us away from our true selves and make us false. We are false when we disguise or bury our vulnerability by becoming aggressive, or when we try to please others because we have long ago lost the ability to take the risk of speaking our truth and perhaps being judged or rejected.

When we choose to live the process of conscious suffering, we finally allow ourselves to totally feel and meet what we used to bury or hide. It is one of the most essential creative processes in a human life, and we exercise this power of awareness without any certainty about the outcome. We let ourselves be led deeper into life by being present with what *is*, rather than by trying to control and direct ourselves and our lives. Imagine the possibility of learning to make space for feelings like hopelessness and despair without attacking ourselves for feeling them, and without gravitating toward some imagined relief or reward. To meet such difficult emotions in this way goes against all the survival programming that has sustained our false selves since early childhood. In the fire of such excruciating internal intimacy with what we each individually, and as a culture, have always run from, we awaken faith in our true selves. We can stand right in the fire, exercise the power of awareness and realize: "I am more than this."

I believe Walt Whitman is speaking directly to both the potential freedom and the inherent uncertainty of this process in these final lines of one of my favorite poems, "As I Lay My Head in Your Lap, Camerado":

> And the threat of what is call'd hell is little or nothing to me,
> And the lure of what is call'd heaven is little or nothing to me;
> Dear Camerado! I confess, I have urged you onward with me,
> and still urge you, without the least idea what is our destination,
> Or whether we shall be victorious, or utterly quell'd and defeated.[1]

Whitman is, in the words of D. H. Lawrence, the best poet of the "unrestful, ungraspable poetry of the sheer present."[2] But his poetry is not merely romantic or rhetorical exhortation; he was a man who worked tirelessly at the bedsides of dying soldiers during the Civil War, comforting them and writing letters home for them. He spent years in a wheelchair, paralyzed from a stroke, and never lost his indomitable capacity for enjoyment and reverence for life or his profound appreciation of humankind. He lived the path of which he wrote, and he knew that ordinary heroism, as great as it may be, is not the essential heroism of each soul facing life's "aged fierce enigmas" that lie within. He understood that so much of our suffering and tragedy comes about because we do not let our souls turn toward the inner terrors and "strangling problems."[3] He knew that, until met within, they are inevitably projected outward and become the nescient forces underlying warfare, conquest, and our incessant survival quest. But once we take our stand in conscious relationship to our own suffering, while there is no certainty that we will overcome the pain, it no longer is something that spreads from us to others. That we develop the capacity for conscious suffering marks a quantum leap in the emergence of the soul.

Let me be clear that there is no intent here to ennoble suffering. We are rightfully afraid of pain, but when pain — especially emotional pain — is what *is*, then to continue to rely on a self-avoidance survival structure created in childhood is to remain barren of potential. When we can at last turn toward our pain and fear, rather than fleeing, we become spiritually fertile, and the fruit we bear is wisdom and greater self-acceptance. We gain empathy for our own suffering, and this grows into compassion for the suffering of others. We become more forgiving, more tolerant. We realize that we are stronger than we knew; we can bear far more reality than we imagined. Because we become less afraid of our own humanity, we naturally become more human.

It is important to distinguish between conscious suffering, neurotic suffering, and the denial of the reality of suffering. Neurotic suffering is a closed loop in which individuals see themselves as the source of their own pain. Even attributing their troubles to their upbringing or to the actions of others doesn't dispel their sense that they themselves are the root problem, and thus neurotics create a victim identity that thrives on the endless rejection of themselves. In many of his films, the actor and director Woody Allen humorously characterizes this kind of neurotic suffering. Since neurotics can't escape their suffering by projecting it outside themselves, eventually it can become too disabling and they may seek help. Any genuine help will lead them to a conscious relationship to their suffering, and they may eventually find themselves on a path of conscious self-healing.

The greater problem for society, however, is not our neurotic members, but rather those Carl Jung termed *normal*. These are people who might not understand why I bother to address suffering. "Suffering! Stop complaining and get on with life!" they might say to someone who admitted to being in emotional pain. They pride themselves on their stoic ability to withstand suffering. Their survival structures function by projecting anything that threatens their identity outside themselves onto the *other*. Whereas the neurotic is obsessively self-reflective and his own worst enemy, for the normal person self-reflection barely exists and the enemy is potentially anyone or anything else: a neighbor, a foreign country, terrorists, rogue states, commies, blacks, Jews, government regulations, taxes, even cancer, and so on. So-called normal people are generally less unhappy than neurotics, because whatever the cause of their unhappiness, it is never their own fault. The suffering that normal people experience is so thoroughly rationalized, so completely attributed to something external, that it never destabilizes their basic sense of identity.

Normal people also always project their own self-transcending potentials outside themselves, onto the savior, the guru, the leader, the sacred scripture. Therefore, to be normal is to be a follower of others who are almost unquestioningly believed to have the answers, the power, the truth, even the Divine truth. Normal people are so thoroughly embedded in their dreams, so thoroughly defended by survival structures founded upon their lack of self-reflection, that any information that might challenge their internalized presumptions is automatically dismissed, and a true exchange of ideas is virtually impossible. The emotional buck never stops in front of normal people; they pass it on, because others are always to blame. In this way violence and unhappiness continue to generate more of the same, while these normal people are never seriously perturbed.

CREATING A CONSCIOUS HOLDING ENVIRONMENT

When our souls are ready, conscious suffering simply means there is nowhere else to go, and that we will face something right here, right now. We assume full authority to remain present, at the beginning of ourselves, for what we feel. In this relationship, we gradually become substantial human beings.

Being present and attentive to our feelings without collapsing into them, and not identifying with our suffering, is analogous to the way a loving, empathic mother relates and responds to her baby (see chapter 3). She brings her whole presence to the infant, both practically and empathically. In a similar way, we can give our feelings our total attention and empathy. We can tenderly hold our own inner experience, recognizing how we are and softly releasing any judgments or reactions that are contributing to our suffering.

The symbol of the Madonna and Child is one of the most potent in Christianity. It is a symbol of a "virgin" relationship — one lived fully in the Now — to our most vulnerable feelings. The Madonna is always shown with a nimbus around her head signifying that her attention to the Child is not merely that of her ego but of her deeper being, her Self, the source of unconditioned, nonreactive attention. This quality of presence is the most crucial element of the inner relationship we can create with our vulnerability and suffering.

This relationship restores a sense of wholeness, because in it we return to the Now, to the beginning of ourselves. Just as empathic parents are aware of their children's distress but do not lose themselves in it, we can be our own parenting consciousness. By being nonreactively present, we are holding our own suffering in a way that mimics a mother's unconditional love. We are not telling ourselves that our misery is the result of the past, or that future redemption requires that we change. We are not judging our feelings or rejecting them. We are not dismissive or impatient or fed up. We do not tell ourselves to feel some other way and then we will be better. If a mother approached her baby in this way, its distress would only intensify; it would become even more lost, more alienated from its feelings and sensations. Like a loving mother with her baby, we must hold ourselves exactly as we are, with complete, unblinking, empathic attention. Our actual experience, as we nonreactively attend to our suffering, will show us that the Self — the part of us that is always more than whatever we're feeling, and which is always present — is an empathic, ever-patient companion.

At first it will be all that we can manage simply to stay present with the difficult feelings and not flee within seconds. To nonreactively hold these feelings requires strengthening the muscle of attention, and ultimately the muscle of faith, so that we do not become identified with the feelings. But as it says in *A Course in Miracles*, "Nothing real can be threatened."[4] It is the false self, the survival personality, that constantly feels threatened. As soon as we pause and return to the Now, the survival programming must gradually weaken its grip on us, because without the support of thoughts and stories, it does not exist.

As we increase our ability to create a conscious holding environment for all our feelings and experiences, the intensity of our emotional distress fades, and we begin to feel spontaneous gratitude for life as it is. We see that our souls are like ships that have carried us deeper into the great ocean of being, and that eventually we have had to make passage, as Walt Whitman counsels, for all of our "strangling problems" and "aged fierce enigmas."

We are heavily conditioned to flee from unhappiness and pain. We keep postponing a relationship with our suffering, imagining that we can escape it or overcome it elsewhere. We pretend that our possessions and wealth, or our diplomas and positions, are proof of how much more than survival we have achieved. Yet fear continues to pull the strings, dominating not only individual lives but also modern society as a whole. We always want a pill, a magic formula to fix things. We thrive on endless forms of escape, and what has chased us from the beginning of time we refuse to finally face.

THE NATURE OF CONTRACTION AND THE BODY AS TEACHER

The psychic movement away from a difficult feeling, which breaks the continuity of conscious relationship to ourselves, is signaled immediately, even before we are aware of what we are thinking or why we are reacting, by a physiological state of stress or tension. As soon as our minds move into opposition with reality, or simply distance us from what *is*, our bodies are the first to recognize this conflict. It is felt as a process I refer to as contraction.

Suddenly our bodies are uncomfortable, tense, on guard. The nature of the psychological threat can be minimal, even a momentarily worrisome thought or occurrence, but if we perceive the threat as a challenge to our identities, our bodies instantly respond as though we were being menaced by a predator. Our breathing becomes faster and shallower, our hearts might pound in our chests, stress hormones course through us, our muscles tighten, our facial expressions turn wary, and our voices become strained. Only then do we begin to *think* about what is happening and inevitably begin a story: "What if my stock shares lose value?" "He is so pompous and insulting." "She doesn't care about me." Once we are off and running with our stories, we have thoroughly disconnected from the beginning of ourselves and are truly lost, although we don't know it. But our bodies *do* know it, and contraction is how our sensual consciousness reports this disconnection.

Because we tend to live so far from our beginning, and consequently remain out of touch with our body consciousness, many of us function in an almost perpetual state of stress, to some degree. We may not recognize that we are contracting until we have driven ourselves to extreme misery. To recognize contraction much earlier, we must first learn to consciously inhabit our bodies in a state of calm. This is why in my work I focus a great deal on body consciousness and on simple things like breath awareness. I do not, however, reduce stress by employing conventional relaxation techniques, but rather by using practices that bring us fully into the present so that we can recognize our bodily states. By familiarizing ourselves with the sensation of contraction and how it differs from the way our bodies feel when resting in the present, we can choose to release the tension. When we do so, we are actually learning how to come into the present and surrender our thinking minds. Since our bodies are always in the present, much more so than our minds, the key to achieving this level of relaxation is to gradually go beyond any form of directed mental surveillance and rest in a felt sense of being. It is not an easy state to describe; it must be experienced. Think of it as a body-centered presence of awareness.

This is what athletes learn: in the midst of an activity such as surfing or skiing, they cannot think about how to move, or evaluate how they are performing, because this kind of self-consciousness results in a loss of coordination. Learning to keep our awareness fully present in the activity, and not letting it split off to become a spectator, commentator, or judge, is essential to being fully embodied and free from the sluggishness of thought. In this state, subtle fluctuations of bodily sensation act as a kind of near-instantaneous feedback mechanism for our states of mind. They tell us whether our thinking is placing us in opposition to our true selves or the reality of the moment in some way. When we learn to listen with the body, moment by moment, we develop the ability to rest in a felt sense of openness, stillness, and presence. Understanding and deepening this state is fundamental to progressing in consciousness.

By learning to rest in this kind of body consciousness, we can immediately recognize an incipient contraction, such as fear, before we are completely lost in a reaction to it. It becomes possible to recognize the thinking that is in conflict with reality as it arises, even before the full story has presented itself and led us into stress. We can recognize even a casual *I* thought and choose whether to join it or not.

Often, as soon as I hear my mind say "*I*," and before the thought has even completed itself, I am already amused, knowing that there is no need to give it any further attention, for doing so will only lead me down some familiar delusional path. Instead *I* remain in the felt current of the Now — the paradoxical fullness and emptiness of being in the present moment.

When we are attuned to the signs of contraction in our bodies, they become early signals that we have lost contact with our essential selves. Then the first thing that we must do is identify the unpleasant symptoms of contraction as something other than a statement of who we are. They are, instead, feedback telling us that our minds is no longer resting fully in the present.

If I am getting angry and I feel my solar plexus contracting because someone is challenging my ideas, I can immediately recognize that I have lost contact with who I am — the self that exists prior to any ideas with which I have become identified. Then I can pause in whatever thoughts my mind is generating, return my attention to the present, bring my awareness to my breathing, and let my awareness open to the point of view the other person is expressing. But this requires constant intention. It is like a conversation between the infinite possibility of the soul and the course I am charting toward it.

In relaxing a bodily contraction, I turn directly toward the tension in my body and soften my awareness by touching whatever I am feeling with a steady, tender, nonreactive attention. As I become more transparent in my being, the contraction recedes and I can usually recognize the self-protective story I was implicitly telling myself. From my initial judgments of the other person, perhaps I realize: "I am feeling insecure." As I remain attentive to this sensation, I can often discover the core illusion underlying it: "When someone disagrees with me, they are taking something away from me." I can see that it is this sense of loss of self that really threatened me. Yes, they are challenging or potentially "taking away" my identification with "my" thoughts, but nothing more. The absurdity of the belief that someone can take something real away from me simply because they have a different opinion becomes obvious. In that moment of recognition, I return to the beginning of myself. This is when my heart spontaneously opens and any other person, no matter how different they are from me, or how much I actually disagree with them, becomes interesting and important in their own right. This listening to a contraction, and following it back to its root in a counterfeit identity or untrue assumption, is the journey home, one that all of us can learn to travel.

When we observe our own minds, we soon see that most thinking is reactive. When we learn to recognize in our bodies the consequences of reactive thinking, we have an excellent motive to stop giving energy to such thoughts. Instead we can return our minds to the Now and begin at the beginning of ourselves, where any further delusion that our thoughts might otherwise lure us into simply dissolves, and immediately we feel open and clear once again. There are, however, some thoughts, stories, and beliefs that don't readily lose their energy. Once we engage in them, we might feel incapable of bringing ourselves back to the present, so they continuoually suck us down into emotional suffering. This most often happens when we're about to face one of the untamed emotions, and this is where we do the deepest and most challenging work. We must gather our attention fully and turn to face directly into this suffering.

No matter how difficult a feeling may seem at first, I find that when I eventually bring my full attention to it and hold it there, suddenly there comes a moment when I am not resisting it. In that moment the whole structure of suffering shifts and becomes a door into a larger consciousness. Almost miraculously the oppressive thoughts and feelings fall away and I am restored to the beginning of myself.

This movement of finding our way back to the beginning can be only partially described, but we can remember that it starts with recognizing contraction in the body. We must learn that, when we are powerfully contracted, we must turn our attention fully toward the sensations of angst and despair instead of toward the thoughts that such dark feelings always generate.

I have learned that I must stop thinking *at* the feelings, which means I stop trying to interpret or explain them. I intentionally resist letting my mind race with thoughts that invariably begin to generate stories about why I am feeling this way and what I should do. Instead I enter into a pure relationship, a profound intimacy with this suffering, and simultaneously sink into the Now of my body as though falling into infinite space. My attention never breaks contact with the bodily sensations. When my energy moves back into my reactive mind, as it always does for a while, I just renew the single-pointed attention to the feeling. Suddenly, whether it happens at once or after many long hours, the darkest place becomes stillness, and even bliss. It is as if I suddenly become transparent, so that both the terrible feeling and the self that hosted it disappear, and there is only openness and presence. I return to the beginning of myself, the Now. How this final shift happens can only be understood as grace. I make the fullest effort of conscious relationship and conscious suffering, but grace brings me home.

As you read this description of a process I have lived many times, I must caution you that it would be a mistake to consider it a method. Every time I face an untamed emotion, it is always the first time. If I remind myself that I have faced this or similar feelings before, this simple thought means I am in the past, using memory to try to guide and encourage myself, and therefore I am not in the Now, which is the only place where I can really meet such a feeling. Wanting a method to overcome what threatens us is just hope; and hope means we are in the future, not in the immediacy of relationship to what we are feeling. Hope is a reaction to fear: it offers the illusion of control and is the continuation of our survival projects. To approach the darkness in this way only makes it darker.

OUR LIVES ALWAYS BEGIN *NOW*

To come to the beginning of ourselves is to cease to be victims of circumstances, the actions of others, or even our own mistakes. The true story of who we really are begins now. We are no longer tossed willy-nilly from one desire, thought, or worry to another in a futile process of trying to escape the nearly infinite forms of "this isn't it" and especially "I am not sufficient as I am." If we realize that we are truly originating ourselves over and over, we have the power to claim a relationship to ourselves that begins right now. Then we are capable of responding to our own feelings or to our situations rather than reacting. When we react, we contribute to the problem. Our judgments are quick, poorly considered, and generally defensive or self-negating. We feel divided from ourselves as well as from others. It becomes difficult to know what to do next. When we are far from the beginning of ourselves, our reactions envelop us in unhappiness and distrust, which follow us well beyond the moment. In contrast, when we respond from the beginning of ourselves, our relationship to ourselves and to others always begins anew. We can take the time to appreciate what we are feeling and see our own states of being, and the behavior of others, in a larger context of empathy and compassion. There is no lingering misery, and no sense of being lost and afraid. Instead there is a growing space of trust.

But to have this kind of personal authority, we must focus our attention directly on the immediacy of ourselves. We have to learn to stay right here and wait with our minds stilled until the waters calm and we sense the deeper current of our lives once again. No one has described the subtlety of this conscious awareness better than the poet T. S. Eliot, when he wrote:

I said to my soul, be still, and wait without hope
For hope would be hope for the wrong thing; wait without love
For love would be love of the wrong thing; there is yet faith
But the faith and the love and the hope are all in the waiting.
Wait without thought, for you are not ready for thought:
So the darkness shall be the light, and the stillness the dancing.[5]

This waiting without hope or love or thought is the essence of creating a conscious holding environment, especially when we face the untamed feelings. It is the essential process by which we depart from the awareness field of fear and survival and enter the far larger field of love. Then we too can experience what all the great souls understand: that human beings are truly the sons and daughters of God. We are not and never have been inherently deficient. Despite endless stories and feelings that can, when we identify with them, convince us that we are unworthy or some-how not good enough, there is a deeper part of ourselves that can hold all this self-doubt. To awaken to this deeper part of ourselves and learn to let it hold our suffering selves is the fun-damental relationship that our souls are calling us toward.

SACRED ATTENTION

One way that I approach the challenge of teaching the art of creating a conscious holding environment is through a practice that I call sacred attention. Attention, as with awareness, can be understood as a relationship. It is the relationship between the one who is aware, or the "awarer" (whom we know as "me" or "I"), and the object of awareness. Generally, we are unconscious of the power we have to influence the quality of our attention — the actual way in which we, moment by moment, *offer* our attention. When it comes to the quality of our attention, we are like a child who, when he or she initially picks up a hammer, just smashes away at the nail without having yet understood that there is a way to hold a hammer and hit a nail that uses no excess energy and affords an extraordinarily high degree of accuracy. In our ordinary consciousness, our attention clumsily and often even aggressively hammers away at our experience, making judgments and demanding that things be different.

Until we begin to explore the power of awareness, we haven't the least idea that we can, moment by moment, offer our attention with a quality of exquisite receptivity and softness, no matter what the circumstance may be, and in so doing significantly transform the experience. Exquisite receptivity is a refinement of attention that automatically brings us into presence, because to be aware of the quality of our attention is to be in the present.

Attention is not merely a passive medium linking us, as aware beings, to what we are aware of: it is a dynamic, mutable medium. But before we can influence the dynamic of our attention, we first have to understand what it means to "offer" our attention. One way to do this is through the practice of sacred attention.

To teach sacred attention, I ask people to make an intentional effort to open to the present moment with a quality of exquisite receptivity and welcoming. I begin by asking them, as they invite this possibility, to become aware of their breath. This immediately tends to bring our awareness into the present. I then suggest that the breath can be used to sustain our attention: we can adhere to breath awareness and attend to each breath as a means of choosing a new relationship to the present moment.

I suggest that each time they breathe in, they experiment with the sense of being exquisitely receptive to the fullness of the moment, which of course means to their own sense of self as well. After a while, I suggest that with each inhalation they are not only being exquisitely receptive but also opening to this exact moment as though it were their beloved, and they the lover. This adds a quality of feeling, or felt attention, to their relationship to the present. Correspondingly, I ask them to, with each exhalation, imagine the most profound sense of relaxation and acceptance and of resting themselves in the presence of the beloved.

The in and out of breathing becomes a cyclical movement of attention that opens us to a sense of connection and love in the present moment. As we breathe, we begin to experience an alteration in consciousness. The quality of the light becomes more vivid, and the air seems to grow more dense. It is an atmosphere that we naturally tend to experience as sacred. Invariably when we are reverent and conscious of our attention in this way, we experience our minds becoming still and the space both within and around us becoming suffused and energized with presence and love that seem to be holding us.

The experience of this kind of presence is common to all religions and known to anyone who enters into deep contemplation.

When we consciously direct our hearts and minds in the name of Jesus, Mary, Buddha, Adonai, or Allah or toward Spirit, the Universal Source, or the White Light, the actual movement of attention is always the same. We reverently open to something we consider universal and ever present, in the immediacy of the Now. In effect, what we are doing is returning to the beginning of ourselves.

We have been holding the key to our own freedom all along without realizing it. It lies in the quality of our attention, moment by moment. Energy-awareness work, and specifically a practice like sacred attention, teaches us how to create a sense of living presence at any time through a shift in the quality of our attention. Although energy work is generally taught in relationship to healing, I purposely refrain from emphasizing healing. As a physician, I initially learned energy work specifically as a complementary healing modality, but as I explored it I began to understand the fundamental power of awareness itself. I believe that when we do emphasize healing we tend to take the vast potential of unconditional attention and, once again, collapse it into the smaller awareness field of survival fear. Then the energy work becomes a means to an end in which there may be success or not, and we have missed the deeper understanding: it is the quality of our attention that opens the door of the present into the awareness field of love and wholeness. Healing energy is simply derived from this greater presence.

Not long ago in one of my gatherings, I found myself facing a dilemma. For a week we had been inquiring into the "architecture" of our untamed emotional states, what I also call "the monsters." These emotions, including despair, hopelessness, and a sense of impending dissolution, tend to engulf us and submerge our sense of self. But if, when not actually caught in them, we examine and describe how they make us think and feel about the future and past, or about ourselves and others, we use the power of awareness to differentiate ourselves somewhat from these states. This is not easy work to do, because to scrutinize these daunting monsters in detail is, to some extent, to energize them; they feed on attention. Even brushing the edges of these feelings is threatening. We want to pretend they are gone and will never come back. But they do come back, and even if we manage to keep them at bay, they lurk nearby, requiring us to ceaselessly energize our survival structures.

Bringing our conscious awareness to these abysmal feeling states when we are not actively caught up in them can help us to remain consciously present later when we find ourselves ensnared once again. Trying to intellectually understand, interpret, or explain these states is not the point. We need only see what specific stories they engender and how they make us feel about ourselves, others, life, the past, the future. Whatever we are aware of, we are also more than.

In the retreat I mentioned, we were at a stage where much of the work had been done in the form of writing answers to specific questions about the experience of these untamed emotional states, and people in the group had written volumes. I was uncertain how best to bring the work to a close. In the past I had at times used a ritual fire — we had cast into the fire something that symbolized the limiting or negative traits we wished to transform. We could also toss in a river or the ocean something that represented what we were ready to let go of, to symbolize its return to the universal consciousness. But in view of what I had come to understand about the intrinsic wholeness of the psyche that inherently includes the monsters, neither ritual seemed appropriate. We cannot simply let go of untamed feelings or metaphorically burn them or cast them into the sea, because that kind of metaphor is itself a form of rejection. It is in effect a kind of violence toward these feelings, in which we are actually dividing ourselves. We are making the circle of our consciousness smaller by excluding them, rather than transforming our capacity for relationship to them and, in the process, increasing our circle enough to let them in.

What then is a wiser and more compassionate way to respect the power of the untamed emotions? After a dream composed of troubling imagery took me to a place of difficult self-reflection, I became so vulnerable that I spontaneously held myself in sacred attention. After that, it was obvious what I wanted to invite the participants to do. I asked everyone to bring all the pages they had written and place them on a table in the center of the room. Then we gathered around the table and entered collectively into the state of living presence. In this way we invoked a conscious holding environment that included our darkest fears. The ritual symbolized a new relationship to these primal fears, one that created the possibility of a more conscious, nonreactive attention.

THE LIGHT BODY

Once we understand that, no matter what is happening, the true center of power is always Now, we naturally start to orient our awareness to the immediate present. The moment we do, we become aware of our bodies in a new way. When we live in our heads, it is almost as if we have no bodies. The body becomes no more than a mundane vehicle, a source of pleasure or problems, or perhaps an obstacle to the spiritual freedom that we imagine requires being released from the constraints of the physical body. Most of the time, the body is just an object of the mind. But as we begin resting more naturally in the present, we become what I call "radically alive." Immediately we notice that our body consciousness becomes much more pronounced. We have the sensation of being vibrant with presence and at the same time transparent. It is as though our familiar sense of self — our separate *me* — has a quality of opacity analogous to a movie screen, and onto this ego our whole psychological reality is projected. But the moment we come back to the present, this opacity diminishes and even vanishes; the screen becomes transparent so the movie doesn't show. Suddenly our stories about past and future, and about ourselves and everyone else, pass right through us.

A hallmark of coming back to the Now is this sense of vibrant energy and transparent presence. Because our senses, when they are not being filtered by the ego, always reflect our states of consciousness, every sense becomes more refined and precise. Sounds become clearer, colors grow more vivid, and the light seems alive, imbuing everything with immediacy and luminosity.

This is often described in spiritual literature as the energy body, the subtle body, or the light body. Light is a good analogy, because we know from physics that light has a paradoxical nature. According to how we examine light, it appears to us either as discrete quanta (particles) or as waves, which are an unbroken continuum. Similarly, the light body is experienced both as a discrete locus of awareness — our individual point of view in the Now — and simultaneously as a field of timeless, boundless awareness.

One of the most immediately noticeable qualities of this transparent aliveness is how intimately it is connected to breathing. It is as though I am not breathing but am being breathed. Yet at the same time I can join the breath with "my" attention and ride with it as though it were a doorway between the finite nature of my physical form and an infinite state of being. The more "my" attention rests softly with the awareness of being breathed, the vaster, more transparent, and timeless the sense of being becomes. I can best describe it as a current that is both independent of the breath and subtly evoked by the breath. In this current, everything is still and the moment is complete as it is. There is a presence that holds me and extends far beyond me. The quality of this presence is fullness, acceptance, and love, and it conveys a sense that *all is well*, even though I also recognize the difficult issues in life. Over the years I have become well aware that this presence influences the state of consciousness of those around me. At certain times in my work, I intentionally amplify it to help induce others to move toward the beginning of themselves.

Because of the connection between presence and breath, I always include breath awareness in my teaching. We are learning to live in the Now, and our breath is never elsewhere. In the hubris of the ego we habitually think: "I am breathing," or "This is my breath." Yet each night we fall asleep and lose all sense of *me*, while obviously we continue to breathe. Thus, it would be more correct to say that breathing is a function of the body prior to me-consciousness. Breath awareness can act as a door between the opaque ego and the immediate Now, where who we really are always begins anew.

As I discussed in chapter 4, I call breath awareness "the friendship." As long as we can rest in friendship with our breath, we can never be completely lost in our minds. There is a thread forever connecting us to the present. We can always say, "Here am I," and return to the sense of a more spacious awareness. When we are present in our bodies, we can never be far from the beginning of ourselves.

As we move closer to our beginning, our egos have less opportunity to infiltrate our self-expression with the stuff of our personal psychologies, so we naturally become more spontaneous and authentic. Eventually, we can't help but develop a sense of humor about ourselves, because the potholes of Self-avoidance we fall into over and over again become so familiar.

The moment we recognize the contraction that comes as we lose contact with the Now, we return to our beginning. Immediately we are, once again, resting in the transparent presence of the light body, being breathed, connected to a larger intelligence, and seeing with new eyes. If we join this breath with our awareness, gradually the stress releases and we resume a state of peaceful alertness. Of course, if we congratulate ourselves for not falling into the pothole, we have just fallen into a different one. The basic understanding always remains: if you can conceive of yourself — anything whatsoever about who you are or are not — it can't be your true self. Relax even deeper.

The more we return toward our beginning, the less we project outside of ourselves from a sense of insufficiency. As we come to feel more and more sufficient as we are, the sense of needing to change falls away. We discover we are already *that* which we have been seeking. When we talk of a "spiritual path," what we are really doing is projecting that path, and this projection forms as a result of the distance we are living — in that moment — from our beginning. Unaware that the distance to be traveled is really within us, we are saying to ourselves that there is a path of some kind that we must travel *before* we can know our essence. But when we are no longer continually being driven away from our beginning by the thoughts and feelings that we were once unable to hold, there is no more path. The distance dissolves. We *are* the path, the beginning and the end.

Discovering the fullness of our beings does not require an

experience of spontaneous awakening. We can awaken gradually, through hundreds and even thousands of moments of grace. Moment by moment, we can learn to draw from the richness of our beginning in the midst of all that life demands of us. To support this potential, which is actually a process of returning to the Now in the midst of daily life, I have created an inquiry process called the Mandala of Being. It is not difficult to learn, and with practice you will find that it becomes a compass by which to return to your true self, again and again.

PART TWO

Utilizing *the* Power *of* Awareness

WELCOMING OURSELVES HOME

The Mandala
of Being

Where Do We Go When We Are
Not at the Beginning of Ourselves?

All of us, in moments of grace, have been imbued with a sense of wonder, gratitude, and love. This is not something we have to work toward. These feelings are far more than the welling up of satisfaction that might come from achieving a goal, getting a great new job, winning the lottery, or even falling in love. Deep joy and contentment, "the peace that passeth understanding," is actually our innate experience whenever we rest at the beginning of ourselves, unconflicted in awareness, not arguing with or resisting what *is*. This is our natural state.

Yet so pervasive is the self-protective conditioning that distances us from our feelings and the immediacy of our perceptions that we almost inevitably revert to the basic survival strategy of projecting our minds away from the present moment. This does protect us, to some extent, by removing us psychically from the place in which we can be most hurt: the present. But at the same time, leaving the Now distances our awareness from the Source and we lose energy — the power to consciously meet and hold whatever feeling is present. This self-protective reflex makes us like a computer that reverts to its default settings every time there is an overload. When we are overloaded, when there is something we don't want to experience directly, we default in a split second to our survival programming. We do this by moving into psychological time and psychological identities that we mistakenly believe to be who we are. The process is so habituated in us that we don't even realize what we are doing.

To learn to live from our innate fullness and greatest natural authority, it is necessary to understand the nature of the psychological realities we default into again and again. As it says in the Tao Te Ching, "If you want to shrink something, you must first allow it to expand."[1] By expanding our awareness of the ways we flee from the present and lose connection to the essential Self, we begin to "shrink" the process of Self-avoidance and thus learn to live more consistently as who we really are. We can frame our inquiry this way: Where do we go when we are not in the Now?

THE MANDALA OF BEING: A MODEL FOR SELF-INQUIRY AND RETURNING TO OUR ESSENCE

Ask yourself, "When I am not right here, right now, in the simple fullness and presence of my being, where have I gone?" If you consider this question carefully, you will see that there are only four possible directions your mind can carry you at the instant you leave the here and now of yourself. These four directions can be represented as poles of two intersecting, fundamental continuums that form the basis of our human experience: time and subject-object consciousness (see figure 1).

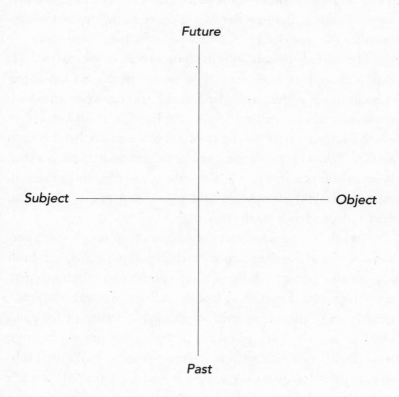

Figure 1.

Time intersecting subject-object consciousness.

The time continuum is generally the easiest for us to grasp. We all comprehend that time flows from past to present to future. When our awareness leaves the timeless Now-moment and enters into time, then our minds can be in either the past or the future. This is not the actual past or future but the past or future viewed through whatever identities are governing our psychologies at that exact moment. Past and future as we can know them are always psychological experiences of time, the imaginings or attitudes of the particular identity through which we are looking. Because they are a continuum, the way we remember the past determines how we anticipate the future.

The second continuum is the form of our basic consciousness that philosophers have termed "subject-object." Subject-object consciousness is the particular level of consciousness in which there must always be a subject — the knower — and an object — the known. It is the basis of what we mean by the term *duality*: When there is a me, then simultaneously there is a you. When there is self, there is also other, observer and observed, experiencer and experience, and so on. No one of these can exist independently of the other.

I think of subject-object consciousness in much more personal terms, as the continuum of relationship, because it is built around our point of view as a separate self in relationship to everything else. From this place we call *me*, we ceaselessly participate in relationships with an infinite diversity of forms of *other*, or *you*: there is *me* and my thoughts; *me* and my feelings; *me* and everyone else: friends, enemies, insects, molecules, subatomic particles, quasars, galaxies, and so on, infinitely. What is crucial to understand is that *me* and *you*, as two poles of a continuum, are always influencing each other. In the psychological domain, how you feel about yourself — whether insecure or confident, embarrassed or proud — will influence how you perceive another person or a situation. Conversely, how you judge any object, or "other" — for example, whether you praise it or denigrate it — instantly influences how you feel in yourself. Likewise, how you react to any so-called outer circumstance, such as a financial setback, determines how you feel in yourself.

Even at the level of our most basic perceptions of so-called outer physical reality, the reciprocal relationship between subject and object is inescapable. Our perception of a tree actually has an effect on that tree, and the tree has an effect on us, although we are rarely aware of the effect because, at this macro level, the influence is minimal. However, this continuum of relationship between subject and object becomes much more obvious in the domain of quantum physics, where the manner in which an experimenter envisions and structures an experiment actually influences the results of the experiment.

By drawing the time continuum and the subject-object (relationship) continuum as two perpendicular lines that dissect a large circle, and which intersect in the center of a small inner circle — the Now position — we create the model that I call the Mandala of Being. Because we don't usually think of ourselves as subjects, and others as objects, I use here the more familiar *me* as an equivalent to the "subject," and *you* as an equivalent to the "object" (see figure 2, page 162).[2]

In the Mandala of Being, the large circle represents the totality of who we are, with our complex and often perplexing ability to be grateful and resentful, trusting and fearful, peaceful and violent, loving and hateful, from one moment to the next. The center of the Mandala is the Now-moment, where, through the quality of our attention, we constantly create ourselves anew. In any mandala, whether the center is shown as a point or a lotus flower or a Buddha resting in profound self-possession and repose, the true center is always the Now, where all the opposing forces in our lives have a common origin and therefore can be integrated. In the present, through the power of our awareness, we exercise direct conscious relationship to our thinking and feelings instead of being victims of them. In our own now-ness, we touch the Source from which our essence radiates. This is presence.

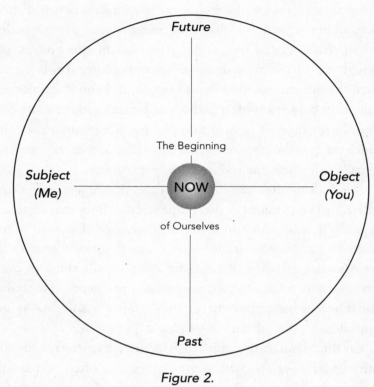

Figure 2.
The Mandala of Being.

The four positions on the circumference of the circle — the Past, Future, Subject (Me), and Object (You) — are the four directions our minds are drawn in when leaving the Now. These four are the foundations of our psychological consciousness. The moment we lose sufficient connection with the Now, we collapse into our own peculiar psychological realms in which everything we perceive and think (about ourselves, others, past, and future) is distorted in accordance with the particular adaptation of our survival personalities and enculturation. It is a personal psychological dream world. When our minds are conditioned to live close to the perimeter of the Mandala — away from the Now center — we have a false sense of self and a mistaken view of others that blinds us to their essence and us to our own. When we learn to rest within the now-ness of ourselves, we are better able to express our essence. In our lives and in human affairs in general, our psychological realities, not our essence, betrays us.

The Mandala of Being reflects two very different levels of conscious human functioning. Some of us live almost exclusively turned away from the Now. Psychologically we are wholly oriented toward the Past, the Future, the Me, and the You positions of the Mandala. Others of us are awakening to our true selves and have begun to orient ourselves toward the Now position. This simple shift, though few sustain it with any regularity, nevertheless has enormous consequences for how we understand ourselves and how we can choose to live.

The Mandala of Being provides a model for self-inquiry into the specific emotional dynamics that govern our lives at each of the four outer positions. At the same time, it provides a practice of Self-remembering, reorienting us toward the Now, where we can live as our authentic and spontaneous selves. In chapter 9, I discuss how to engage this practice.

By becoming acquainted with the four positions of the Mandala — Past, Future, Me, You — and understanding their crucial relationship to the central Now position, we can each learn to recognize the unique ways we abandon the present and lose contact with the immediacy of our beings. We can come to understand how we sustain false identities through the beliefs we hold about the past and the future and through the recurrent stories we tell ourselves (and believe) about who we, and others, are. Inevitably we recognize that much of what we constantly tell ourselves through our thinking is false. We can learn to appreciate what each of these stories or beliefs does to our states of being and recognize the actual sensations they create in us.

A simple demonstration can convey the impact of our stories on our sensations, on the way we feel in our bodies. Imagine a clear plastic bottle filled with water, to which we add a handful of dirt. When the bottle remains undisturbed, the dirt settles and the water becomes, if not fully clear, then close to it. However, if I pick up the bottle and shake it, immediately the water becomes turbid, and it can take a long time for the dirt to settle again. We can imagine that the bottle of water is our body and the dirt represents sensations of anger, tension, anxiety, and so on. When our attention is resting softly near the beginning of ourselves, our emotions and stress "settle" and we become calmer and clearer in our beings. If our true selves are emanating from the cores of our being, and by analogy from the center of the bottle, then when our "mud" settles it can shine forth freely. This is when we experience so much gratitude and really feel the blessing of life.

However, the moment we tell ourselves a story, such as "I have to be more loving" or "I'll never be happy in my work," those very thoughts are equivalent to picking up the bottle and shaking it. Instantly our sense of self becomes muddy with feelings of guilt, shame, anger, and anxiety. Stress hormones go streaming though us, our breathing becomes tight, and our musculatures become armored so that our beings become opaque with tension and negative feelings. At such times we are likely to think reactively, behave poorly, and make bad decisions.

The idea of the bottle as a visual cue came to me from a line in Stephen Mitchell's translation of the Tao Te Ching: "Do you have the patience to wait till your mud settles and the water is clear? Can you remain unmoving till the right action arises by itself?"[3] As we begin to understand that we do not have to live as victims of our own thinking, the muddy water is a helpful and wry reminder of what we are doing to ourselves, and that there is always another choice: to let our mud settle. Sometimes in a group, when someone is talking about himself or herself, or about others, the past, or the future, in a way that stirs up "mud," I actually pick up a bottle — with compassion — and shake it, turning the water murky. This demonstration graphically makes the point that every thought that judges or rejects what actually *is* has its revenge on our physiologies. When we can understand this and begin to let our bodily states guide us toward well-being, we have discovered the real work of liberation.

I have taught hundreds of people to use the Mandala model, and for many of them it has become the basic foundation of their spiritual paths. By elucidating how we "leave ourselves" and what this actually feels like, it also shows us how to return to the Now, where our real selves begin again in each moment. In this way the Mandala work gives us what so many of us lack: a true place to start from, states of being we can know in our bodies that links us to a universal source we can always return to.

The Center of the Mandala of Being:
The Now Position

T. S. Eliot referred to the Now-moment as "the intersection of the timeless with time."[4] This intersection point in the Mandala of Being can ultimately be understood as a place of pure awareness or pure being, in which subject and object, as well as past and future, coalesce, and there is only a state of pure, unitive consciousness. This is, in each of us, our true beginning.

Of course, nothing at all can be said about the true Now. As in talking about the true self, to talk about the Now we have to enter into some level of subject-object duality in order to use words and concepts.5 In Buddhism, this state is termed *nirvana*, which literally means "extinction," as in the extinction of a candle flame when it is blown out. Nirvana is the highest mystical experience of changelessness, inner peace, and freedom obtained through the extinction of the self. Obviously it is not the presence of awareness that is extinguished but the dissociated point of view of the separate self — the ego-I. Once there is no separation between experiencer and experience, we are one, and this is the most profound realization of wholeness and of union with all of existence. All mystical traditions have their own way of describing this state of absolute fullness or pure consciousness. Entering this state spontaneously, as I described in chapter 6, completely changed my life. It shifted the referent for my identity from me-consciousness to the sense of emptiness or ineffable being that is pure awareness itself.

But working with the Mandala of Being does not require any previous mystical realization. The Now is still the Now however we understand it and whatever degree of mystical connection we may or may not have had. I like to think of the Now as an ever-shifting continuum of presence. Looking at the Mandala, we can visualize that, as we move closer to the center, we are becoming more present, and each moment has greater depth. Moment by moment, we have the sense of meeting and being met much more fully in all our relationships. Colors are brighter, the light seems to be alive — every perception, every sensation is much richer. As we move toward the center — the Now position — life surprises us and we find ourselves all the more frequently falling into love, forgiveness, gratitude, and compassion.

The beauty of the Mandala work is that, regardless of our level of spiritual experience and understanding, we can use it to bring ourselves closer to our own essence and a deeper meeting with life. All we need to do is use the power of awareness to grasp where we actually go when we leave the Now of ourselves — what kinds of thoughts link us to the past, future, me, and you, and what kind of sensation takes over as we "stir up" our mud. This nonreactive attention to the sensation itself will automatically begin the process of differentiation that frees us to realize more clearly who we really are.

Orienting awareness toward the present has profound consequences for how we live our lives. We gradually recognize in our bodies and hearts that the closer we are to the Now of ourselves — the intersection point at the center of the Mandala of Being — the more spiritual and creative energy we have. To move toward the center of the Mandala is to return to the Source. Our minds become stronger; we have greater powers of attention and awareness. This automatically enables us to regard ourselves with much greater objectivity and to be inherently less identified with our old stories. As a result we become spontaneous and authentic. We carry true authority, the authority that comes from a growing connection to our essence, not that which is borrowed from diplomas or other culturally sanctioned achievements. It is an authority that is not imposing but humble, amused, kindhearted, and forgiving. I refer to this as higher-self functioning.

In contrast, the further we move from the center, the less adapted we are to the present and the more we actually contract into an unshakable identification with our own separateness. This sense of separateness manifests as various identities that then have to be defended. Our basic psychologies become strategic and are always to some degree dominated by fear, distrust, calculation, and survival. Because we are moving away from the Source, we lose spiritual energy and become weak-minded. We become more and more susceptible to identifying with our stories and emotions, defining ourselves according to our cultural conditioning, and becoming addicted to the reinforcement of group mind. I refer to this as lower-self functioning.[6]

The crucial reason for learning to return to the beginning of ourselves is that here we gradually build the spiritual muscle — the power of our attention — needed to meet the difficult and even untamed emotions that have driven us away from ourselves all our lives. We can observe the stories we use to avoid core feelings, and can disengage from the tamed emotions these stories create in us. When we are truly present in the Now-moment, thoughts can seem to happen in slow motion. In the film *The Matrix*, when Neo awakens to himself as The One and can see the bullets coming, he simply says, "No," and the bullets suddenly slow down in their trajectory toward him. This reminds me of the slowing of thought we experience in the Now-moment. When we are resting in our beginning, we don't even have to say "No." We are at-one in ourselves and can actually watch the stories emerging and dissolving before they ever become *me*. This disinterest is not the denial or repression of these stories, or the feelings they create; it is Self-realization. We know these stories are not who we really are, so they are not relevant. As we learn to easily recognize the stories that have in the past lured us away from our essence, and we see that they have lost their power to do so, we can regard them with amusement when we see them arising. They are like old friends, and it is hard not to smile at an old friend, especially when you know that this friend will try to take you right back into an all-too-familiar struggle that you now know better than to give any energy to.

Nothingness, the extinction of the self, is our egos' deepest fear. As long as identification with me-consciousness remains strong, there will eventually be a kind of dark night, a profound despair or sense of annihilation. When this occurs, even if our capacity to meet these feelings has become greater as the result of our spiritual work, our basic defense will be the same. We will throw ourselves fiercely back into the intense mental activity that fabricates a perpetual stream of stories in order to maintain some familiar level of our sense of self. Generally this is a state of despair, as we ricochet between fear of annihilation and compulsive thinking. We are seeking comprehension of something that can never be resolved at the level of thinking. But even if these thoughts create further confusion and suffering, it is always a form of suffering that does not fundamentally threaten our sense of a separate self to the same extent that the core feeling does. Therefore, we like our stories, and we defend our stories, because, we feel, at least this is *me*, whereas the core feeling, being untamed, threatens to unseat our sense of *me*.

When we ask, "Where do we go when we leave the Now, the beginning of ourselves?" we are inquiring into how we keep defeating our own self-transcending impulses because of our egos' fear of nonbeing. We could call it avoiding enlightenment. Understanding how we do this is an essential part of the path of Self-realization. Learning to come back to our beginning is also necessary to truly heal the wounds of early childhood so that we do not have to keep fleeing from our untamed emotions and externalizing our fears.

The Continuum of Psychological Time: The Past Position

This position of the Mandala of Being is composed of the beliefs or stories we have about our pasts or the past in general. These stories are about what we regret, blame, feel guilty about, feel ashamed of, feel nostalgic about, or are proud of. These stories are memories about ourselves, or specific situations, and especially about people whom we recall in an especially positive or negative light. These stories become the emotional basis for interpreting the present.

Some people tend to be more identified with the past than others are. If I am one of these people, then when I disconnect from the beginning of myself, I have a tendency to land in the past and use the past (by means of the past stories I bring into my consciousness) to rationalize or explain what I am feeling or believing right now. I project the past onto the present, and regardless of how happy or unhappy I may have been then, the effect is always to diminish the living presence of the Now.

The Continuum of Psychological Time: The Future Position

This position of the Mandala of Being contains all the stories we imagine about the future. These are what we fantasize in the present about our future health, relationships, work, finances, and every other aspect of life, as well as our fantasies about the future of our children or other loved ones. This position of the Mandala is all our hopes and dreams, plans, fears, and worries about the future, and the emotional atmosphere these create in us.

Many of us tend to primarily identify with the future. When we lose contact with the beginning of ourselves and cease risking being fully present in the Now, our minds predominantly fall forward in time. We use the energy of hope or fear to rationalize our choices. Hope or fear about the future, while seemingly reasonable, is actually the way we sustain the basic survival orientation of our emotional holding environment.

The Continuum of Relationship: The Subject, or Me, Position

This position of the Mandala of Being consists of all the ways that we objectify ourselves. In the Now-moment, we are as we are, and nothing can be said about who we ultimately are. Any *me* that we can think of is always elsewhere. Therefore, virtually anything that we can think about ourselves is just a story or belief about who we are. This includes all our judgments about ourselves, and all our beliefs about what we want or need in order to be fulfilled: our "I am" and "I am not" stories, as well as our "I should" and "I shouldn't" stories. This position contains our fantasies and day-dreams in which we imagine ourselves in different ways.

The Me position is usually the hardest for us to grasp because we are so thoroughly and unconsciously identified with this construction from early in life. It is the basic consciousness of the separate self, and we are so embedded in it that we do not realize that *me* is only a creation of thought, not a thing we can locate and touch or that we actually are. But while *me* is not objectively real, when we tell ourselves stories about ourselves, they have real power to affect us emotionally and energetically.

Me stories always fall into two basic categories: they are either depressive or grandiose. In them, we either berate and negate ourselves or praise and inflate ourselves. Through *me* stories we can create misery or temporary happiness in the Now, but in them we are never looking at who we really are, or living life fully.

Some of us, rather than overly identifying with past or future, tend to fall more readily into the Me position when we leave the Now of ourselves. What we are actually doing is defaulting into our core identities of insufficiency or into identities that compensate for this insufficiency. Here too this simply creates our familiar emotional (third) holding environment.

The Continuum of Relationship:
The Object, or You, Position

This position of the Mandala of Being represents all our beliefs and stories about what we could term the *other*, or simply *you*. *You* can be anything we perceive as being elsewhere. Even our own thoughts and feelings can be considered objects of consciousness. For many people, money and God are among the most powerful *you* stories. But generally and most significantly, *you* tends to be other people. When we inquire into the You position, we look at all the stories we tell ourselves about these people: our judgments about them, what we believe they think about us, and what we believe we need from them in order to feel good about ourselves. The You position contains our beliefs about how others should or shouldn't be, and particularly our beliefs about how they are that angers or hurts us.

How any *you*, whether person or thing, God or money, exists in itself is not what we are considering here. We are considering the power we give to any *you* by means of the stories we tell ourselves about him, her, or it. Our past or future stories can poison or diminish the immediacy of the present with negative feelings or false beliefs (remember the image of the bottle that is shaken and becomes muddy), and our *you* stories do the same thing. Every *you* story injects a particular emotional quality into the present moment — anger, sadness, happiness — and since subject-object consciousness is a continuum, whatever quality is generated by our *you* stories simultaneously creates a specific emotional holding environment in *me*.

USING THE MANDALA OF BEING AS A MAP

At this point it is important to realize that while I have presented these four positions as seemingly independent — and we will be approaching them that way as we consider them more fully — they are actually inseparable because they invariably overlap. For example, the moment we enter a particular *me* story, that *me* has its own bias that causes us to judge others in a particular way, and it has an inherent slant on how it recalls the past and imagines the future. The same happens if our minds, in leaving the Now, leap first to a *you* story: immediately this implies a particular *me* believing the story and, again, an inevitable bias about the past and future. *Me*, as a false self, is really the basic source of distortion in our psychological worlds that determines the tone for the stories in the other positions, and we are blind to it.

As we observe our own thinking, we can see that each thought tends to belong predominantly to one of these four categories, even if it could arguably be placed in one or more of the others as well. More important, our own emotional dynamics, as we will soon see, can be understood in terms of which direction in the Mandala we most often tend to move when we leave our beginning.

The Mandala of Being is a map by which we can begin to understand the reality we constantly create when we leave the Now of ourselves. Take, for example, a situation in which someone has disappointed us or we believe we have been rejected and we feel sad. If we are able to stay in the Now position and experience the sadness as a unique sensation without reacting to it, the sadness will quickly become part of a larger quality of openness and vulnerability, and perhaps will even become compassion for ourselves and the other person. But few of us are so connected to ourselves. Instead what most of us do is collapse into the sadness. But the moment we do so, we implicitly put "I am" in front of it — "I am sad" — and it becomes a *me* story.

We have moved to the Me position of the Mandala. Then, because subject-object is a continuum, this *me* story will inevitably have to rationalize or explain *its* sadness by telling *itself* another story. For example, in a situation like this, I might turn toward the You position and attribute my sadness to my belief that *you* have rejected me: "I'm sad because John [or some other person] can't accept me as I am." Now my sense of self depends on a *you* story that I believe about the behavior of another person. Of course, none of us can ever absolutely know what goes on in someone else; it may be that John is simply choosing to honor his own needs and is not, in his mind, rejecting me. I am telling myself a *you* story that I can never really know is true, but which serves to rationalize *my* sadness by blaming someone else and thereby sustaining *my* (*me* story) identification with it.

Meanwhile, the Me position story ("I'm sad") and the You position story ("because John can't accept me as I am") cannot be sustained without a history and a future. I implicitly require (and so create) psychological time. I turn to the past and, because I am identified with sadness, invariably remember experiences that made me sad, perhaps when I felt judged or rejected by my father. I might then think of a past story: "My father never accepted me either" ("I am sad because John doesn't accept me as I am, just like my father didn't"). I have moved (my mind) into the Past position and let the past, as I remember it, be the basis for how I interpret the present and why I automatically assume John doesn't accept me. And then finally, because time is a continuum, if I believe I was rejected in my *past* story, I will inevitably anticipate a *future* story that creates the same emotional quality as the past. So as my mind moves to the Future position, perhaps I imagine: "I will never find a man who is good for me." Now I have inhabited all four positions of the Mandala: "I'm sad (Me) because John can't accept me as

I am (You), just like my father didn't (Past), and I will never find a man who is good for me (Future). I have completely embedded myself in the energy of sadness and made my identification with this victim-self unshakable.

But all this is more than just a few beliefs or stories; it is actually a self-perpetuated emotional holding environment, very similar to what we internalized in our childhood. Instead of engaging the innate wholeness of myself as an aware being, I recruit my awareness to support an underlying or core identity as an unworthy or unlovable person destined to always be unhappy in some way.

And so, starting with a moment of sadness that I could not meet, feel, and hold, in a split second I become the victim of my own unconscious self-creation story, which saddles me with a false identity of insufficiency and its world of suffering and fear. And this aggregate of *me*, *you*, *past*, and *future* stories can hold us for minutes, hours, days, or most of our lives, because the *me* story "I am sad" can instead be "I am angry, numb, exhausted, afraid, unhappy, guilty, ashamed, wounded," and so on. The *you* story about John could just as well have been about Bill, Liz, an employer, the economy, a lawsuit, the car, the house, or whatever. The *future* story "I'll never find a man who is good for me" could equally be "I'll never be free, fulfilled, safe, able to slow down, respected, understood, wealthy enough, seen for who I really am," and so on. And the *past* story about my father never accepting me could just as easily be about my mother, my brother, my sister, my spouse, or any person or past situation that I blame, feel guilty about, or regret.

All this endless avoidance of who we are right now begins when we are unwilling or unable to risk the full experience of the moment. It first started when we were young and had no idea what we were doing. We take for granted this way of constructing reality, and it continues until such stories create so much suffering that the suffering itself drives us, as adults, to consciously exercise the power of awareness and inquire into how we have become so miserable. When we finally do see that all our suffering stems from the fact that we create our stories from the wrong starting point, we can learn to return to the Now of ourselves and become fully present. We can "let our mud settle" until we rediscover the fullness of our beings. The Mandala work is rich because it gives us a framework that not only makes us conscious of where we go but also always shows us who we truly are — that ineffable essence that we must learn to abide in and trust moment by moment.

In this work, we approach the Mandala of Being first as a conceptual map and tool. But when we begin to regularly use it to reflect our own thinking and behavior, it quickly becomes a practice of Self-remembering by which we bring ourselves, moment by moment, into fullness and presence. By understanding that when we leave ourselves we are predominantly in one of only four possible places — Me, You, Past, or Future — we gain a powerful way of *interrupting* our habit of Self-avoidance. As soon as we realize we have left our beginning, we have already returned to a position of more complete intelligence from which to observe and experience ourselves honestly and respond to life sincerely.

The power of using the Mandala model to recognize that we have left ourselves quickly becomes obvious. To describe what this is like, let me use the example of Cary, a very bright thirty-year-old literature teacher whom I counseled. Cary was dissatisfied with so much in her life. She spoke about how difficult it was at work: the students weren't respectful; they didn't want to learn; parents didn't care or were too involved; she had too many papers to grade at home; there wasn't enough time for herself; the curriculum suffocated her spontaneity and creativity in the classroom; she would never get ahead financially. These were just a few of the stories that regularly plagued her. But the most disturbing one was that she considered this career a compromise. She had wanted to do something with her life that she felt was more adventurous and creative and hadn't because of her survival fears. While all her complaints and desires could be considered valid at their own level, a deeper truth was that they were just stories, and telling them to herself caused her suffering. Each story kept her from living the simple fullness of herself, and each time she told herself one of these stories, she poisoned her Now and drained her own energy.

In teaching her to work with the Mandala process, I suggested that she welcome this period of her life as an opportunity for spiritual practice. Every time she realized that she had left the Now-moment and gone into *me, you, past,* or *future* stories while at work, her task was simply to return to the present and meet whatever she was feeling, without reaction. She was to just breathe, be with herself, and step into the present. I was asking her to slowly grow her faith in her true self. In this way she would hold on to a little of the energy that she usually dissipated by entering the stories.

I explained to her that she needed this energy if her own transformation was to be anything more than running away from the idea that "this isn't it." I told her to think of the Mandala work as simply learning to release the power of just a single story daily, by not giving herself over to it. I pointed out that, by so doing, each day she could return from her job a little less poisoned and with a little more energy, feeling a little more alive. I told her that she did not have to think about changing anything in her life except her own Self-avoidance. I suggested that at the end of a year, the incremental increase in her energy would cumulatively become a significant shift in where, in herself, she lived her life from. As a result she would naturally begin to attract new potentials and opportunities for her life. She would hardly have to make a choice; she would automatically take the right steps.

And that is exactly what happened. She grew stronger and more confident in herself and naturally began to follow her heart. She discovered that when she stopped telling herself stories about having no time, she did have time after all, and she began to take dance classes. Within two years she had shifted to a part-time teaching position and had begun a new career as a dance and movement instructor, something she truly feels stimulated by and is grateful to be doing.

One of the questions I am asked most frequently in my seminars and retreats is "How can we take the heightened state of consciousness achieved during the retreat and maintain it at home?" Many of us have had the experience of arriving at a state of expansion and clarity, but after returning to our everyday lives, soon find ourselves back in our usual moods, worries, and frenzies, and possibly even feel overwhelmed. Whether the heightened clarity was a completely unanticipated state of grace, or the result of a meditation retreat or workshop experience, or it just gradually emerged during a long holiday, the sense of being centered and clear soon wears off. Why? Where does all the energy that we acquire go?

My answer is simple: Past, Future, Me, You. A way to image this energy-loss process is to think of ourselves as sieves. When the energy is coming in from the Source faster than we let it leak away, we become clearer, more balanced, more authentic, and more likely to express love, steadfastness, compassion, and forgiveness. But when the incoming energy leaks away faster than it can be replenished, we begin to contract into our usual irritability, hurriedness, or control issues, and our survival personalities take over once again.

Energy, as I am using the term here, is really our power of awareness, and this is always a product of our proximity to the Now-moment. At the beginning of ourselves, we are united with the Source; the further we move away, the faster we leak away that energy and diminish our capacity for awareness. Our *past, future, me, you* stories are little black holes that continually suck away our energy by creating their own vortices of unreality. This unreality, like a dream, seems real to us at the time, but from within it there is no way to be replenished by the Source. We seem to always be at the edge of exhaustion, wondering why are we so tired, why is there so little (or so much) time. Why can't we seem to pull ourselves together? The answer is simple: we are paddling without putting our paddle in the water. We don't grasp that we are replenished only by the Source, and that for this to happen we must return to the Now, to our beginning. We have to take the risk of staying in the present. Therefore, one of the most important things we can learn is to see clearly the four places we go when we leave ourselves. Then we can wake up from these stories and "re-source" ourselves, moment by moment.

As we enter this work, it is essential to reaffirm that we are exercising the power of awareness to recognize how we leave ourselves and, thereby, learn to return our attention to the present. In making this inquiry, we must resist the habitual tendency to judge our success. Judging means we are using awareness to serve our survival personalities, and this only puts us back in the old holding environment of insufficiency. Skillful use of the power of awareness lets us make our stories conscious and returns us to the Now moment — the central Now position of the Mandala of Being — where who we really are is always inherently more than whatever we are conscious of. In the Mandala work, we automatically abide in our true selves with ever-growing faith precisely as we come to understand how we leave the Self.

To live fully in the present all the time may not be possible. My wife likens it to balancing on the head of a pin and inevitably falling off, over and over. But in learning to ride a bicycle, initially falling off is the very experience that allows us to discover the balance which constitutes riding the bike. As we learn to live more consistently in the Now, we are bound to frequently "fall off" into our stories. But by learning how we fall and where we tend to land, we become more familiar with the place from which we have fallen — the Now of ourselves. We discover a new equilibrium, a centered state of being that has always existed prior to our stories, in which we are at ease, authentic, clear, spontaneous, and loving.

CHAPTER NINE

Experiencing *the* Mandala *of* Being

I invite you to ground and integrate what I have so far presented, by exploring a practice that has the power to guide you to new presence and fullness in your life. You will be exploring the Mandala of Being in the same way that I teach it in my seminars. This work will help you to acquire the means of being a truly self-determined individual. It will show you how to stand in your own light, consistently present to your true self throughout the course of daily living.

This chapter has a workbook format. It moves back and forth between commentary and sections where I guide you through the Mandala self-inquiry process. I suggest that you first read through the whole chapter and then go back and actually work with the questions about the four positions. Follow the guidelines for letting yourself feel the sensations and emotions generated by each of your stories. It is essential that you give yourself the time to feel what it is like to rest in the Now. Take in each of the aphorisms that support remembering who you really are in your now-ness, and let yourself feel the space they invite you to feel.

Your understanding of this work will be much more grounded in you if you give yourself the opportunity to have a palpable experience of your stories and contrast this feeling with the felt sense of who you are in the Now. There is a tremendous difference between conceptual understanding and knowledge that has the opportunity to penetrate every cell of your body. What we know only in our heads is easily overridden by the first feeling that takes us out of the Now and sends us into our stories. But when we actually have the experience of presence, our stories simply have no power.

In my seminars, I divide the group into pairs and have each pair work together with a Mandala arranged on the floor. Each member of the pair takes a turn walking around the Mandala and speaks his or her stories aloud in each position. The other partner takes notes so that the person who is doing the inquiry can refer back to them later. The scribe can also provide additional support by repeating the specific questions that help to focus the inquiry. Exploring the Mandala with a partner, we can gain insight into ourselves as we listen to our partner identify his or her stories. Having the support of another person's attention can also make it easier to stay present with some of the more challenging feelings that the stories may evoke.

If you are walking around the Mandala of Being by yourself, have a pad of paper and a pen handy. You will want to be your own scribe, jotting down brief summaries of the specific stories or beliefs as you recall them in each of the four positions.

To construct your own Mandala, first look at figure 2 on page 162. Next, locate an area on the floor where you can create your Mandala. It is important to choose a location where you can work privately, without interruption. Use a piece of paper or cardboard as your central position marker and draw a circle on it. The circle symbolizes that, at the beginning of ourselves, we are ineffable consciousness — a deep, open state of awareness — so write the word *Now*, or *Beginning*, inside the circle, and set this position marker on the floor. Use four other pieces of paper or cardboard as position markers, labeling them "Me," "You," "Past," and "Future," and orient them as shown in figure 2. (I'm suggesting that you name the Subject pole "Me" and the Object pole "You" for the sake of simplicity and because we do not think of ourselves as a "subject of consciousness" and others as an "object of consciousness.") Leave one or two feet between each of these positions and the central Now position.

By laying out the Mandala in this way, you can walk from one position to another so that your whole body participates in the inquiry experience. I have found this to be especially important. When we combine purposeful physical movement with self-inquiry, the learning becomes more immediate.

As you stand in one of the positions and tell your stories, it is valuable to speak them aloud so that you can hear your own words. Verbalizing and listening in this way seems to create more distance between the teller and the stories, and therefore you can gain greater objectivity about them than would occur if you simply allowed them to surface and be reviewed as thoughts in your head. It is also a much more precise way to connect to the feelings created by the story.[1]

When I am facilitating people in the Mandala work, I always repeat their basic stories back to them using their own words and the same intonation. I also echo their descriptions of what they are feeling as they recognize what their stories create in them. Hearing what they have just said seems to assist them in staying connected to the stories they are working with, because it keeps the mind from jumping away. This increases their ability to feel the current and immediate effect of their stories. As you are working alone (or with a partner), say each story aloud more than once to create these same benefits for yourself.

If for any reason you are unable to physically walk around the Mandala speaking your stories aloud, you can draw the Mandala on paper and then jot down your stories as you move your hand, or a small object such as a pebble, from one position to another, as if the Mandala of Being were a kind of board game. Nonetheless, I suggest that when you have an opportunity, you still read your stories aloud to yourself so that you can hear them and feel them more completely.[2]

After standing in any of the other positions, always step back to the center of the Mandala, the Now position. Each time you return to the Now, allow your mind to begin to sink into your body, into your immediate now-ness. Whenever you are standing in the Now position, it is initially helpful to describe aloud the shift in feeling that takes place, just as you have in the other positions. After a while, however, the more you move into the Now, the quieter your mind will become. At a certain point, trying to describe the sensation of presence may interrupt the deepening connection to yourself, so speaking can become counterproductive. When I am guiding someone standing in the Now position, I ask them to try to describe what they are feeling or sensing. However, as they go deeper, I allow more and more quiet time. I suggest that as you listen into yourself in the Now position, getting in touch with what is happening in your sense of self, you allow yourself to softly describe whatever you are sensing, but also give yourself enough silence to rest and go deeper into that space.

Stepping back and forth between the Now and the other

positions of the Mandala, combined with verbalizing our experience, helps us to feel the difference between how we are in our stories and how we are in our now-ness. Eventually it is this felt sense that guides us, because it is much more immediate than thinking. It demonstrates for us the consequences of our stories in our own bodies, and then reinforces the crucial inner shift of *stepping back from* these stories (as a source for our identities) to the beginning of ourselves.

THE NOW POSITION

Step to the center of the Mandala of Being and stand on the Now position marker.

Grasping the potential to return the mind to the Now is key to the Mandala work. It is the starting point, and ending point, of every inquiry. It is crucial that we remember again and again: who we really are always begins Now. This fundamental truth is the most empowering thing we can ever learn.

Softly say this to yourself: "Who I really am begins right now." Gently "listen to," or feel, the space both within and around you that this recognition invites. With tender curiosity, acknowledge your now-ness as it arises fresh in each instant.

I express this turning of attention into the Now to embrace our own now-ness as "Here am I."

Experience this for yourself right now: Here am I.

Remaining in the Now position, let your mind sink down into your body. Inhabit your body with the presence of your awareness. Feel the humming vibrancy of your physical being. Feel the continuously arising gift of your breathing.

Welcome your breath as your friend. Travel with it, one breath at a time, deeper into the sensation of your being.

As if your breath were the finest feather, "brush" any sensation you find, maintaining exquisite attention. Soften yourself within your body. Keep releasing any tension that develops in your breathing.

Feel how your mind becomes quieter as you become ever more softly present in the here and now. Notice the spaciousness growing in your sense of self.

If your eyes have closed, open them from time to time and let your gaze rest softly on whatever you see around you. Notice any sounds.

Perception is always in the Now. The division between inner and outer is a construct of our thinking mind, not our experience as we rest deeper in the Now.

Come down out of your head and enter into the full spaciousness of yourself. Let go of the inclination to remain a spectator or commentator. Allow your mind to sink down into its essential state as pure presence.

One way to visualize this is to see your "mud" settling and the "water" of your consciousness gradually growing clearer.

Continue to stand in the Now position until you can actually feel, at least to some small degree, that you have gone deeper into your now-ness.

Moving to the Now position is not a question of avoiding anything or changing anything. There is no need to try to stop thinking; this only creates tension. Just as the heart pumps blood, the mind flows thoughts. But as we return to the present, there is less me-consciousness for these thoughts to grab on to, and our minds naturally grow calmer. The thoughts seem as if they are further off, less important, and less able to attract our attention. Likewise, there is no need to try to change or escape any emotion that is present. Just turning our inner gaze directly toward the emotion and steadily brushing it with feather-light attention allows the energy of the emotion to release into the spaciousness of our beings.

At their root, many of our most difficult feelings, even despair and shame, open us to an exquisite vulnerability when we cease to create stories about them. It is this vulnerability that we must begin to trust, rather than avoid or fear. This is where true growth in consciousness takes place.

The moment we inhabit the now-ness of ourselves, we regain the innate understanding "I am sufficient as I am." We break the "this isn't it" cycle of dissatisfaction and the restless chase after "this *is* it." We do not feel as if anything is missing when we come back to the Now. Even if a sensation of lack is present, it is something to experience, to be intimate with in its own right, not something to excite our minds into stories of insufficiency and neediness.

Each moment is full as it is. We can begin to feel that who we are right now is enough. There is no other place we need go to heal ourselves or complete ourselves. In the stillness of our own now-ness, we realize, "I am already *that* for which I have been seeking."

These two understandings, "I am sufficient as I am" and "I am already *that* for which I have been seeking," become abiding truths as we learn to rest in the Now of ourselves.

In this chapter, whenever I invite you to step back to the Now position, I repeat these aphorisms of Self-remembering. At first they may seem to be simple affirmations, but as you spend time moving into the feeling of these essential truths and learn to trust the peacefulness they invite in you, they become foundational blocks for learning to begin anew in yourself, in each moment.

The center of the Mandala is where all our stories are gradually extinguished, and where, in the immediacy of the moment, all feelings can be held and experienced in their purity. In this experience, we grow in spaciousness. The true language of the Now is never words: it is silence and presence. This is the beginning and the end of who we really are.

Take a few moments to rest in the Now of yourself...

I am sufficient as I am.

I am already *that* for which I have been seeking.

By starting your inquiry from the Now position, you have had an opportunity to taste the simple, unconditional fullness of your being. But in daily life, the present is not where we have become conditioned to center our awareness. We live instead in psychological time, and our self-identification is supported by an ever-changing array of stories that rationalize or justify what we refer to when we say *me*.

THE *ME* STORIES

Step to the Me position in the Mandala of Being.[3]

Open your awareness toward anything that comes to mind as you connect to the sense of who you believe you are when you think or say "me" or "I."

The following questions will help you to focus this inquiry:

What are the stories or beliefs I have about myself?

What are my judgments about myself?

What are my "shoulds" and "shouldn'ts" about myself?

What do I believe I need to be, or have to do, in order to feel good about myself?

Let these questions help you become aware of the conscious, and often subconscious, ways you tend to label yourself, define yourself, and set conditions that you believe are necessary for your happiness, security, and sense of being in control.

To ground this inquiry, think about actual situations in your life where your mind has told stories about you.

For example, maybe you feel that you reacted overly critically when your son came home with a bad report card, and then you told yourself, "It's all my fault. I am not a good mother." Generally, when we are so embedded in this kind of thinking, it does not occur to us to see such statements as stories. We automatically assume they are true, even though if we stopped to challenge them, we would eventually see that they are judgments.

To help you evoke some specific stories, begin by recalling a particular scenario in which you felt uncomfortable in some way. Think of a time when you felt insecure, frightened, sad, angry, competitive, or jealous. Or you could bring to mind a situation in which you felt particularly good about yourself, perhaps proud, attractive, powerful, or even superior.

Ask yourself: "What was I telling myself at that time?"

Complete these sentences aloud:

I was telling myself that I am too _____.

I am not _____.

I should have _____.

I shouldn't have _____.

I need to be more (or less) _____.

Jot down as many of these stories as you can, as simply and briefly as possible.

A *me* story is a statement that makes us an object in our own minds. It is not our true selves. It tends to define or qualify who we believe ourselves to be by means of judgments that are either self-glorifying or self-negating. In the above example, the story is: "It's all my fault. I am not a good mother."

Next comes a very important step:

Take a few moments to feel what recalling these stories has generated in you now, as you stand in the Me position.

It may help you to recall the analogy of the bottle of water that becomes muddy when it is shaken. Every story, every conscious or subconscious belief, shakes us up and makes us muddy in some way.

Notice how you are you feeling as you speak and write each particular story.

For example, you may say something like: "When I think about how bad my son's report card was, I feel guilty. I feel sad."

Describe what happens to your energy level.

"I feel heavy and tired."

Describe the sensations in your body.

"There are tears coming."

Be careful not to just stay in your head and think about the feelings these stories would probably create in you.

Actually feel the emotional and physical atmosphere generated as you recall each story. Stay with the feeling long enough to clearly imprint the felt consequences of telling yourself a particular story.

This is not easy to do; we are not familiar with giving ourselves permission to stay present with difficult feelings. When I am working with people, it is relatively easy to tell when they are just thinking about the stories, as if they were watching a movie, instead of really allowing themselves to come down into their bodies and feel them.

Ask yourself: "Am I just in my head, or am I really allowing myself to feel all this?"

If you find you are not really feeling much at first, take a few deep breaths and relax. All stories create some kind of sensation, some kind of emotion. Just give yourself time until you begin to recognize what you are feeling.

To be attached to our stories is to live in a dream in which we create a familiar suffering or self-inflation that limits our ability to see what *is*, and this disconnects us from our real feelings. To awaken from this dream, we must be able to return to the beginning of ourselves. Only in the Now are we able to access the soul's self-transcending awareness.

Now it is time to ask yourself, "Who am I really?"

Specifically ask yourself, "Are any of these stories about my true self?"[4]

Don't use your thinking process to look for an answer to this question. Instead allow your mind to become receptive and turn your attention toward that which is aware of all these stories. Let your awareness observe the stories and the feelings these stories create. Attune yourself to whom or what is present for this.

Ask yourself, "Do I believe that any of these stories describe the fullness of my essence?"

When you become receptive in this way, you immediately recognize that who you are, is more than any thought or feeling.

Step back to the center of the Mandala of Being, the Now position.

With this physical movement away from the Me position, begin the internal shift of attention to the immediate present.

Let your mind sink down out of your head and into your whole being. Feel your breath. For several breaths, follow the collapse of your chest as you exhale and then carefully observe the momentary gap and relaxation before the next breath arises. Enter that gap with your attention. Let your breathing become soft. Try not to control your breath, but rather let it lead you deeper into your body, your now-ness. Be alert and passive at the same time. Let your breath breathe you.

You don't have to force yourself to give up any story.

Simply ask yourself, "Who am I?" and move your mind toward that which is aware in you (and not toward a specific answer, which would only start more stories). Breathe with this deeper space of awareness.

Give the emotional mud that your *me* stories created in the earlier inquiry a chance to settle.

If this isn't sufficient to release the sensations created by the me stories you uncovered in the inquiry process, ask yourself, "How would I feel right now if I were not telling myself these me stories?"

Simply imagine how you would be if you were just your-self in the same situation but without the stories.

Perhaps you would feel open and relaxed. Maybe you would feel uncertain and anxious.

Whatever you feel, let yourself feel it; don't just think about what you might feel. Speak aloud so you can hear yourself saying what you are feeling right in this new mo-ment. Rest in this felt sense of who you are in the Now, having shifted your awareness enough to have some dis-tance from the stories.

The moment you do so, you restore connection to your true self and regain the power of awareness.

Continue to take advantage of this shift and deepen your connection to the present. Become aware of your breathing, and let your mind sink down into your body, into the fullness of yourself. Become aware of your per-ceptions: the quality of light, the details of your sur-roundings, any sounds, the temperature of the air. Aware . . . alert . . . calm . . . open. Rest in the present: Here am I.

Sensations and perceptions are always in the Now. There is a palpable change of presence as we return to rest where our true stories always begin. It is essential to familiarize yourself with what this feels like.

Remaining in the Now position, turn to face the Me position.

From the vantage point of standing at the beginning of yourself, rooted in the power of awareness, feel compas-sion for the self of your me stories. Empathize with all the suffering these stories have created in your life. Feel compassion toward the you who experienced this suffering

and softly hold that aspect in the larger awareness of
your true self. See if you can find a way to speak to this
smaller you.

This invites the healing potential of the Self-self relationship.

But if as you rest in the now-ness of yourself, the feelings that have been evoked by your *me* stories do not release, or are replaced with ones even more disturbing, then before you can feel compassion for yourself, you must use the power of awareness to continue to be present with whatever remains.

This is the most crucial work of all. The mud created by any strong emotion begins to settle the moment we reconnect to our essential selves and realize that these *me* stories are not truly who we are. A sense of clarity is restored. But when this does not happen, it means that our stories, and the emotions they create, are actually protecting us from a deeper feeling, a core sense of insufficiency or wrongness invariably associated with an untamed emotion. At such times, even more presence is called for.

Rather than describing the feeling aloud, at this particu-
lar point in the work just look directly at it.

Trying to explain or describe the feeling actually amounts to "blinking" and sidestepping. Even slightly wondering when the feeling will stop is also a way of distancing and avoiding direct conscious relationship to the feeling. Believing you have felt this way before is drawing a comparison to the past, and is just another form of avoidance that only gives the feeling more power. Any of these strategies will carry you right back into more stories and trap you in the world of that feeling.

Continue to touch the feeling with total attention one
breath at a time.

Even if you are crying, bring your attention to your breath and your immediate surroundings.

When you are crying, your breath is erratic and you never think to focus on it right then. But no matter how you are breathing, your breath is always a Now sensation that will gradually bring your mind to the present. As this happens, the feeling will begin to change. Untamed emotions always seem at first to be overwhelming and global. They seem much larger than who you are. But as you keep looking directly at them and keep using your breath to hold your attention in the Now, even the untamed emotions must surrender to the power of awareness. Gradually the feeling begins to become smaller and more localized in your body. Perhaps it will feel like a heavy stone in your belly, or a pain in your throat. Now you can be present with it; it is not bigger than you are.

Soften around the feeling, but don't, even for an instant, let your attention leave it, or it will tend to become global once again.

Gradually let your attention rest on the feeling even more delicately.

Any feeling that is met with full attention and exquisite softness inevitably begins to weaken and shift.

Stay with your breathing, and bring your attention gently to your heart. As you become aware of your heart — a space in the center of your chest — bring a soft smile to this space. Be present with whatever you are sensing in your body with your gently smiling heart. Maintain this until you can actually feel the sensations calming and your mind becoming quiet and receptive. Now you are in a fresh relationship to yourself:

My true story starts Now . . .
I am already that *which I have been seeking.*

Now you have felt the contrast between being identified with *me* stories, which determine your emotional state, and the actual experience of who you are in the now-ness of yourself. Of course, few of us have ever been taught that we are conscious beings, that awareness is our essence, that we are always more than who we tell ourselves we are. We live in the holding environment of our *me* stories, and because Me and You are a continuum of relationship, if we don't see ourselves truly, then we cannot see others clearly either. Therefore, it's time to take a step out of the Now position and move to the You position, where we can inquire into the stories we tell ourselves about others.

THE *YOU* STORIES

As you step to the You position marker, allow yourself to call one significant person in your life to mind. Open yourself to any thoughts and feelings you frequently have about this person.

If you want to focus on a different category of "other," such as your job or money or God — all potentially fruitful explorations — I suggest you postpone this until later and begin instead with a specific person who plays an important part in your life, especially if you often find yourself with angry or hurt feelings in relationship to this person.

(As a reminder, if you are undertaking this inquiry process by yourself, it is helpful to write down each story that you tell yourself about a particular person. Then, for each story, one at a time, speak about the feeling this story creates in you. Pause to feel it, and then return yourself to the Now position.)

To help uncover the stories you tell yourself in the You position, the following are questions or statements that can focus your inquiry:

What are the stories I tell myself about_____? (Name a specific person.)

What are my criticisms or judgments about this person?

I believe this person should _____.

I believe this person shouldn't _____.

I need this person to _____.

I believe this person thinks I am _____.

If only this person would_____, then I could _____.

Don't try to hide yourself from the full extent of your judgments. Don't dismiss stories about what you need from someone because they seem unfair or unrealistic. There are times when we are all experts at being unfair and unrealistic. It is important that you not edit your stories to make them more self-flattering. Expose your stories no matter how petty or ashamed they may make you feel.

Always name the specific person as opposed to speaking of others in general, and be as specific as possible about the circumstances in which the stories occur. When we start to tell ourselves stories, words like *everyone, all, no one, they, always,* and *never* are so global that they hinder our ability to get in touch with what we are actually feeling. For example, when a woman tells herself "All men are insensitive," she poisons her Now with anger. The story is obviously untrue because the specific people or situations in which insensitivity has been an issue for her are being generalized into a global condemnation of men. Even if she eventually recognizes the falsehood of this generalization, and can temporarily release the feelings of anger and hurt that her story creates, the underlying emotional dynamic remains in place.

This suggests that the individual making the inquiry is not willing to deeply examine her life by looking at specific people and incidents. The emotional holding environment is sustained despite the questioning process. A far more useful story is "Bill is insensitive when he makes plans without consulting me." Now it is clear that this is a specific judgment of Bill's behavior, and the next step is to see what feelings this judgment creates. Then she can return herself to the Now and decide whether to remain a victim of these feelings or join with her true self. If she chooses the latter, new and more authentic behaviors become possible. As the Tao Te Ching asks, "Can you remain unmoving till the right action arises of itself?"[5]

Another common way we confuse ourselves is by disguising a judgment as a feeling. For example, we frequently make statements like "I *feel* he is too controlling," when what we are actually saying is "I *believe* he is too controlling." This is a judgment, not a feeling. As such, this is a story, the truth of which could be debated. The feeling itself has yet to be named and made conscious. An actual feeling is a sensation whose reality cannot be challenged, but it can be held in the power of awareness. When we understand this distinction, we no longer victimize ourselves with our own hidden judgments by calling them feelings.

Take the risk to let yourself fully feel what these stories create.

Again, it is important not to just think what these stories would likely create, because this would provide a mental buffer against the actual sensations generated by the stories. Go beyond this level of defensiveness and thoroughly experience how each story about a specific person makes *you* feel now. What happens in *your* body? What emotions are present? What are the actual sensations of these emotions? Can you imagine what is happening to your blood pressure and stress hormones as you tell these stories?

The feeling and emotional climate created by these stories is how, right now, you are holding yourself; it is your self-created physiological and psychological holding environment.

Fully taste the poison of these thoughts, how destructive so many of these stories are for you and for your relationships.

Once again, step back to the Now position.

To help you make the transition back to the Now, you can ask yourself: "How would I feel if I were simply present with this person and not telling myself these you stories? How would I behave?"

Just as you created a potential space of unknowing about yourself by asking, "Who am I really?" ask yourself, "Can I really be sure my judgments and beliefs are true?"

Having acknowledged the possibility of unknowing, you are moving closer to the Now of yourself.

There is no need to reject or let go of the stories unless you can clearly see that they are not true. But even if they feel true, simply imagine who you would be right in this moment if you were not telling yourself these stories. Just by imagining this, a space of new possibility opens.

Deepen your passage into the fullness of the present moment by becoming aware of your breathing and staying

present in your body. Let the mud of emotions gener-
ated by the you stories slowly settle and your mind be-
come still, your body easeful. Softly let your attention
rest at your heart and bring a soft smile to that space.

Feel the recognition.

Here am I.

Reestablish the sense that you are at the beginning of
yourself, where your true story always begins.

Claim the all-essential power to bring your attention to
the immediacy of your body and your sensations, rather
than allowing your attention to be captured by your be-
liefs about or reactions to others.

Feel the fullness of yourself right now.

As you go deeper into the sense of the now-ness of yourself,
you are automatically withdrawing energy from identification
with all the stories evoked while you stood in the You position.
Now you may be able, perhaps for the first time, to truly let
yourself see another as "other." We cannot see anyone as they
really are when we are looking through the lens of one of our
identities. Then the other is only the extension of the psychology of that particular identity — someone who pleases us or
threatens us. But when you see others as simply who they are,
then you can regard them with compassion. Just as all of us
have frequently lost ourselves in stories and adopted identities
that transformed others into players in our dreams, so have all
the other people in your life done the same with you.

As you learn to live from the beginning of yourself, you become able to withdraw what you have projected onto other
people. This means you are capable of ever more vulnerable intimacy. Other people will always be who they are and do what they

do. Each meeting with another will bring something new: it will shake us with passion, deepen our gratitude to life, or expose us to our greatest fears. There is no immunity from the other, no way to be certain they will not rock our boats. But when we know ourselves at our beginning, there is no danger of anyone ever sinking us.

As you withdraw your projections, people change because you have changed: you are living from the energy of your fullness, not inhabiting the identity that created those projections. The bonding energy of the Me-You continuum can hold us in limiting and even destructive patterns of relationship, but when one person comes back to the beginning of himself or herself, the other is freed as well, and the energy of the relationship is liberated to a new potential.

Demanding that someone change (including ourselves) is fruitless; in fact, it is a form of violence. We all have the potential to change, and it happens completely naturally the more we realize our essential selves. In the absence of this fundamental understanding, requiring someone to change is a weapon used against that person. It is a means of attacking what *is* and an attempt to protect ourselves from feelings we are not meeting in ourselves. It is ignorance of the fact that we are already whole, already *that* for which we have been seeking. We must not attempt to manipulate other people to protect us from our core fears. Who they are, as they are, is the reality of them. To fight against this is to suffer. Telling yourself that someone else needs to change is a story. Let the emotional mud of this demand settle.

Come back to the Now of yourself.

I am sufficient as I am.

At the beginning of ourselves, we are never victims of what others think or do. Quite naturally, without us having to do anything, all these *you* stories lose their emotional charge.

Learn to feel the choice between the old, contracted holding environment and the simple fullness and clarity of your true self. Where is it decreed that there is less grace, less beauty, less God in this moment than any other? Notice how it feels to recognize that when you are at the beginning of yourself, no one else is needed for your happiness, and yet you are so connected, so grateful for the people in your life. Love and gratitude for others can never be really full when we believe we need them in order to feel whole; they can always leave us and hurt us. But when we come home to our beginning, we experience real gratitude and no fear that someone can take something of ourselves away from us.

> Standing in the Now position, in the power of awareness, turn toward the You position and feel compassion for the person or people involved in the stories you have been thinking about. Speak to these people. See them for whom they are without the overlay of your beliefs about how they should or shouldn't be. Offer your attention without any agenda, without wanting anything from them.

If, as you step back to the Now position, you cannot find the compassion to see others as they are and accept them that way, if instead the old stories keep pulling you out of your beginning and into resentment or hurt, it is because underneath these painful feelings lurks an even more threatening feeling, one of the untamed emotions. Perhaps it is a core identity of worthlessness, or a terrible sensation of abandonment that has crystallized into a belief, such as "I am nothing without this partner." This primal fear will not go away simply because you can recognize the falseness of your *you* stories. You cannot truly come back to the beginning of yourself until this feeling is fully met and held in the Now.

Turn your inner gaze directly toward the feeling rather than toward whoever you imagine is responsible for causing it.

Bring your awareness to the friendship of your breath and let it carry you deeper into the feeling.

Remember not to think *at* these really difficult feelings; this just keeps you separate from them. It is essential not to put words with them or interpret them; this will just lead you back into your stories once again. Realize that you are meeting one of your untamed "monsters" — that this is a sensation within you, not who you are — and begin to make room for it in the fullness of yourself.

Breath by breath, continue to sink deeper into the now-ness of this feeling so that your mind is not moving away from the present.

Without stories to reinforce them, most disturbing feelings simply dissipate immediately. Those that don't are your teachers, "worthy opponents" as Don Juan taught Carlos Castaneda.[6] They are ones that, as you meet them, build the muscle of faith and true self-worth.

Restoring the sense of resting at our beginning in the Now position can take time, but time like this is precisely what we too rarely offer ourselves in ordinary life. When we begin to consciously face feelings that do not immediately dissipate even when they are no longer reinforced by thought, it means we are uncovering fears that our faith is not yet great enough to allow. We are getting to the root of our present survival structures. This is deep work, the darkest hour before the light of dawn. But even at the darkest times, the power of awareness abides: we are always larger than what we are aware of. By trusting this truth and resting in the Now of ourselves, embracing anything at all that we feel, we steadily build muscle until we are no longer accepting our limited identities, no longer the victims of our stories about others. More and more, we live authentically in the fullness of our beings.

The tenacious power of our stories about others usually has little to do with the present. Their power over us comes from what we believe about the past and unconsciously project onto our present relationships and circumstances: "I was never wanted as a child." "When my father left us, I lost my trust in love." Therefore, now we must take our inquiry to the Past position of the Mandala of Being.

THE *PAST* STORIES

Physically step to the Past position marker and allow your mind to open toward the past.

Begin at first with a broad invitation: "What do I find when I turn my attention toward the past?" Let specific stories, whether from the recent or distant past, flow spontaneously into your awareness.

The past is so vast that it holds innumerable memories, but trust that your soul knows exactly what you need to become aware of at this time.

You can use the following questions to help focus the inquiry:

What are the stories I most frequently tell myself about the past?

What do I regret? Blame? Feel guilty about? Feel ashamed of?

What are my most potent memories, whether positive or negative?

Who are the most important people in these stories, and what did they model for me?

What do I believe my parents should or should not have done?

Speak (or write) all the stories that come to mind.

It is wise to view our memories as if they are stories rather than facts. Therefore, even though we may believe that our memories represent irrefutable facts, for the sake of this work regard them as stories. (See chapter 10 for further discussion of this point.)

After you have identified as many of these stories as you wish, allow yourself to thoroughly feel what each of them creates.

Sink your attention into your body and observe what you are feeling: What sensations are present, what emotions? What is the quality of your energy?

As you stand in the Past position, realize that everything you are presently experiencing is being filtered through a mind that is comparing the immediacy of your Now to something lived before. When our minds leave the Now and move into the past, these stories impose their own emotional energy onto the present, perhaps making us feel guilty or regretful or unsafe. This can close our hearts to being simply present with what *is*. It is not written anywhere that we have to be victims of the past. To continue to live in this way is weak-mindedness. We can decide to have a more open, "beginner's mind," a quality of attention in which our true stories always begin Now. Of course, there is greater vulnerability in moving toward unknowing and in experiencing a less familiar sense of self. But doing so is closer to participating with reality, and it permits us to live our own fullness right now.

> *Having allowed yourself to realize what these past stories create in you in the here and now, take the crucial, conscious step back to the Now position.*
>
> *Ask yourself, "Who am I right now? Am I, in this moment, in the power of my awareness, the person whom I have believed myself to be only because of my past?"*
>
> *Standing in the Now position, sink your mind into your body. Notice the sensations within you: the weight on your feet, your breathing.*
>
> *Observe the residual emotions from your past stories and touch them softly with your larger awareness, breath by breath.*
>
> *Let your awareness fill your hands and observe the sensations that begin to be present in them. Turn your palms toward each other and begin to breathe your awareness into the space between your hands. Attune to this space. Gradually let your mind become still and present.*
>
> *Release the tendency to be a spectator. Fully join your experience. Immerse yourself in it completely.*
>
> *Continue to rest your attention in the virgin quality of the present moment, and in the fresh sensations arising in your hands and throughout your body.*
>
> *Gently release the emotional environment of your past stories.*

Whether our *past* stories are true or not isn't really the issue. Who you truly are in the present moment is a conscious being capable of an entirely new relationship to yourself. Who you are in the now-ness of yourself is not determined by the past. Simply feeling and acknowledging this creates a chink in the armor of an old identity that thrives on habitual ways of remembering the past.

> If simply moving back to the Now position and deepening your sense of self in your body, and deepening the presence in and around your hands, isn't sufficient to let your mud settle, ask yourself, "How would I feel — who would I be — if I weren't telling myself these past stories?"

Is reclaiming your now-ness like taking a heavy pack off your back? Perhaps suddenly you feel light, even buoyant.

> Release any thoughts and move into this space. Allow this sense of space to generalize throughout your sense of being. Stay with your breath and gently let everything go, all the thoughts about the past, all the emotions, until you sense that your mind is entering a state of stillness.

> *Here am I.*
> *I am sufficient as I am.*
> *I am already* that *for which I have been seeking.*

> Continuing to stand in the Now position, turn toward the Past position.

> Open your heart to all that you have lived, and all that you have been, which has led you to this moment.

Could you appreciate the fullness of this moment if you had not lived all that you have lived? Hasn't every single experience contributed to whom you are now?

Being released even momentarily from the burden of the past, while at the same time being aware of the past, you are experiencing *forgiveness*. Forgiveness is our natural response to the past when we are realizing our innate fullness in the Now. Once there is forgiveness, we are no longer victims of the past. Memories no longer have the power to capture our attention in ways that pull us into story. In knowing who we really are, any memories, no matter how traumatic they once seemed, are now part of the grace of our lives. This is the essence of forgiveness.

Let your attention rest in your heart and stay fully present for each breath until your mind becomes quieter and you feel gratitude for the gift of life itself.

If, in making this inquiry into your *past* stories, you encounter highly charged memories and emotions, turn your attention directly toward them and remember that you can remain present with any feelings without collapsing into them. The art to doing this is to let your breath awareness bring you fully, but very softly, into whatever you are feeling. Let your body become soft, not resisting the sense of exquisite vulnerability.

In the Mandala inquiry, we are not trying to eliminate any negative feelings or resolve any problems. Rather, we are becoming intimately acquainted with the places we go when we leave the Now of ourselves. If we encounter strong feelings in the process, this is valuable. The most important thing we can learn is how to hold these feelings instead of letting them drive us again and again into stories.

Now you are ready for the last phase of inquiry: witnessing the power you give to the future. We anticipate the future according to how we hold the past. Most of us live by chasing after the life we imagine will make us happy, or by struggling to prevent ourselves from arriving at one we don't want. While we do this, we miss our lives. We sacrifice them to the future by handing our power over to it.

THE *FUTURE* STORIES

Step to the Future position marker, and allow your mind to move toward the future. Notice what you immediately feel.

Do you want to turn to the future? Is it exciting for you, or disturbing for you?

See what comes to mind, and then focus your inquiry with these further questions:

What do I frequently tell myself about the future?

What am I hopeful about?

What am I anxious or worried about?

What is my vision of the future?

What are my plans, my dreams?

What are my hopes and fears for my family and friends?

Remain alert to how you are feeling. Check inside: What do these stories that I tell myself about the future create? What happens in my body? How do I feel?

Let yourself fully experience the physiological and emotional reality generated by what you envision about the future.

This is the holding environment that you create with your imaginings about the future.

Don't just recall how you have worried about the future or excited yourself with hope. Bring the full emotional intensity of your thoughts into the present so you can really taste the influence of your future stories. Stay with this inquiry, and be as thorough as you can in noticing the consequences of the different stories you have about the future.

Then take the intentional step back to the Now position.

Remember, the *Now* is the only time in which you have any real power to influence your future.

Again summon the energy of self-inquiry: "Who am I right now? Am I the person I imagine in the future? Can I really know how I will feel then, how I will think, how I will act?"

Realize that the future is, after all, always a fantasy. No one can really know the future with any certainty. Therefore, invite the energy of doubt:

Ask yourself: "Can I really know that these stories are true?"

The issue isn't that we can or cannot be assured that certain things will occur in the future, but rather that we cannot know how we will be at that time, how we will feel, how we will behave. Of course, our bodies eventually die. This we know with our intellects. Consider, though, that it could be possible to live the process of aging and dying from the Now of ourselves, liberated from all the different stories we tend to tell ourselves as our bodies change. The future we imagine is a psychological future — in the instant we imagine it, what we imagine creates our present-moment psychological states. Do you want to be the victim of how your mind imagines the future? Do you want to be determined in this way?

Take hold of the understanding: "My true story starts Now."

Having felt the sensations these stories create in you, how they poison or obscure your sense of Now, ask yourself, "Who am I if I don't tell myself these future stories? How am I in myself, right now, without them?"

Attune yourself to your breathing, and let your attention rest gently in your heart. Keep sinking into your body, into the now-ness of yourself. Let the "mud" of the emotions stirred up by the future stories settle, until you feel your mind become open and receptive and you are fully restored to the now-ness of yourself.

Here am I.

Don't try to force any thoughts or feelings away, but instead bring your awareness into the present until you are calm and clear in yourself.

I am sufficient as I am.

While we would be fools not to live today in a way that creates the best potential for us in the future, we must be careful not to exhaust and demoralize ourselves chasing after imaginary lives. It is possible not to obsess over our successes (this is really survival in disguise), and not to lose touch with the immediacy and beauty of our lives. We can consciously anticipate our needs for the future without becoming attached to the results of our actions.

As you stand in the Now position, turn and face the Future position.

Consider that the state of consciousness which holds the greatest possibility for the future emerges from being fully present right now, and let yourself trust who you are. Put your trust in trust itself.

Now is the eternity that connects us with everyone and everything. Now is when we attract all that we really need to further our lives.

None of us can control the future, and trying to do so only creates distress. If we cannot enjoy life now, how do we imagine we would enjoy ourselves even if we should attain our goals? When Self-avoidance becomes habitual, we delude ourselves into thinking that this will cease in some make-believe future.

The survival personality is like a castle made of stones of Self-avoidance laid one on the other for years and years. To deconstruct this structure, we must take each stone, each story, and look at it while we familiarize ourselves, moment by moment, with who we really are and always have been.

I am already that *for which I have been seeking.*

In this moment, let your life surprise you.

THE GENERAL SPIRIT OF THE WORK

In your first experience with the Mandala of Being, you have had an opportunity to realize that everything you think about yourself, others, the past, and the future is just a story. This is the first crucial component of this work.

As the conscious being who has just made this inquiry, you have already begun to separate your true identity from the stories. This is the process of differentiation inherent to utilizing the power of awareness. You have taken a step in the direction of Self-realization.

Your mind has believed these stories for a long time. Some have been passed on to you from previous generations so that you are completely habituated to the emotional environment they create. In working with the Mandala of Being, it is essential to realize that the whole range of sensation within you, in any moment, and the stories you are telling yourself, cocreate each other.

This leads to the second crucial component of the work: to actually feel what each story creates. It is not sufficient to merely think about or speculate about what you might feel, or to remember how you felt at an earlier time. You must actually *feel* the effect of each story in the present and accept responsibility for the emotional environment you have created within by believing and repeating these stories to yourself. You are the creator of this environment, no one else. It is your psychological survival paradigm. The more you believe it, the more real it seems and the more attention it commands.

To prove to yourself that these stories have emotional power only as long as you are *not* living in the Now requires making the shift between any of the positions and the Now position many, many times. By feeling what these stories create, and then experiencing who you are when you rest in the now-ness of yourself, your whole being begins to understand the difference between the delusional reality of these psychological constructions and the innately healthy and full quality of who you are at the beginning of yourself.

You spend your life building one story upon another without a consistent starting point for whom you really are. It is like navigating without a polestar that provides a fixed reference point. Your thinking is compulsively sequential, moving from story to story so fast that there is hardly any gap through which you can escape from the confusion, distorted values, and frequent misery you yourself invoke. What the Mandala work offers you is a process by which to create that gap.

In the Mandala work, you are the one who is looking at these stories and feeling what they create in your field of sensation and energy, so they can't represent all of who you really are. More important, the Mandala work always begins from the Now as you feel it and breathe it in your whole being. The Now provides a starting point for recognizing your own sense of fullness and presence and a way to acknowledge the suffering you formerly took for granted.

You have now consciously experienced the psychological suffering that ensues when you leave the beginning of yourself. When you return and give the stirred up mud a chance to settle, you encounter an entirely different feeling: calm, clarity, and even gratitude and joy. If you continue to suffer, however, you are likely troubled by a long-buried or long-ignored distress that can now be met with compassionate and healing attention. It is a pain no longer exacerbated by the emotional and psychological overlay of stories that can drag your mind away from the present and deplete your energy. By being more fully present with your pain, you eliminate unnecessary suffering.

In life there are always difficulties, but when you learn to return to the beginning of yourself, you stop polluting yourself with self-generated misery or false, unsustainable consolation. By walking through the different positions of the physical Mandala and inwardly shifting attention back and forth between whom you always are at the beginning of yourself and what your stories create, you can begin to see that you have a choice whether to continue to live in them or not.

In this exploration you have moved systematically from Me, to You, to Past, to Future, but as you continue to utilize the Mandala you will see that you actually bounce all around it. One moment you may be in a *past* story, the next in a *me* story, then a *future* story, then *me* again, then *you*, then back to the *past*. Round and round you go in psychological time, making false self-identifications and inaccurate judgments of others. But now you have a tool which enables you to recognize that all of this is a way to avoid what you are actually feeling and to distance yourself from what *is*. Now that you understand how to come back to yourself, you can take the steps to do so and become fully present again.

For each particular process of inquiry using the Mandala of Being, it is essential to start from and always return to the Now position. The work entails both identifying how you leave the Now by believing the various stories you tell yourself and, equally important, learning to take all the necessary time to really return to the Now and to trust this ever-renewing space. Identifying with the fullness of yourself in the present is what gradually releases your psychological identification with the stories. In returning to the Now, you regain the capacity for spontaneous, intelligent, nonmanipulative, authentic self-expression and presence. In the Now, you have a chance to begin a new relationship with yourself and everyone else.

Engaging in this work can at times bring you to disturbing feelings and sensations, and you may find yourself afraid to continue. If any part of the process evokes strong emotions, step back to the Now position and focus on your breathing. You can then decide if you want to continue the work or take some time out and return to it later. If you find it necessary to step back from the Mandala inquiry, then you can appreciate just how powerful these stories have been — and continue to be — in determining your sense of self.

When you work with a process of inquiry like the Mandala of Being, your mind may trick you into thinking you are working with something abstract. But in reality the dynamic of the Mandala comes from your life. You live only in the Now, yet your mind is continually leaving it. Take, for example, the situation where the Mandala work becomes too threatening to continue. In the Now, this is simply a strong sensation. But when your mind leaves the Now, you unconsciously return to the past and endow your present feelings with the power over you that you remember them previously having. At the same time, you jump into the future, fearing that these feelings will continue to haunt you and worrying about how to make them stop. You do not turn your attention directly toward the feeling itself, and you do not stay silently present with the pure feeling. As a result, you cannot come back to your beginning, and instead you remain a victim of the feeling.

This work is never about judging any of your stories or feeling ashamed for having them. And it is not about trying to eliminate them. Attempting to do either just reinvents the same old negative holding environment. This work is about the power of awareness through which you implicitly transcend what you are aware of and thereby transform your consciousness. Inquiry into yourself necessitates that you learn how to be present with nonreactive awareness. You learn to regard your stories and the sensations they generate as signposts that you have lost contact with your essence, and then again and again bring yourself back to Now, back to your beginning. Awareness itself is the engine of change.

The heart of the work is to recognize how it feels to be contracted as a result of your false stories, and how this differs from resting in the fullness and openness of your true I-Am. Throughout your life, without realizing it, you have become addicted to the emotional holding environment of your stories. To heal, you need not oppose these stories but, rather, to become familiar with the felt sense of openness and presence at the beginning of yourself. You must understand that your true story always starts Now and learn to return over and over again to the felt sense of your now-ness.

In time, and much more quickly than you might expect, you will develop a sense of amused disinterest in these stories and the emotions they create. You will get to know who you really are so well that when you find yourself caught once again in your old (third) holding environment, you'll often just shrug, laugh, breathe, and begin your life anew.

BECOMING NOW-WEIGHTED: A VISUAL REVIEW OF THE MANDALA OF BEING

A visual teaching tool that I often use helps people grasp what the Mandala work accomplishes. First, I describe the plastic toy punching bag I had when I was a child. This conical figure had a smiling face painted on it and, when inflated, stood about three feet high. The bottom was rounded and had a separate compartment filled with sand, which acted as ballast so that no matter how hard I hit or pushed it, it always returned to upright.

To demonstrate one way to visualize the Mandala work, I improvise a sort of punching bag by using a pole or tube that I can move around like my toy moved. I place one end of the pole on the Now position of a Mandala of Being laid out on the floor, with its four cards marking the four peripheral positions: Past, Future, Me, and You. The bottom of the pole, which remains fixed on the center, represents how our bodies always live in the Now. To show the various possibilities of what our minds may do: I let the pole totter this way and that — toward the Me position, then toward the Future, then perhaps over to the Past, or to You — *but I do not let it become vertical.* Eventually I let it fall over completely onto one or another of the four positions, explaining that this is how most of us live: bouncing chaotically from one story to another, identifying with one position or another, without ever standing upright in the now-ness of ourselves and becoming still at the center. The further from upright you tilt in any direction — toward Me, You, Past, or Future — the further you are from Now. The farther you tilt, the less presence and energy you have, and the less your true self is expressed through your personality.

Then I demonstrate the crux of the work: I tilt the pole from one to another of the four positions, but always swinging it back up upright, passing through vertical — directly over the Now position — as the bottom-weighted punching bag would do. This is the way we can learn to live: we can always return, however briefly, to the beginning of ourselves. The pole swings upright, across the Now position, dipping into the Past, Future,

Me, and You positions, until gradually I decrease its arcs and let it wobble ever closer to the vertical, to the Now. This demonstrates how our minds can become more consciously adapted to the present so that we more often express our true selves.

In martial arts, balance is essential, and there are terms that refer to how our weight is distributed through our legs and onto our feet. In certain moves, most of our weight is on our leading leg and foot. This is referred to as being "front-weighted." If our weight is on our back leg and foot, then we are "rear-weighted." What the Mandala work teaches us is how to become "Now-weighted."

Of course our minds inevitably live in psychological reality. We are always, except perhaps in deep meditation, operating on some level of me-consciousness. We each function as a separate individual with a unique point of view. As we live out various roles — professional, parental, or spousal, for example — we are constantly being challenged in unpredictable ways that can put us off balance by throwing us into stories. The Mandala work increases the extent to which we can remain Now-weighted: present in our bodies, aware of but not reacting to our sensations, and remaining directly aware of disturbing feelings without being thrown into stories.

We are learning to live from our true selves, spontaneously and authentically expressing our essence in the midst of daily life, rather than having our points of view, role functions, and sense of self co-opted by false identities built upon false *me, you, past,* and *future* stories. By learning to live this way, we become far more emotionally and spiritually intelligent and much more connected to our intuition. We have a means — the quality and fullness of our own beings in the Now — by which we become more at ease in ourselves, trust life, and have compassion and respect for one another.

CHAPTER TEN

The Nature *of* Emotional Reality

Lower-Self Functioning, Part One

As a teacher, and as a student of my own emotional nature, I long ago realized that it was relatively easy for me to guide people to heightened and expansive states of consciousness, particularly when working in a retreat amid the amplified energy of a group. The challenge was to sustain an open, full heart when I returned to the demands of daily life.

Our ability to enter states of expansiveness, clear-mindedness, and centeredness is always the cumulative result of living more in the Now. The reason people quickly leave these higher states is that without the constant reinforcement of consciousness work to refresh the mind's connection with the immediacy of the moment, its habit is to move away from the present.

I was fascinated to finally understand that *where* the mind moved to when it left the Now invited the specific (negative) emotions that emerged. Emotions like anger, fear, and guilt do

not cause our states of being but are themselves the effect whenever our minds move into *me* stories, *you* stories, *future* stories, or
past stories. As illustrated in figure 3, when our awareness is not
rooted in the Now (as indicated by the arrows pointing away
from the Now position and not originating in the center of
the Mandala), we feel specific emotions that correspond to the
predominant direction in which our minds have moved. When
the mind is in the *past*, we tend to feel regret or nostalgia or guilt.
Anger or hurt tend to come from our *you* stories, hope or anxiety

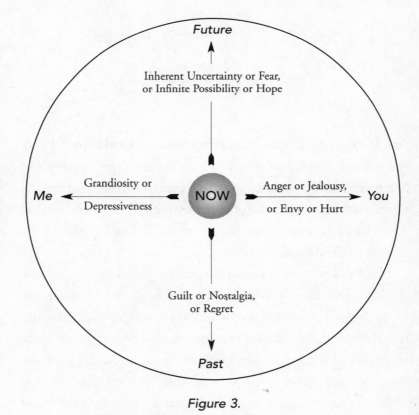

Figure 3.

The Mandala of lower-self functioning: what we feel
when our awareness is poorly adapted to the present.

or fear from our *future* stories, and grandiosity or depression from our *me* stories. Our level of emotional functioning is a direct reflection of how far from, and in which direction, our minds have moved from the Now. I refer to this as how well or poorly we are adapted to living in the present.

There are specific emotions or feeling states that occur when we are truly resting in the present. A sense of simplicity is the dominant one, along with feelings of gratitude, connectedness, empathy, compassion, tolerance, forgiveness, and love. We can also experience a pure form of anger in the present, but unlike the kind of anger that tends to ferment into bitterness and resentment, this anger cleanses like a storm, maintains our dignity, and leaves no destructive emotional residue. In contrast, the emotions we encounter as our minds move further from the Now are much more toxic to us and to others.

I have come to think about our usual way of living in *past*, *future*, *me*, and *you* stories, with the false or limiting identities and the destructive emotions that accompany these, as being trapped in "lower-self functioning." This is not a specific way of being but rather a continuum of emotional dynamics and behaviors that may be extreme depending on just how far from the present our minds remain.

The power of the Mandala of Being is that it provides a way to understand that these negative emotions are not the problem, but are signals of the manner or direction in which our minds have left the present. Instead of remaining victims of these emotions, or fearing them, or feeling ashamed of them, we can begin to appreciate that their onset reflects our degree of adaptation to the present, and that it offers us the opportunity to return our attention to the Now. The moment we do, most often these emotions quickly dissolve, or at least we can face them directly in a creative and transformative manner.

THE ME POSITION:

The Emotional Consequences of the Stories We Believe about Ourselves

As noted earlier, when we refer to ourselves as *me* or *I*, this is a kind of conditioned laziness. If we actually turn our attention to find this *me*, we discover a space of awareness that is neither not-*me* nor *me*. It is a space through which thoughts, feelings, and sensations flow, and by identifying with and objectifying the "experiencer" of these, we construct the concrete notion of *me* or *I*. If we really try to discover this experiencer, we quickly see that we face an infinite regress, such that whatever we identify as *me* is always preceded by *that* which is aware of whatever we are calling *me*. This understanding leads to one of the most important insights about ourselves and one of the most difficult to actually grasp: who we really are cannot be comprehended by thought. Said in another way, when we are fully present in the Now, we do not have any thoughts about who we are; we simply are. Thus, when we refer to the Me position in the Mandala of Being, the *me* in question can be any one of various identities we unconsciously assume in order to rationalize whatever we are thinking and feeling, moment by moment. *Me* is also the way in which we objectify ourselves by identification with whatever we are doing: our actions, roles, careers, and so forth.

The most immediate way to recognize that we have left the Now and moved to the Me position is to become aware of the stories we are telling ourselves (or others) about who we are. As previously mentioned, these stories create one of two possible emotional dynamics, either grandiose (self-glorifying) or depressive (self-negating). (See figure 3, page 220.) For example, perhaps we tell ourselves in a certain context or situation: "I am unattractive, not smart enough, unlovable, too ambitious (or not ambitious enough). I make myself into what others want." Such stories, in the moment we think them, are negative self-judgments, and even if they seem true insofar as they characterize some aspect of ourselves, identification with them creates an instantaneous depressive feeling state. When we live in a recurrent constellation of *me* stories, we are likely to feel sad because we are unconsciously defending an identity that does not represent our true fullness. We are compelled to be inauthentic, and at some level we know it. It creates a sorrow with no one specific cause that we can discover. It feels global, and we are literally dispirited.

Alternatively, we may tell ourselves endless stories in which we'll beat the odds, overcome some daunting obstacle, walk away unhurt from a truly dangerous situation, triumph over some other individual, or automatically expect others to accept and support our points of view. In this way we create a positive self-identification and grandiose feeling state: "I am the best; my ideas are the most creative; I am a great lover; I am invincible."

Day after day we objectify ourselves, believing we are this way or that, swelling or shrinking with every validation or judgment. We develop an intense self-involvement that blinds us to what we are really feeling and experiencing, to the needs and realities of others, and to reality itself. We naturally prefer to feel good, so our grandiose stories are generally considered preferable to the depressive ones. But regardless of whether our stories are positive or negative, they invariably defend against present-moment feelings that we are unwilling or unable to turn toward and relate to directly. When our minds throw us into *me* stories, we are not truly connected to ourselves. Grandiose appraisal of our strengths can lead us to distrust softness or avoid vulnerability; our creativity can become a compulsion without which we feel lost. Depressive stories become the way we hide

in a shroud of victimhood and refuse to risk expressing ourselves directly or opening to new situations. Identification with
any *me* story limits our ability to be spontaneous or authentic.
Any kind of belief about ourselves can pass through our minds,
yet none of this is really who we are.

The *me* stories are the key leverage points for our personal
psychologies. Once our *me* stories create an identity, all of our
you, past, and *future* stories are conditioned by that particular
identity: they support and rationalize it. Each identity constantly
conjures up different provisional realities: transient scenarios
about ourselves, who others are, and what we do or don't need
from them. Each ephemeral scenario determines how we interpret the present, colors the manner in which we recall the past,
and decides the flavor of hope or fear by which we anticipate
the future. Although we don't perceive them as fantasy until we
bring our awareness into the present, these are ways of rehearsing an imaginary sense of self and imaginary relationships, or
they are ways of rehearsing for situations that we either desire
or fear. But in this fictional world, our actual immediate experience goes unseen, and in this blindness our false sense of self
remains protected. While we rehearse the imaginary, we are
missing the real. The pervasive element of distrust in all this —
the core feeling of insufficiency — and our inability to truly live
in the present, goes unrecognized. And while this continues,
our survival personalities relentlessly place us in either a depressive or a grandiose false identity, whichever we have learned to
use to defend against our deeper feelings. In the Me position,
we emotionally hold ourselves in continuous anticipation of a
life that is real only in our minds, and by so doing we falsify our
actual lives. It is a fantasy in which we pretend our lives are
working, but because we are not initiating relationships from
our authentic beings, very little love or joy is possible.

When we work with the Mandala of Being, we become aware that in the Me position we tell stories about ourselves that are actually a way of avoiding our true selves. Just to think the words *I* or *me* as we tell ourselves a story can become a signal that we are not really present, that we have moved into psychological reality and lost connection to a fuller level of awareness.

For example, a forty-five-year-old woman whom I counseled was distraught because, in her mind, her husband wasn't grieving their separation, whereas she was sad and disoriented. She had been telling herself various versions of "I have never really known this man, and now I have wasted years of my life." What a devastating thing to think: "I have wasted years of my life." Can someone waste years of their life? Of course, in the psychological reality of that story, she was literally creating the misery of wasted years. But as I guided her around the Mandala, she could clearly see that this was a *me* story, and that it was not intrinsically true. She could feel how it created despair and dragged her down as though there were a hundred pounds on her back. I then had her stand in the Now position and shift her attention to the open, new, unknown moment. As she connected to her breathing, she gradually became present for all the sensations in her body, especially the sensations of sadness and disorientation. Without the *me* story "I have wasted years of my life," these feelings are sensations in the body that can be met and held. Like anything else we are capable of being aware of, what we experience in our bodies is not who we are. It did not take her long to arrive at a much fuller and more open state of awareness, in which she realized that what was happening between her and her husband was not the immediate issue, and that what she was doing to herself with her stories *was*.

We don't have to stop the *me* stories or fight against them, because this just perpetuates the ongoing warfare inside us. Nor should we try to create an alternate, more desirable story. The more we seek the positive, the more we flee from whatever we consider negative, and vice versa, which is just another prison.

In each of us, this is the heart of the third holding environment. Rather than trying to change these stories, we can simply start becoming aware that they exist: "Hey, this is a *me* story, therefore it cannot really be who I am." Then, remaining non-reactively present, we can automatically shift our awareness closer to the Now. It is as though our attention moves from the foreground, where everything is created by thoughts and all the emotions they engender, to the background, where there exists a quality of mind that is not thought, that is the presence of awareness. Immediately we gain a felt sense of ourselves, and we are once again grounded in our bodies. As we become aware of our breathing, and our minds remain softly alert, we may have the sense of being breathed; we are just awareness, just who we are. If the *me* story creates a particularly strong emotional quality, such as a feeling of hopelessness, this may linger. But if we turn our attention directly toward this immediate feeling, without letting the mind be carried off into further *me, you, past,* or *future* stories, the hopeless feeling will gradually subside.

Moving our attention back to the present and disengaging from identification with a *me* story can feel like a gentle "coming home." We feel as though a weight has been lifted from us, and our energy flows much more fully. At other times it can feel as though we are entering a space of unknowing, or a deeper, wordless knowing about ourselves that can make us feel disturbingly vulnerable. As a result, I call the choice to return our attention to the present "a movement-in-faith." To remain identified with our *me* stories and the emotional environments they create is to cling to the familiar. These are our psychological worlds, and we don't really know ourselves in any other way. Therefore, who we are prior to these stories, and when freed from them, even though it is closer to our essential beings as consciousness, often feels unfamiliar. We must have a little faith when we begin to embrace this unknown and vulnerable quality of being.

Who indeed are we when we relax our false or limited identities and return our minds to the present? What we return to is not itself an identity, something we can name, something we can make concrete and call "me." It takes experience with this curiously vulnerable quality of being before we begin to trust that it is a psychologically healthier, more relational, and more empowered state. But as we begin to remain more consistently in the present, our own deepest wisdom spontaneously asserts itself. We connect to a universal intelligence that encourages us to naturally tend to think inclusively and holistically. We gain greater emotional clarity and can be much more intimate and authentic.

What the Mandala of Being invites us to understand is that any time we recognize that we are telling a *me* story, either we are caught in the habitual cycle of Self-avoidance that begins early in life, or we are unconsciously reacting to or compensating for something in that moment which threatens our identities. By returning to the Now position, we have a chance to consciously suffer these feelings and thereby speed our process of self-healing.

Being in the present and recognizing the patterns of our old, habitual emotional dynamics, we have the opportunity to choose new responses and new behaviors and thereby interrupt and begin to change these patterns. For example, in a discussion with your spouse in which you might typically adopt a grandiose mode, believing your point of view is the only valid one and then becoming angry or dismissive, you could instead bring your attention to the present and see that, in this moment, you are in a room with a person you know well; you are breathing;

you are filled with adrenaline; your heart is pounding. Yet you are not, despite the intensity of your feelings, in any real danger simply because your partner doesn't see things your way. There is a threatening, angry feeling *and* the reality of simply being there with your spouse. Then you might choose to act in a different way. You might admit that you brushed aside your spouse's point of view, and ask him or her to repeat it. If the situation is an argument in which you have told yourself a *me* story, such as, "I can't stay in this marriage," and you have moved into a sense of hopelessness and despair, then instead of allowing your depressed feeling to prompt you into a habitual behavior such as withdrawing, you might risk offering to help your partner with whatever he or she is doing. Or you could ask what might make things easier in that moment. Again you are creating a new potential for relationship in the present.

Acting in opposition to what we are feeling, and deciding to behave in an unfamiliar way, creates a highly vulnerable space. We break the old covenant, the reality of our familiar *me* world. With this discontinuity, we can feel as if we will be overwhelmed or annihilated. We might argue that not obeying these stories and the feelings they create is being inauthentic, but this is only inauthentic relative to our *me* stories and their psychological worlds. This *me* isn't real. In fact, by choosing a new behavior, we are being authentic in the present, to an unknown self, and opening up space for something entirely new to emerge in that moment. When we grasp the message of the Mandala, it leads us to a whole new level of possibility and to true freedom.

It is important to understand the distinction between clearly seeing our own behavior and entering into self-negation. "I see how I could do this better" is a valid perception. "I never do anything well enough" is a story supporting a depressive identity. Essentially, if there is a thought that qualifies who we are and creates either a grandiose or depressive emotional reality for us, it represents a movement away from our true selves, a poor adaptation to the present and to life. This is what epitomizes lower-self functioning.

In contrast, if we turn our attention in the Now toward our *me* stories and identify the feelings they are creating, staying fully but softly present and gradually ceasing to react to these feelings, in that moment we might have a sudden realization, such as, "The reason I have been so judgmental and impatient is that I have been making myself the victim of my own grandiose expectations." This realization is a clear and true insight, not a *me* story. In this moment of seeing, we are liberated from a false identity, and we feel the emotional environment that it has been creating dissolve. Then we can see the situation much more clearly and relate to others with more empathy and patience. The power to choose how to respond is fully back in our own hands.

THE YOU POSITION:

The Emotional Consequences of the Stories We Believe about Others

The You position has to do with the stories we tell ourselves and generally believe, at least in the moment, about others. The Mandala of Being illustrates that, when our minds lose connection to the Now position and fall too far toward the You position, we lose ourselves in the *other.*

In our thoughts and daily interactions, we imagine we see others objectively and clearly. But because subject-object consciousness is a continuum, whatever psychology dominates the identity through which we interpret our experience turns everyone (and everything) into an extension of that psychology. It is as though we are unknowingly looking though a lens, and the lens is distorting everything we see. People become objects, to a greater or lesser degree, of our own design — not truly *other*. Until we take the lens off — which means returning to the beginning of ourselves — we cannot see other people as they actually are. We lose the ability to empathize with them.

Objectifying people in accordance with our own identities, we unconsciously inflate or diminish them. When we are grandiose, other people become diminished in their significance to us. When we are depressed, in our minds they become much more powerful. Conversely, in the subject-object continuum, when in the You position we inflate the importance of another, we generally invalidate and depress ourselves. Likewise, if we discount the other person, we implicitly glorify ourselves. In this way, the other person becomes a mirror for our own grandiose or depressive *me* world. When we are not truly present, we have no center and are constantly changing our psychological states with each *you* story.

One of the greatest causes of persistent human suffering is our tendency, when we feel threatened, to look to another person as our savior or to perceive this person as our enemy. We are conditioned to believe that we can, and indeed *need*, to be saved by some other person — by his or her love, attention, power, or money — or that the other is the *source* of our pain. We learn early in life to continually modify ourselves in an attempt to ensure the love and approval of the other or to diminish feelings of threat. Because we are dependent on others in childhood, we continue to imagine we can't live without the other, even if we perceive that person to be a source of pain.

If our parents were unable to leave their *me* world and really meet us from the now-ness of themselves, we have never felt recognized in the now-ness of ourselves. It becomes impossible to internalize a sense of self that is truly our own essence, independent of our parents' psychologies, particularly our mothers'. The psychoanalyst Alice Miller has written that every child is gifted in its own unique nature, but when that nature cannot be recognized by the mother because of her own self-involvement, the child's world can never be its own.[1] In such circumstances we grow up without a real sense of self other than what we get as a result of unconsciously agreeing to let ourselves be formed by the expectations and needs of our parents and, later, either by others or by our jobs. We are alienated from ourselves and, in extreme cases, even develop self-hatred, because we have never really been seen as ourselves. This is the psychological inception of what later in life will become codependent relationships: relationships in which adults are bound to each other out of unconscious fear that without the other they cannot survive or don't really exist. The power we give to the other to complete us, and the tendency to be inauthentic rather than risk disapproval, are both symptoms of not living from our own now-ness.

If we perceive distance and separateness from the other, it is always a reflection of how far from our own beginning we are, not something inherent in the other. If we feel too enmeshed and fused with the other, this too is an indication that we have lost contact with our true selves. It is easy to become lost in the other when we have no real sense of self.

As noted earlier, the "other" is not always a person. God is a powerful other. Money is one of the most potent others, with its almost archetypal power over us. Often when people lose money, they feel they have lost their "self" and feel threatened. Conversely, individuals who win a lottery may become expansive, elated, and filled with gratitude. Yet studies have shown that in a year's time many such winners revert to their original emotional states.[2] The power to change our lives in some essential way is not inherent in money or in any other person. We *give* that power to money and to people and to God as we lose the power to remain in our true selves. Certainly the circumstances of our lives change with our financial fortunes, as they do in accordance with our health, with the temperament of those who share our lives, and with our beliefs in God. But nothing external to our true selves, including our finances and anyone's love or approval (or the lack of it), has the power to complete or diminish us in any essential way unless we grant it that power. To underscore the point: the further we are from the now-ness of ourselves, the more important the other — in any form — becomes in determining our states of mind.

Whatever we are in relationship with, be it our ideas about God or money, catastrophic events such as earthquakes or tsunamis, or the ceaseless interactions with people that make up our daily lives, how we respond and behave depends on our ability to appreciate the true uniqueness of the individual and the situation. When we move to the Now position, the other becomes distinct, the situation becomes just what it is, and all of this is less and less the extension of our conditioning or survival psychologies, and less and less a reflection of ourselves from which to derive our identities.

ANGER AND HURT:
The Basic Emotions of the You Position

When we have given away some of our sense of self to another and have moved into the You position of the Mandala of Being, there are two primary emotional qualities that signal this: anger and hurt (see figure 3, page 220). Both have many disguises and secondary forms. Anger might appear as resentment, jealousy, possessiveness, envy, impatience, or the tendency to be judgmental. Any of these forms of anger taken to the extreme can become hatred. Hurt ranges across a whole spectrum, from sadness, to feeling betrayed, to a sense of abandonment, to a desperate woundedness.

The more inauthentic we have unconsciously made ourselves in our attempts to ensure the approval and attention of the other, the more angry or hurt we become when the behavior of the other does not bring us what we believe we need or deserve. The more we have suppressed ourselves in order to avoid threatening the other, the more furious we are when they grant themselves the freedoms we have denied ourselves.

When we do not live at the beginning of ourselves, our predominant mechanism for relating to others is *control*. Just as we seek approval and try to avoid disapproval in order to protect our survival personalities, we also use approval and disapproval to control others. We please or we threaten. We demand that the other person live within the same limits we have unconsciously placed on ourselves. We become possessive and jealous because unconsciously we have attached our sense of self to the other and believe he or she has the power to give or take away our essence.

This is the nature of negative attachment: it is based on fear. There is fear of loss of the other and, accordingly, an escalating need to control the other. There is fear that the other will abandon us, that they will find happiness elsewhere and carry away our happiness with them. No power resides in what the other does or who the other is; the fear simply indicates that we have accepted an identity of insufficiency or worthlessness and are not living from our I-Am. Choosing people who treat us in such a way that we remain caught in a constant power struggle with them, which is characterized by anger and woundedness, is our third holding environment. This struggle permits us to maintain the continuity of a familiar sense of self.

Because of the bonding imperative in early life, the assumed existence of the power of the other — as an extension of our survival structure — has been deeply conditioned in us. Consciously resisting this early conditioning is not easy. Any behavior that cues even the slightest suspicion that the other is neglecting us or withdrawing from us can be experienced as a threat and can prompt fear equivalent to a child's fear of abandonment by its mother. Before we can even think about what the other is actually communicating, our survival personalities become alert and our immediate reaction is some form of anger, or hurt. Then, whatever manipulative strategy we have learned will let us regain a feeling of control — whether attempts at pleasing the other person, or submissiveness, or attack, or withdrawal — immediately comes into play. In the You position, we are profoundly dependent upon, and constantly make ourselves referent to, the attention of others. Inevitably, we do this in ways that continuously hold us in an emotional milieu similar to that of our early childhood, regardless of how painful or destructive to us that early environment may have been.

When we unconsciously lose ourselves in another, the actions of the other have a deep impact on our feelings. The real or imagined withdrawal of the love of the other can feel like the most profound dread. Long before we ever consciously face this kind of feeling in ourselves and claim the power to be in relationship with it, we unconsciously give to the other the power to protect us from it. Inevitably a battle is waged in the form of an atmosphere of ongoing conflict within the relationship, marked by repeated episodes of our impatience, frustration, irritability, and anger. These emotions signal that the other is not being obedient to our needs, not protecting us from feelings we don't know how to hold by ourselves. He or she is violating the rules by which we have already unconsciously compromised our own authenticity. For us to be authentic means risking the loss of relationship, and when we have unconsciously projected so much of our self-sense onto the other, we feel this loss as if it were the loss of our true selves. Of course, it is impossible to lose one's true self, but we become so identified with a false and insecure self that we cannot know the difference. To be inauthentic becomes the norm, the basic survival strategy, and we don't even realize it.

If anger grows into hatred, we want the other to suffer what we've suffered, to feel what we've felt, and to feel even worse if we can somehow arrange it. In this state we are surely poisoning our own hearts. Why would we do this, rather than come back to our own sense of presence, right here in our own bodies, where we begin anew in the fullness of our true selves? The answer is painfully simple: as soul-poisoning as anger, woundedness, and even hatred are, these emotions are still less difficult to tolerate than the sensation of complete unknowing akin to nonbeing, which we may experience if we let ourselves come back to the Now. Also, if we have never known a true sense of self, we are unlikely to suddenly develop one on our own and to spontaneously learn to consciously hold in ourselves the sense of utter desolation, worthlessness, and despair: the core feelings underlying our negative attachments to others. If we seek wise, compassionate guidance and make a deep commitment to a path of Self-realization, we may learn to do so. But until this happens, unconsciously holding ourselves in misery and generating misery for others is familiar and feels safer than meeting the untamed emotions.

· This third holding environment is not merely a re-creation of the second holding environment of our early lives; we can, as adults, create far more terrible environments. When we cannot bring ourselves back to the present and face the core sensation of nonbeing in whatever guise it takes, we have no choice but to generate a mental state that reifies *some* sense of identity, no matter how miserable or cruel. If we do not see the problem in ourselves, it can become our truth, our raison d'être, to see the problem as being outside of us, in others. And the more we create this awareness field of anger, judgment, and hatred of others, the more we are created by it. The poisoning of hearts can easily occur over generations, as so much history tragically illustrates.

The key to understanding this is to recognize that the reality of all this anger, rage, woundedness, and envy is directly proportional to the degree to which we are not living from the beginning of ourselves. The closer to the beginning of ourselves we are, the more we are the disciples of our own lives facing into our own feelings, not victims holding others responsible for what we feel. The awakening soul realizes that others have whatever power they have over us precisely to the degree we are unwilling to be in relationship to these difficult feelings within ourselves. All our relationships with others mirror our relationships with ourselves and indicate our depth of presence in the moment.

When we really are in the present, there is no "other" external to us whom we need to complete us — whom we can't live without or, worse, whom we need to diminish, control, or even destroy in order to make ourselves superior and secure. When we start from the You position, we are already disconnected from ourselves, and we constantly tell ourselves stories about the other: "He doesn't care about me." "She is too picky." These stories are virtually endless. We demand that the other change so that we can be happy or safe, and the result is a relationship based on distrust. This distrust, in turn, diminishes each of the participants.

At the beginning of ourselves, no longer do we stand in the territory of an old conditioned *me* world, but instead meet the other in a consciousness that exists prior to it. Each of us is innately free, open, spontaneous, trusting, and ultimately a mystery. We cannot ever fully comprehend this mystery. Our task is to free ourselves from our own limiting identities and distorted ways of seeing the other, and to live and meet one another in the fullness of ourselves. Then the relationship that is created is intrinsically based on trust. In a milieu of trust, the energy of the relationship itself may actually elevate the consciousness of each person in ways that transcend what each brings to it. Together they create and evoke a wholly new relational kingdom.

CHAPTER ELEVEN

The Nature *of* Psychological Time

Lower-Self Functioning, Part Two

We all live embedded in the phenomenon of time. Dawn gives way to sunrise, and dusk to night. Our bodies age, and we may watch our children grow and age in their turn. Without time, there would be no growth or change, no beginnings or endings. But whatever time may be when we view it abstractly, the reality of time as we experience it is psychological. Depending on which identities dominate our sense of self at any given moment, we may look at our pasts as enemies or friends; we may welcome or fear the days to come. When our awareness leaves the Now and moves into the past, we give our memories the power to determine how we feel in the present. Likewise, when we lose contact with our now-ness, what we anticipate about the future can fill our present with anxiety or hope. For this reason it is essential that we understand the emotional consequences of what happens to our sense of self when our minds become lost in the past or future.

THE PAST POSITION

The most fundamental quality of the past is that it is absent. As vivid as a memory may be, we cannot touch it; we can never relive a past moment. Yet despite its absence, through the action of memory the past can take hold and burden us with a sense of irretrievable loss. We can consciously or subconsciously remember wounds and therefore expect the present to hurt us. Equally, we can remember experiences of such joy and love that the present moment seems to pale in comparison. For good and ill, the past conditions our appreciation of the present.

The past never fully leaves us, and this is necessary and good. Without the past, there would be no way to function in the present: to learn from the past is essential to our survival. And from our past experiences we gain our depth of humanity. What we have lived, the mistakes we have made, the lessons we have learned — all this and more increases our wisdom, empathy for others, and gratitude to life itself. But there is a price to pay for this gift, and it is our constant tendency to compare. All of the things we perceive and think, and the choices that lead to our actions, come from comparison with past experiences.

For the interpretative mind, there can be no understanding of any experience without comparison to previous experiences. For this reason, comparison is inherent in all forms of ordinary learning. But because comparison is a continuous and generally unconscious attribute of mind, the originality and spontaneity intrinsic to each moment can be lost. Thus it becomes difficult for us to have an original perception in the present moment — to see things as they are, what in Zen Buddhism is called "original mind."

Thought itself does not exist without the foundation of the past; therefore, thought can never enable us to meet anything and experience it as truly new. To think about our feelings or about a situation is reflexive: we instantly stop seeing what *is* and convert it to something familiar. This diminishes our aliveness and our intelligence. The moment we think about what we are experiencing and put words to it, we are trapped in the past and don't realize it. We live by means of a myth of certainty: this is how things are because this is how things were, and therefore this is how they should be. But a great deal of this supposed certainty rests on imagined and often unreliable or even fictitious memories of past experience.

Nostalgia

Without memory, we could not function. Our lives would lack purpose and meaning. We would fall into the same holes over and over again, the way Bill Murray's character did in the movie *Groundhog Day*. It is essential that we can learn from our mistakes and thereby improve on earlier and inferior reactions and responses. But it's hard to discern memory from reality: memory *becomes* reality. If we experience a deep romance at some point in our lives, it may become the standard by which all new relationships are measured and perhaps found wanting. If an experience was particularly positive or meaningful, we tend to create an idealized memory of it. Then nothing again may seem as good or as alive, giving rise to nostalgia: "Those were the good old days." We can spend our lives trying to recapture a past feeling, in effect refusing our immediate experience in favor of a futile pursuit. Thus nostalgia signals that we are not having an original relationship to the present moment, that we are viewing and interpreting our experience through the lens of the past.

Guilt and Blame

Whenever we are faced with a feeling that threatens our sense of self, and we do not have the power of awareness to remain with the feeling, our minds flee from it, often into the past. Then, whatever we are currently feeling, especially if it is threatening, appears to be the *effect* of some previous *cause*. This leads to guilt, another primary emotion linked to the past, and to blaming (see figure 3, page 220).

Guilt and its cousin emotions, shame and regret, all work like this: "If I hadn't done *that* (in the past), I wouldn't be feeling *this* (now)." *That* can refer to almost anything — an action taken or not taken, a momentary lapse of judgment. Perhaps we said too much to someone and now regret it. We think, "I would have prevented this if only..." To experience guilt shows us that we have violated our own sense of values, and that an apology or behavioral change is required. But to allow guilt to live beyond the first moments — in which it guides us to a new relationship to ourselves and others — is to attack ourselves and create a negative holding environment. The presence of guilt signals that we are overly identified with the past and are not at the beginning of ourselves. At our beginning we do not experience guilt, only compassion and forgiveness for so easily forgetting our true selves.

Blame works in a similar way. It, however, is not based on our own behavior and does not lead to an attack on ourselves, but is based on someone else's behavior and precipitates an attack on them. "If only they had been different, then I wouldn't be suffering in this way now," we tell ourselves. Parents are favorite objects of blame and so are spouses. But assigning blame to a particular person, the government, the communists, the health care system, the universal *them*, and so on hurts the blamer more than anyone else. When we blame, no matter how legitimate our grievance may be, we are the one who contracts. Our hearts close, our blood pressures rise, and our bodies course with stress hormones. When we do not meet our present feeling with our full attention, blaming someone or something else for what we are feeling is, for our conditioned identities, safer and far easier than taking full responsibility for our own relationship to our feeling states.

At the beginning of ourselves, we do not blame others for the feelings they "cause" in us. We can tell them that we feel hurt and ask them to change their behavior. We can choose not to expose ourselves further to disrespect, neglect, or abuse if we perceive ourselves as exposed to these. We are in charge of our own relationship to what we are feeling. We give no one else this power. When we do begin to assign blame, we can immediately realize that we are not at the beginning of ourselves, because we have placed the cause, and therefore the power to meet our feelings, outside our own immediate beings and onto others, as well as into the past. If we do not grasp this, then in extreme cases we might choose to seek retribution. Then the emotional misery will enter into a self-generating cycle, which could keep it alive and growing, even for generations. In this way we make ourselves victims, and victimization by blame tends to be highly contagious. At its root, there is always someone unable to meet a difficult feeling and who chooses to see the cause of that feeling as external to himself or herself.

To step out of this cycle is to break a covenant with *me*, with a habitual or cherished identity. Who feels guilty? Who is blaming? Who needs to take revenge? Who wants the other to hurt like I hurt? *Me*! To live with these feelings is to suffer, but the identities that thrive on them are not really threatened by emotions such as guilt, blame, nostalgia, or regret, since they are the very emotions that support these particular identities. This is why I refer to them as tamed emotions; we suffer with these emotions, but this suffering is a cocoon in which we barricade ourselves and feel the continuity of our beings. The appeal of the familiar, even if painful, is that it steadies us and is unbroken. And it is unbroken because we continuously recreate it.

If instead we hold these feelings without empowering any specific identity — by not entering *me, you, past,* or *future* stories — we may have a conscious encounter with a deeper level of feeling, where the untamed emotions reside. At the beginning of ourselves, our questions are not about whether these emotions are real, but rather along the lines of: "Who am I if I remain non-reactively present with a feeling instead of defining myself by it? Who am I if I see that the source of my guilt is not what I did, but how far from my true self I have been all along? What if I realize that I have never been completely authentic in my life?" Suddenly what was mere guilt becomes a genuine abyss, a shocking revelation of the dream in which we have been living. By comparison, guilt is easy to bear, and blame is a downright relief. When we are unconsciously identified with the past, we are protected from facing and being penetrated by feelings that might challenge and even crack open our survival identities — and lead us to a fuller, more vulnerable, and richer level of our humanity.

This is not to deny that guilt and regret serve a valuable purpose when they indicate to us that we have betrayed our own sense of what is right. Blame also serves a purpose if it shows us an injustice that we can remedy. The complete absence of these emotions, which occurs among sociopaths, is certainly not healthy, and denying or wanting to escape or transcend them is not the point. But guilt and blame are tamed emotions, and if we dwell on them it is because doing so maintains some particular identity, usually one built upon depression. In Mandala work, the presence of these emotions invites us to leave the Past position and return to the Now, where we can discover ourselves anew.

Unless enough of our awareness remains in the present, we will keep living the same patterns, keep reengaging the same emotions, and continue rationalizing with the same thoughts that we unconsciously carry forward from earlier experiences. Without the nonreactive attention of an open awareness, which recognizes that our true stories always begin Now, we cannot accurately interpret feelings as they arise in the present. We don't have enough space between the feelings and our past conditioning to permit them to take a different pathway in us and bring us to a better understanding.

This is a problem of differentiation once again. Just because we become angry doesn't mean there isn't a more complex or more subtle quality to our emotion. How often do you get angry? How long does it last? Suppose the next time you become angry and begin to blame someone else for your feeling, you were to stop all your *past* stories for a moment? What if you brought the feeling fully into the present by focusing all your attention on it? Maybe you would find that there really is an element of anger in how you felt, but by resting at the beginning, you might touch your feeling more receptively and realize, "I see, I'm not really angry. I feel unseen." As you continued to observe this feeling with soft, nonaggressive attention, you might further understand that feeling unseen actually frightens you.

The moment we accurately recognize what we are feeling, the feeling shifts, and often this can restore our sense of clarity and fullness. Recognizing that your real feeling is fear, and having the insight that it comes from feeling unseen, you may actually remember that this is an old feeling from early in your life that has nothing to do with what another person has just said or done in the present. With this understanding, you narrow the gap between who you really are and what you are feeling, and it becomes possible to express what you need, or what is bothering you, more directly and less reactively. This points to the danger of being in the past: it moves us too quickly into an old analysis or interpretation of our immediate sensations, so that we tend to be reactive rather than let each moment be received in its *own* fullness.

As long as we continually compare our new experiences with those of the past, we dull our ability to be innocent, to have a fresh and immediate relationship to the present. Each moment could be a doorway into the ever-changing fullness of ourselves, but instead we crystallize ourselves into static identities. The act of comparison is automatically the extension of a previous *me*, and the origin of our first *me* is consolidated by about age five. Yet even as adults we often automatically employ the primitive defenses that worked for us in childhood, because we unconsciously assess our present vulnerabilities as if we were still children. The self-protective patterns of striving for control, approval, and security that were necessary in childhood continue into the present, where we, as adults, no longer require them. Yet we continue to believe that we do. We make ourselves into robots whose reactions and expressions are predetermined, instead of having original relationships, as conscious beings, to the immediacy of new experiences. This ensures that our ways of being will not be new and fresh; they will be predictable, conditioned, and as a result, dead.

One of the clearest indicators that we are living in the past is the sense that things are taking too long, dragging. When we live unconsciously in the past, boredom and impatience become frequent defenses against facing the deeper feeling of our emptiness.

We have to return to the beginning of ourselves to view the past intelligently, as a source of depth without which we could not fully appreciate the present. To take this crucial step, we must recognize that guilt, blame, nostalgia, regret, boredom, and impatience do not have to be engaged, interpreted, or "fixed," but can be welcomed as signals that we have left the now-ness of ourselves. When we experience any of these emotions, we can ask ourselves the question "What am I not meeting in my-self?" Having asked this question, we can release our thought processes and become quietly present, receptive to whatever might arise. Our deeper awareness is not conditioned; it has no *me*, no *me* world. When we listen with this quality of attention, we are always at our most responsive to a greater intelligence.

The Unreliable Nature of Memory

Most of us assume that what we remember is real, but as more and more research demonstrates, memory is unreliable. Take, for example, a study of specific memories of the explosion of the *Challenger* space shuttle in January 1986.[1] Within hours of the actual event, a group of psychologists presented a questionnaire to several hundred students, asking them to describe where they were, how they felt, and what they were doing when they heard about the tragedy. One year later the same students were asked to answer the same questions. The results were fascinating: researchers found that there was no statistically significant correlation between the students' initial responses and what they described a year later. Perhaps it is even more fascinating to note that, when asked which of their two responses they believed to be more accurate, the vast majority chose the more recent recollection.

We can draw the conclusion not only that memory constantly changes, but also that how we regard something today seems more real to us than what we thought about it before. It is questionable whether any of our early memories are accurate. Furthermore, the phenomenon called "verbal overlay" can distort even short-term memory. In a study documented in *Science News*, volunteers watched a video of a staged robbery, and twenty minutes afterward, half of them were asked to write a detailed description of the robber's face. Five minutes later, only about one-third of those individuals were able to accurately identify the robber from a lineup of suspects. In comparison, those who had not been asked to write the description were twice as accurate in identifying the robber.[2] Engaging the verbal mind in describing a recent event can cause us to "overlay" our own fantasy picture onto the event, which, it turns out, is less likely to accord with reality. Moreover, around 66 percent accuracy is not very convincing when eyewitness testimony is used to determine the guilt or innocence of an individual. This is why many courts now allow expert witnesses to present the research that challenges the presumed accuracy of eyewitness testimony. Yet despite growing evidence of the unreliability of memory, especially when it concerns emotionally charged events, most of us continue to believe that what we remember is accurate, and we treat it as truth.

The Implanting of False Memories

Not only is memory inaccurate, but according to the researcher Elizabeth Loftus, memories can be changed by things we are told. Loftus asserts that facts, ideas, suggestions, and other forms of postevent information can modify our memories. Her research suggests that merely asking someone to consider the possibility of an event having occurred in their distant past can cause the implanting of false memories in certain individuals. These memories can be highly detailed and completely believable to the individuals who possess them, even though the events they are "remembering" never actually occurred.

In one of her experiments, Loftus presented subjects with questions about actual experiences from their childhood, which had been determined through interviews with the subjects' parents. In addition, they were questioned about an event that had not actually occurred. The imaginary event involved being briefly lost in a supermarket and then found by a kind, loving older woman who helped the child find his or her parents. The false memory was intentionally benign so that evoking it would not induce a traumatic memory. When first asked about this event, none of the subjects remembered it, because it had never occurred. But when asked again a few days later in a follow-up interview, several interviewees reported that the event might have happened, but that they had forgotten. By the third interview, some days later, approximately 40 percent of the total number of subjects believed they had been lost in the supermarket, and could describe the older woman and their reunion with their parents in significant detail.[3]

Although some of the research is controversial, the potential for the implanting of false memories is generally considered to be a real phenomenon with serious consequences in certain legal situations, and especially in psychotherapy. There are therapists who have been sued for allegedly implanting false memories in their clients. When the therapists purportedly suggested that early abuse could explain the patients' symptomatology, some patients began to "recall" these events, causing them, their families, and others severe distress. In some cases, lawsuits against family members, teachers, and clergy later judged to be completely innocent of the charges against them added even greater distress.

We now know from brain imaging research that the areas of the temporal lobes of our brains that show increased activity on PET scans as we recall an event are the same areas activated during the use of imagination. This may explain why it is difficult for us to recall memories, especially those that are emotionally charged, without embellishing them with our own fantasies. This also suggests that objective memory of certain lived events may not be possible, and that all of us, in varying degrees, are living in a dream about our pasts that we only imagine being objective historical truth.

We can understand the link between imagination and memory, as well as why we can be tricked into "remembering" things that never happened, if we consider that memory is inevitably colored by our subjectivity. Depending on whichever identity or *me* story is dominant at the time we live an event, the experience of that event will be influenced and even distorted by the subjective nature of that particular identity. If we meet with a boss at a time when we are feeling insecure and doubtful about our own authority, we may remember the boss as having seemed dissatisfied with us, critical, or even dismissive. If, on the other hand, we are feeling good about ourselves during that meeting, we might remember exactly the same exchange as one in which the boss seemed to be supportive and appreciative. The insecure identity remembers a demoralizing event, while the secure identity remembers an encouraging one. The consequences of this are profound.

The *me* stories we are living at the time of an actual event do inevitably influence how we experience and recall it. Moreover, the identity dominant at the time of recall, whether hours or decades later, reimagines and reinterprets that specific past event in accordance with its present emotional reality. If an event was originally traumatic for us because we had assumed a victim identity at the time, it may remain that way if we continue to invoke that memory while in a victim state. If, however, we are in a more open and secure state — closer to the beginning of ourselves — and our minds recall that event once again, it may no longer carry a traumatic quality. We might recall it with acceptance, understanding, and even poignancy, remembering how easily we used to become insecure. Even if we have experienced a traumatic situation, as soon as we return to the Now we have the power to heal our relationship to our pasts.

Right Remembering

A crucial point about memory and the past in general is that *right remembering* requires living at the beginning of ourselves. Right remembering means being capable of accurately recalling an event because, in the now-ness of ourselves, we experience what *is*, unhampered by the distorting lens of our lower-self functioning. Expectations and desires distort our memories. Fear, guilt, and shame do the same. It is probably wise to assume that our pasts are always, to a certain extent, imagined pasts. When considering the past, we should, at the very least, take the position of unknowing, of recognizing that we can't ever be fully sure of what happened then. This way, the door is left open in the Now for forgiveness.

When we return our minds to the Now, we have the capacity to differentiate our present states from our memories. We are far less likely to be captured by a past identity, and therefore we are no longer inclined to unconsciously interpret memories in ways that ratify that particular identity. We instead assume a witnessing consciousness that is already whole and full in itself and has no investment in altering perception to fit a particular kind of psychological conditioning. The old meaning and significance of a memory, with all the feelings that have been part of it, are therefore no longer needed, so it is spontaneously set free: it is *forgiven*, and its energy is returned to us.

When we identify with the past, less of our energy is available to us. How much less depends on how *closely* we identify with the past. Using the Mandala of Being, we can visualize it this way: the further from the center, the lower our spiritual energy and the more extreme the perception of separateness. When we live further from our beginning, we are increasingly dominated by lower-self functioning. Accordingly, we are inherently more grandiose or insecure about ourselves, more defensive, controlling, and needy with others, and more distrusting of everything in general. Inevitably, our egos' survival strategies will work overtime. Our minds will be spinning thoughts, analyzing, interpreting, judging, and so on, trying to rationalize our feelings — which will tend to be negative — and trying to find some resolution.

In contrast, when we step away from the Past and move closer to the Now position, we are moving toward pure consciousness and are increasingly infused with universal energy. This gives us more spiritual muscle, more capacity to exercise the power of awareness and remain nonreactively present with what *is*. Therefore we have more innate faith in the wholeness of ourselves. As we move toward our beginning, we increasingly perceive wholeness and feel related to everyone and everything, and every moment feels immeasurably full.

Nostalgia, guilt, boredom, regret, and blame all indicate that we are living old stories and not refreshing ourselves in the fountain of infinite renewal, where our new stories begin each moment. In ordinary psychology based on wanting to understand our personalities, we think of these emotions as negative and we work to modify ourselves in order to find a more positive way of being. This is an appropriate early stage of consciousness growth, but it still rests on a perception of ourselves that is concrete: we continue to imagine that we exist as exclusively private, separate psychic entities. At this level we have the power to partially shift the so-called negative patterns. But we still identify with our bodies, our feelings, and our ideas and do not yet know who we are in our true selves. In a sense, working only at the level of emotional reactions is still only rearranging the furniture within the *me* world, not perceiving the relative illusion of that world itself.

It is essential to understand that all tamed emotions — anger, hurt, and guilt, to name a few — have a positive effect in the sense that they maintain the existence of some identity and therefore protect the basic integrity of the ego-I. Once the consciousness of *me* consolidates, all emotions — regardless of their consequences — support the primary imperative of preserving that basic identity. Thus the myth of the separate self remains unchallenged. Within that myth we can hope for a utopia where all behavior has been properly modified so that human beings live forever in peace, harmony, and sustainability, but this can never actually occur where the survival of false and limited identities is the unassailable priority.

For the awakening soul, the presence of nostalgia, blame, guilt, or regret is a way for us to recognize that the tug of lower-self functioning is holding us in the past. Rather than seeing these emotions as negative, we can understand that they are compassionate signposts urging: "Wake up; be in your body; find the friendship of your breath. Let your mind sink down into the now-ness of yourself. Discover who you really are, right now."

These emotions are calling us to engage the power of awareness and make ourselves vulnerable to the present. This is their gift to us. When we let our yearning for truth lead us into the fullness of each moment, these emotions repeatedly point the way home. They are, as they do this, a blessing.

THE FUTURE POSITION

Because time is a continuum, to a very large degree our expectations for the future are determined by how we remember the past. A traumatic past relationship may make us leery about future prospects. A positive experience in the past may make us feel hopeful about the future. But as the Mandala of Being shows, whether we retreat into the past or the future, the emotional quality of our memories or future prognostications instantly affects our current *me* world. We can scare ourselves, depress ourselves, or inspire ourselves with these stories. Whatever identity (or, actually, core feeling) is operational in our *me* world at any moment determines the emotional meaning we attribute to the past and simultaneously determines the emotional quality we anticipate in the future.

Expectancy

Imagine you are sitting in the center of the Mandala, right on the Now position, and you want to observe the influence of psychological time on this virgin moment. Attempt to set aside any tendency to compare what you are experiencing now to any previous experience. What is this Now, without the nearly ineluctable element of comparison? Next, consciously try to diminish the influence of the future on your Now awareness. Can you discern that your mind wants to tilt toward the future? Do you sense a certain quality of restless expectancy? It is as though you are always looking at the Now with a question: "How much longer will this last?" "Where is this going?" "Okay, what's next?" The mind is like a child in a car asking incessantly, "Are we there yet?"

Expectancy is a natural attribute of the mind, but unless we really anchor ourselves in the Now and can make the pull of expectancy conscious, we do not recognize the presence of expectancy itself. In that case, we live unconsciously identified with our expectations for the future.

Uncertainty and Fear

The unique psychological architecture of the future is notably different from that of the past. Whereas the past is remembered but forever absent, the future is imagined yet forever *withheld*. It is like the horizon: we endlessly approach it but never arrive. To be overly identified with the future is to be always on our way *to* life, not actually *living* it.

By its very nature, the future is inherently uncertain and, at the same time, offers near-infinite possibility. These qualities give rise to the two basic emotional states that occur in us as we move away from the beginning of ourselves and become overly identified with the future: fear and hope (see figure 3, page 220). It is the uncertainty of the future that causes us to fear: "Something terrible could happen." "What if I don't succeed?" Anxiety and worry are forms of fear which tell us that our minds are overly caught in the uncertainty of the future.

We try to compensate by being vigilant and prepared: "If I take care of this and watch out for that, then everything will be fine." We spend our lives trying to guard against or forestall anything bad we fear might eventually occur. We always try to stay one step ahead of the game. But we can never be fully prepared; something unexpected can always happen. The more we try to anticipate every contingency and the more we try to accomplish, then the more we think about what needs to be done and the more pressured we become. When our minds are unconsciously in the past, time seems to drag; but when we unconsciously live in the future, there is never enough time.

The fear engendered in us by the uncertainty of the future can also take other disguises, such as pessimism and cynicism. Instead of trying to choose our futures and risk failure and rejection, we may refuse to take any real responsibility for them. Unwilling to live in the present and proactively create the greatest potential for our futures, we instead defend ourselves by being pessimistic and cynical: "It won't work. Nothing will ever change. It's always going to be this way, so what's the use of trying?"

Pessimism and cynicism are emotional rationalizations for refusing a fuller involvement with life. They are defenses of a depressive victim identity that will not allow us to muster up the courage to risk facing all the uncertainty and possibility of the future.

Often we have no idea how thoroughly we have identified with the future. It seems so normal to us to be always on our way to our lives, always almost there. Then suddenly we receive a call from the doctor reporting worrisome test results. With the specter of illness or even death before us, all our assumptions about what we would eventually be or do, all our dreams and plans — the picture of everything yet to unfold that we have taken for granted — can collapse in seconds, and with it our sense of self. The emptiness of the present in which we so rarely live can leave us in a state of desperation as we face the fear of nonbeing.

Some people continue to displace this fear into the future, imagining nonbeing after they die. Others forestall it with beliefs about life after death. But the terror that grips most of us when our imagined futures are stripped away is really the sensation of nonbeing that we have never truly faced in the present. Death is the ultimate humiliation of all of our ego-based identities, and its approach ends the delusion of immortality in which these identities cloak us. But for our egos and our whole *me* world, coming back to the Now without a real sense of our true selves is just as much a death as physical death.

The eventual confrontation with physical death is one of the most basic experiences of human life; it is the one absolute certainty about the future. Yet, as noted in the Mahabharata, a Hindu sacred text, even though death surrounds us everywhere, no one really believes they will die. Of course, intellectually we know we will die, but we do not allow ourselves to be *penetrated* by this knowledge and thus to confront the actual feeling of loss of self. By denying death, by living in a culture that worships youth and considers it morbid to contemplate death, we ensure more or less complete identification with our *future* stories. As a result, we are sitting ducks when reality takes a shot at us.

Possibility and Hope

The uncertainty of the future tends to generate fearfulness, but its promise of unlimited possibility makes the future exciting and full of endless reasons to hope: "This marriage is a match made in heaven." "Our team is going to win the World Series this year." "My book has every chance of being a bestseller."

Fear can cause us to contract and revert to our primitive survival strategies, thereby severely diminishing our intelligence. Hope can make us expansive and can propel us into enthusiastic action. This can be good, such as when a doctor tells us that with our cooperation and appropriate behaviors, we will heal and make a full recovery. But often hope is a form of escape from feelings we need to embrace; then, escaping into a *future* story that offers hope is actually self-destructive.

A wise character in the science-fiction television series *Taken* makes the observation "Hope is the lie we all need." Certainly, in a culture rooted in survival, distrust, and fear, hope is virtually mandatory: we believe that without it we cannot live. As a physician I learned that hope can be an important part of the healing process, but when physicians feel compelled to provide hope to their gravely ill patients, they leave many of them in a state of misinformation and ignorance. Politicians do much the same, playing on our fears and offering unrealistic and even unattainable promises instead of encouraging their constituents to face the challenging issues that must be addressed if humankind is to reach its fullest potential. And throughout our consumer society, inspiring hope about becoming more attractive, desirable, successful, or popular is a basic marketing (survival) strategy for many businesses.

Since escaping from feelings that we can't seem to address head-on does make us feel better and temporarily decreases stress, no doubt there are certain short-term health benefits to many of the hopeful lies we tell ourselves. As a result, popular culture considers hope a psychological necessity. But at what price? There is no question that it's better to have hope than to collapse in despair if we are not yet ready to consciously suffer and learn from it. In certain situations, offering and encouraging hope is a form of compassion, almost like extending a rope to a drowning person. Yet the only life we can extend with hope is the life we know; hope is generally hope for the continuity or improvement of our *me* world.

I once heard a radio commercial for a hospital that specializes in cancer treatment announce that, at this facility, they know that people want treatment that will change their lives as little as possible. This may seem understandable, yet if we do have cancer, perhaps this means it is time for us to fundamentally change. The hope that we can treat cancer without changing our lives or being inconvenienced might actually limit our potential to heal.

When hope pulls us away from the Now, where we might face difficult decisions or distressing truths, then hope amounts to denial of the soul's capacity to discover a new and deeper connection to life in the midst of suffering. Being present with what *is*, without hope, and facing into despair without hope, is a fundamental initiation, the dark night of the soul that is a basic means for the evolution of consciousness. In contrast, indiscriminately offering hope is a form of cynicism and lack of faith in the transformative capacity of the soul.

Whether hope is more destructive than it is constructive, or vice versa, depends on our maturity and how deeply we have wanted to know ourselves. But our culture's tendency to blindly value and encourage escape into hope keeps us from facing the difficult feelings that we must learn to hold if we are ever to live with greater freedom from fear.

Perhaps much that we hope for is delusional. Why would we need or want hope if we are living in the fullness of ourselves? Certainly the soul does not "hope" that the inherent self-transcending nature of awareness will lead us to ever-greater authenticity and intelligence. It just does. We need not hope that things will change, that everything is impermanent — it just is. What we might call innate hope is the natural expression and fullest working out of life's inherent wholeness. And facing directly into life's ferocious moments does not take hope. It takes courage, determination, and self-surrender.

False hope is always a movement away from the beginning of ourselves, usually to escape some sense of threat. We temporarily attain a degree of succor through such hope, but our culture's indiscriminate encouragement of hope weakens our collective spirit. Humankind is constantly escaping into the future, not just to imagine and build a better world to come, but also to save itself from an unacceptable Now. This flight from the Now decreases our energy and diminishes our intelligence. It is an ancient psychological survival strategy, but its collective expression is colliding with the capacity of our planet to support human life. We make poor choices when hope is driving our actions.

False Enthusiasm

Anyone who is unconsciously identified with the hoped-for future believes the best is yet to come and compulsively works to reach predetermined goals. This is a form of blindness. The present becomes merely the means by which to attain our personal ends. More to the point, when our minds are unconsciously in the future, the present disappears; it is simply not available to us. We substitute heading toward our lives for actually living.

When we are overly identified with the future, one of the disguises that hope can take is false enthusiasm. True enthusiasm is "god-inspired" — the root meaning of the word. False enthusiasm is an unconscious autoerotic game, a way of exciting ourselves with the intensity of our own ambitions and aspirations. It uses possibility as a kind of narcotic. In some people it propels a life that requires a nearly continuous adrenaline high, "beating the odds," having an "edge," and always looking toward the future. False enthusiasm is a kind of drivenness, an unrealistic optimism that we can "make it work." In our culture such an attitude is highly admired, and fortunes have been made from this success-oriented form of Self-avoidance.

The reason false enthusiasm is unrealistic is not because these goals can't be met; all too often they can. But false enthusiasm is inevitably born of an insecure *me* world, and when we are engaged with this enthusiasm, we tend to use people and natural resources as a means to achieve our own ends. Because it does not emanate from the beginning of ourselves, false enthusiasm is rooted in a more limited intelligence. As a result, while under its sway we are much less capable of seeing the intricately interconnected nature of all things. What we do and accomplish through our false enthusiasm, no matter how brilliantly executed, will inevitably be in greater conflict with, and ultimately more destructive to, the wholeness of the world than actions born of a deeper intelligence and truer enthusiasm.

When we are overly identified with the future and living in hope, we convince ourselves that we must postpone truly enjoying life until our conditions for happiness are achieved. But since we are unconsciously fleeing our own sense of emptiness, those conditions can never be met. There is no level of success that makes the heart feel successful before we learn to hold feelings such as emptiness and hopelessness themselves. Whether entrepreneur or workaholic, we pretend to ourselves that we are working of our own free will, but the deeper truth is that some of us can't step off the fear-hope treadmill, because our identities and our emotional survival is built around it. In our culture, the necessity for achievement is a primary form of Self-avoidance. Hope and fear are the carrot and the stick, as philosopher George Jaidar has written, used to entice and enforce the survival mythos expressed through the drive for success.4

When we rely on hope to avoid subconscious fears, we postpone having a direct relationship with ourselves. As T. S. Eliot wrote, if we are to know the "stillness of God" — the fullness of ourselves — we must "wait without hope / For hope would be hope for the wrong thing."5 And when it comes to finally facing the untamed and disowned feelings that humankind has been fleeing virtually forever, hope *is* the wrong thing. We must understand this clearly, because the whole human survival project rests on a hoped-for future that never comes. It never comes because we don't really want it to. Our identities are sustained by remaining in the fear-hope dynamic, not by arriving at the wholeness of ourselves right now, even though wholeness — or in our culture, "happiness" — is what we keep telling ourselves we do want.

This is the nature of the third holding environment: We live inside a psychological structure of insufficiency and unworthiness, a pervasive waking dream in which we have to prove to ourselves and the world that we have a right to exist and are worthy of everything we can get. This psychological structure makes us perpetually unhappy, but sustaining this unhappiness — using it to motivate ourselves while in the pursuit of happiness — is what we unconsciously assume is the key to our survival. We sustain our waking dream as though our lives depend on it. In reality, this way of holding ourselves actually threatens our survival.

To be sure, the future will become the Now, and there will always be challenges. But why should the future represent any inherent threat or hope if right now we are living from the fullness of ourselves? When we arrive at the beginning of ourselves, which is not possible until we have at least begun to face and hold the untamed emotions, then we have developed a sense of trust in ourselves. Indeed, we have actually created an authentic sense of self, not something resting on external achievements. Once we have *this*, then why not trust the future as well?

Hope is a weak counterfeit for real trust and fullness. If we are overly identified with the future, hope is our antidote to the distressing feelings we have not met in ourselves. We externalize this unmet fear and forever try to conquer it *out there* by battling natural terrorists like bacteria, prions, viruses, and cancer or human terrorists who strap explosives onto themselves or hide behind corporate interests or global economic policy. But no matter what wonderful progress we make in countering or defeating the external threats, we are never safe, because we will continue to externalize our untamed fear of nonbeing. There will always be a new threat and always the antidote of new hope.

As history shows, our efforts sometimes accomplish more than the results we had hoped for. Through vaccinations we overcame smallpox, until the disease was so rare that immunization was no longer necessary. Now, with nearly everyone having lost their immunity, the whole world is vulnerable to a terrorist attack using organisms preserved by military research to create biological weapons. Similarly, as we manage to make significant progress against cancer, the technologies we will inevitably develop to do so, such as genetic engineering, may over time become just as perilous as cancer. Creating runaway genetic anomalies can potentially disrupt whole ecosystems. We are already enmeshed in the predicament that synthetic chemicals used in food and energy production and in new technologies are linked to a growing epidemic of cancers, mental disorders, and birth defects, not to mention global warming.

Given the excess food-production capacity in First World countries, farmers sometimes let food rot or dump it in the ocean rather than put it all on the market and depress prices, which would decrease profits. Simultaneously, governments in these same countries spend billions to subsidize farmers, thereby artificially driving down the cost of foods and making it impossible for farmers in developing countries to compete in the world market. The practices that provide hope for one group of people can steal hope from others.

It is crucial to our survival to let ourselves finally see how reflexively we flee from fear and follow the lure of hope. When we project ourselves toward a hoped-for future, anything that happens in the present moment that is even slightly threatening to our desired futures causes us anxiety, worry, or fear. Anxiety and worry are immediate reminders that we are not at the beginning of ourselves. Anxiety tells us that we have made our sense of self contingent on something that has not yet happened. If we will not come back to the beginning of ourselves and face our fears, then inevitably our minds will be thrown into some kind of hope process. Hope, therefore, is also an immediate reminder that we are not at the beginning of ourselves.

Money and the Future

Money is a means of exchange of energy between people, and so it is an essential part of many of our relationships. As with any relationship, the consciousness and potential of the relationship depends on where we start from in ourselves, and when it comes to money, more often than not, our minds move to the future and we start from fear. It is the fear of scarcity, or of being cheated, or of feeling out of control, or that our needs will not be met, or that we won't be able to take care of ourselves or our loved ones, or that we will be perceived as failures or at least not as successful as others. In short, money becomes an extension of our survival psychologies. It gains its great power from the future that we imagine it can protect us from, the uncertainty we believe it can cushion us against, or the rest time it promises us.

But if we take some money and hold it in our hands right now, we will see that it gives us nothing. There is no joy, no peace, no fullness. It is not intrinsically beautiful like a flower or a smiling face. It has no energy at all until we attach it to our grandiose or depressive *me* stories and especially to our *future* stories.

Consider how much money you would need if, right now, you were resting in a sense of your own innate wholeness. How many possessions would you need, how big a house? How many of the counterfeit fulfillments and forms of escape of modern culture would really matter? Consider what you would do with your money, what you would invest in, how you would share it.

True wealth is being who we have always been at the beginning of ourselves. Material wealth, once our basic needs for food and shelter are met, is the power we imagine we can use to control the future. But since the character of the future is inherently uncertain, we can never have real control. This is why even abundant wealth cannot provide true peace of mind or an open heart. Having money does not change the basic survival mythos. In fact, it can reinforce it, because the more control we imagine we have, the more we are afraid of losing control. The more opulence and comfort we surround ourselves with, the more identified with it we become, and the more afraid we are to live without it. The more exclusiveness our wealth can ensure, the more security systems we need to protect it. In service to fear we use money as insulation from life's vicissitudes, and this means from other people as well. Wealth tends to isolate us and makes us distrust those who have less, because we are afraid they will take advantage of us. Wealth and our grandiose *me* stories often go together, and as a result, we can think ourselves better than those who have less than we do.

Whether we are rich or poor, there can be no true freedom until we can face all our *future* stories about money, feel what they create in us, and return to the beginning of ourselves. Believing money will make us safe or give us special authority is false hope and grandiosity. It puts the power to gain security and our self-worth outside of us; we become defined by how much money we have, instead of by who we really are. This is poverty of the spirit.

If we are authentically seeking to know ourselves, it is essential to consciously examine all our *me* and *future* stories about money. We will see that fear of loss of money is really a disguise for the fear of nonbeing. Whatever hope money promises, it always leads us away from ourselves. Therefore we cannot *hope* to know the fullness of being — to cross over from a survival-based existence to a genuine spiritual life — unless all the hope attached to our money stories is released. An acorn does not have to hope to become an oak tree. Neither does a human being need to hope for money or anything else to become a human being. The soul is calling us to our unlimited potential for a consciousness that is not contingent on our circumstances.

God and the Future

I often turn my mind toward God, without the least idea of what I am doing. Generally, I just feel a deep sense of gratitude, but there are times when I feel scared and spontaneously ask for help. When I do, I often wonder why. I know nothing about God, except the one certainty that I am creating a conversation with "something" that I am imagining exists because I am threatened by the sensations present in me. Usually when I think in this way, I stop my conversation with "God" — I even find it amusing — and just surrender my mind into a deeper sense of listening into whatever I am feeling and into the fullness of the moment. I have no idea how to cross the abyss to that Source that some part of me intuits and forever yearns for, and which seems to forever remain out of reach. Oddly, even the notion of such a Source may itself be born from the inexplicable quality of feeling that I have just called *yearning*. The feeling is unquestionable, but to imagine an ultimate Source — some place of final succor and belonging — is, like speaking to "God," suspect. Perhaps because there is no real foundation to our egos, we need to imagine that foundation, and we call *this* God. Knowing that at the level at which all thinking takes place there can be no truly satisfactory resolution to this feeling, I have learned to embrace a sense of unknowing and even gentle helplessness that has become for me a source of exquisite tenderness and gratitude.

It seems to me that, once we are able to face directly into the immediacy of our moments of primal aloneness, there is little to ask from God. Yet I understand our tendency to supplicate for assistance; at times, life's suffering is daunting. So, many of us turn to God to ask for help, to ask God to change our destinies, to heal us or those we love. I don't know anything about this God, but I do not question the psychological effect of such "prayer." Prayer can be healing, but I doubt it has as much to do with God as it does with the depth to which we have brought our minds into the Now. To me, it is our knowing of ourselves in the Now that is our only true means of knowing God and is the essence of prayer.

If we are continually running away from fearful sensations, what God can we possibly have except one that we allow to infantilize us, and that we use as a source of false hope? You might disagree and point out that it is not false hope to believe in healing through prayer, that miracles do happen. And I would agree, miracles do happen and prayers may heal. But as wondrous as it is that sometimes a person is suddenly healed of advanced cancer or another disease or affliction, wouldn't the greater miracle be that the enormous amount of fear that dominates the lives of most of us, and leads to most of our praying, were finally healed?

For that to happen, our understanding of God has to change. By believing stories that place him beyond us, we also place his intervention outside us and in the future or, in the stories about God's miracles, in the past. Turning toward God is, for many of us, a means of never truly coming to the beginning of ourselves, where we might actually know God directly. Instead, we keep imagining we must postpone such a profound relationship, because God is so great and we are so insignificant by comparison. (These are *you* and *me* stories.) We postpone it until our final breath, imagining that at last God will come to greet us and forgive us. But will we know fullness or forgiveness then, when we rarely allow ourselves to know it now? When the disciples asked Jesus to "tell us how our end will be," he responded: "Have you then discovered the beginning, so you inquire about the end? For where the beginning is, there shall be the end."[6]

When we unconsciously identify with the future, we live in a constant battle with anxiety and fear. As we attempt to compensate by deluding ourselves with hope, we may coerce our thinking to make it "positive," because a positive story invites a positive feeling. "I am a beloved child of God" is a far more pleasant and uplifting belief than "I am unlovable." But it is impossible to establish a genuinely sustaining feeling state solely through the agency of positive thinking, because even if the stories are *about* our true selves, they do not arise *from* our true selves. Positive thought is not the language of the Now: all thoughts interrupt the flow of deeper awareness. Direct awareness is never static or repetitive. Unless the feelings that we deem positive, such as joy, gratitude, and forgiveness, arise within us spontaneously from the quality of our relationship to the present moment, they are not authentic. Any intention to use thought to change what we are feeling is a rejection of what *is*, and is a form of manipulation that inevitably invites us back into reaction and negativity.

If hope takes the guise of an effort to think positively in order to bring about a future of our own design, then a step has been missed. It is the step of faith, in which we face into the fear and distrust motivating our desire to create this positive change. Knowing that at the beginning of ourselves "we are already *that which we have been seeking*" and "we are already sufficient as we are," we turn toward the now-ness of ourselves, to what *is*, not to what might be.

This is the step that is rarely explained: that we must again and again face fear until we can do so without being thrown back into the pattern of lower-self functioning. Then we are united with a far greater wholeness, and whatever we have genuinely asked in our souls to know and to live comes toward us more or less effortlessly. All we need do is stop avoiding our true selves. In relationship to our fear and distrust, we can, as mentioned earlier, become like a wise mother who takes a distressed child and, receiving the child exactly as it is and holding it in the steadiness of her love, helps this child return to its own innate faith.

When we no longer react, we have become transparent. It is a sacred transparency, an exquisite vulnerability in which our beings holds the moment completely. Then we are the world, and it lives in us and holds us perfectly.

There is a wonderful paradox in all this. The vendors of spiritual magic, those who promise that we can have the future we want just by changing our expectations, without having to face fear and despair, are not entirely wrong. We live in a generous, reflexive universe. If what we need in order to learn faith is to change our thinking and take positive action, and then see a beneficial change in our lives, the universe grants this happily. But if we continue to do this, imagining we have found a way to manipulate life, the universe sooner or later reflects back the fear underlying our new strategy for control. Then we discover that positive thinking and quasi-spiritual tricks no longer work, and that we will have to learn faith even in fear itself. This is the "dark night," the no-man's-land each of us eventually has to cross if we are to become fully human.

It is as though, when we are spiritually youthful, we are generously allowed to see that we live in a universe of infinite possibility that responds to our beings. We have our first conscious experience of faith, and we see that, indeed, we are held by existence: our distrust ultimately is unfounded. But it is the ego and its survival project at the helm of our initial, youthful spiritual experiments, and inevitably we are called to maturity. Since the last thing we are willing to trust without "hope" is a relationship with the untamed fears, we find it difficult to redeem these dark places, and we postpone doing so.

After any awakening or any new opening into a state of expansion and new vision, these darker aspects are always the next energies that come forward and ask for our acceptance. If we do not turn away, do not keep reburying the darkness over and over again, then we can, at last, rest in the fullness of ourselves, and the limiting conditioning of the fear-hope process no longer enslaves us. We can finally let fearful feelings be safe inside us.

Only in the present moment do we have any true power over the future, for if we experience ourselves as full and whole now, we intrinsically trust whatever the future may bring. We do not exercise this power with thought alone, but with the full strength of our awareness and the whole of our beings. True change comes about through the nonreactive gaze of attention that deepens us into the present and thereby opens us to a new vision of life.

CHAPTER TWELVE

The Natural Emergence *of* Essence

Witnessing the nobility of the human spirit in acts of kindness, courage, or self-sacrifice, we have every reason to feel inspiration and gratitude for the rich potential of our humanity. I remember reading of a Hutu woman who in 1994 risked her own life by hiding a dozen Tutsi tribespeople in her home to save them from certain death. In Rwanda at that time, Hutu extremists killed some eight hundred thousand people, mostly Tutsi and moderate Hutus. When she was asked why she had taken such a risk, she said simply, "I was taught that we are all human beings."

Why are deep values more important for some of us than even our own survival? I believe the answer is that values like the ones this Hutu woman demonstrated with her profound act of courage and compassion represent the true foundation of our being. Empathy with the feelings of others, forgiveness and compassion for them, and deep trust in life — these are emanations of the true self. To be surprised by love in any moment, or to find ourselves filled with gratitude, wonder, and joy, is natural at the beginning of ourselves.

I know that many of us, when we see or hear of selfless and noble acts and acts of genuine kindness, are suddenly moved to tears. I think of these as tears of recognition: they confirm what we know deep in our souls about who we truly are and about what is most noble and good about us. To be the recipient of someone's openhearted caring, to feel truly seen by another, to really be listened to, to be forgiven after years of guilt, and to find forgiveness after years of rage: these are among life's greatest blessings.

A friend once described her experience of attending a brief talk by Mother Teresa. What stayed most in her memory was that, as Mother Teresa walked into the auditorium, the whole room became silent and filled with presence. My friend attributed this to Mother Teresa's personal emanation, but I believe it was far more than just the presence of one individual. I believe the consecration of her life spoke to the hearts of everyone attending and invited a quality of respectful attention that, itself, unified the energy of the audience. She transmitted faith in what is good and whole in a human life, and everybody present, having the same in themselves, began to vibrate to her music and amplify it. It was a moment of mutual blessing. Mother Teresa was surely the catalyst, but I believe the presence that filled the auditorium was the collective radiation of qualities that belonged to everyone.

Fairness, compassion, wonderment: these are innate to very young children. Most children, if given a few cookies, will divide what they have and share them with others present rather than horde them. This kind of behavior begins to diminish as fear-based socialization trains it out of us. But rarely is it fully extinguished, and if our own lives call us to deeper self-reflection, we will find these higher qualities reemerging in us, lifting us, and guiding our lives. They are, I believe, the natural fruit of the soul's innate self-transcending capacity: the power of awareness to bring us closer and closer to the ineffable mystery of our beings. And as we proceed on this journey, we will express these essential qualities more and more, without inculcation.

In my work I have often witnessed love, trust, openness, respectful attention, and other forms of human goodness spontaneously emerging in people. All it takes is an environment in which individuals are encouraged to know themselves and in which they feel safe to just be themselves. Some of the people I counseled were facing difficulties in their lives that might easily have predisposed them to victimhood and self-involvement. But because they were willing to look honestly at their stories and fears, and to set these aside as they learned to become fully present and alive in their bodies, invariably their hearts opened and love, trust, and new creativity flourished. The benediction of a saint is a glorious thing, but it does not take a saint to create a field of mutual blessing; it takes people who are willing to build their relationships by starting from the beginning of themselves.

We have seen how the Mandala of Being models the emotional dynamics of identification with our *me, you, past,* and *future* stories. Assuming that these stories and beliefs are reality, we deny our deeper essence as conscious beings and inevitably limit ourselves. However, reality changes as we become more capable of living in the Now and exercising our power of awareness. Our attention that is habitually pulled into stories changes direction and becomes reoriented to the beginning of ourselves. Immediately, we spontaneously and naturally begin to express our more noble attributes.

THE MANDALA MODEL AND THE NATURAL EMERGENCE OF ESSENCE

Now we can appreciate the Mandala model in a whole new way. It becomes a map describing the emergence of our essential qualities: our identification with *me* stories gives way to discerning self-inquiry; angry and judgmental *you* stories are replaced by empathic and compassionate presence; guilt- and blame-creating *past* stories heal through forgiveness; and the worries and false hopes born of *future* stories evaporate as we learn to trust ourselves. The strategic behavior and contracted emotional climate of lower-self functioning is replaced by a quality of simplicity: we are authentic, and feelings of gratitude, joy and love well up spontaneously. (See figure 4, page 275. Note that the arrows — representing the direction of our attention — which point away from the Now position in figure 3, are directed toward the center of the Mandala in this figure.)

Self-Inquiry and the Me Position

As we consider the Me position, what challenges our false self-identification is our innate capacity for self-reflection, exemplified in the classic self-inquiry "Who am I?" All spiritual traditions emphasize some form of self-inquiry, and a tradition from India known as Advaita Vedanta places this question at the heart of its teaching. Advaita, which means "nondual," was taught in India by the great Indian sage Sankara, who lived in approximately AD 800. In the last two centuries, the philosopher-saints Ramakrishna, Ramana Maharshi, and Nisagardatta have been the most famous exponents of this path.

In posing the question "Who am I?" we are not asking ourselves an intellectual question that has a quantifiable or even qualitative answer. The answer is not a profound or subtle self-conception. Rather, in posing this question we withdraw energy

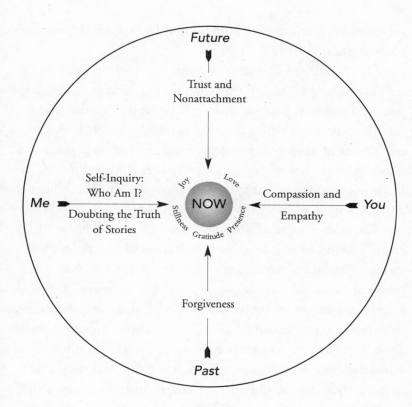

Figure 4.

The Mandala of higher-self functioning: what we feel
when our awareness is well adapted to the present.

from identification with all self-conception, including, most important, from *anything* thinkable about ourselves. We instead attune ourselves to the immediate present (see figure 4). In doing this we are not trying to remain as spectators. By bringing our attention as fully as we can into the Now and remaining open and alert, we merge with the Now moment, really the immediate experience of ourselves prior to thought. One of my teachers, Franklin Merrell-Wolff, himself a great admirer of Sankara, spoke of this as consciousness (he is referring here to me-consciousness) turning back to find its own root as original consciousness.

This practice of opening our awareness to the present — attending fully to what *is*, rather than fleeing from it via *me*, *you*, *past*, and *future* stories — is the crucial work, but whether we actually experience Self-realization is not the point. It is not in our power to achieve this through our own efforts; grace is a mystery we do not wield. One Zen master summed up the relationship between effort and grace this way: "Enlightenment is an accident, practice makes us accident prone."

The realignment of attention through the inquiry "Who am I?" invites us to recognize that *I* arises as an endless, ever-changing stream of sensations — anxiety, happiness, fear, irritation, calmness, joy, and so on — that can be placed before a larger field of awareness. Instead of becoming identified with this flow and our equally endless stories about it, we can look *through* it. This makes each story and the whole structure of sensation that lies beneath it a relative truth and partial self-identification, at most. Thus, the energy of the inquiry "Who am I?" is doubt about the veracity of any *me* stories, and the result of exercising this doubt is transparency.

In spiritual circles, doubt is sometimes called the poison of the heart, referring to how our depressive *me* stories repeatedly undermine our innate sense of what is real and true for us. However, in deep self-inquiry, doubt is essential: if we do *not* doubt the truth of our *me* stories, and indeed all our stories, it is very difficult to disengage from their power over us. Then it may not be possible to return to the Now, allow our hearts to open, and feel deep trust in life.

Of course, I am not speaking here of doubt about functioning within a particular role. For example, to doubt we will get a job because we think "I never do well in interviews" (*me* and *past* stories), or to doubt we can be ourselves, because we tell ourselves the story "I am always so afraid of what other people think" (an amalgam of *past, you,* and *me* stories), only undermines our ability to be authentic and meet the situation fully. This means we are caught in the identity of self-doubt. In contrast, the quality of doubt that is the energy of higher-self functioning is the doubt that questions the basis of such self-doubt, or of any identity. It does so by asserting a more complete awareness that does not deny or reject but that simply rests transparently in the present and realizes: "Here am I, doubting myself."

"Here am I" takes its position in the Now, and thereby we are able to feel the immediate quality of sensation within ourselves and see which stories are operating in us right now. If we can realize "Here am I, building a case with my thoughts about why I may not get this job," *and*, having shifted away from identifying with the self-doubt, we can be present in our anxiety or vulnerability and hold *this*, then we are already more transparent, more filled with energy. Instead of being thrown into devising further stories, we function at a higher level. In comparison, unconsciously identifying with self-doubt, and telling ourselves stories that create a self-defeating holding environment, keeps us at an especially low level of functioning. Alternatively, if we rely on false hope and tell ourselves, "I'll wow them with my charm; they won't be able to resist me," we may disguise our underlying sense of inadequacy, but this is scarcely better.

Even if our stories, when engaged with the energy of doubt, are clearly untrue, they can still feel true. To our core emotional identities, which we developed early in life, these stories seem true because we have subconsciously believed them for so long. They emerge from our third holding environment — our internalized survival psychology — and then re-create that psychology in an addictive loop. But asking "Who am I?" and becoming softly receptive allows us to recognize that who we are isn't adequately embraced by any story. Most of our stories are untrue at a factual level; they are judgments or beliefs. And they are not true in an ontological sense, because they distance us from our immediate sense of being and thereby weaken our ability to know our true selves and express our essence.

To break the stranglehold of our stories, we must bring our attention as fully as possible to the present and, from the now-ness of our fuller awareness, *look* at the stories we are telling ourselves, *doubt* that this is the whole truth, and then *feel* what it actually creates in us emotionally and energetically. When we do this — in effect tasting the "poison" — we can understand the ridiculousness and destructiveness of what we believe about so many things. Then we will automatically want to invite a healthier potential.

Sarah, a counseling client whose husband suffered from advanced heart disease, told me one of her *me* stories: "I have to keep Jim alive so I won't feel lost." I asked her to let her awareness sink down into her body and pose the question "Who am I really?" and then listen inside and feel her story. When she had done so, I asked her to see if the story about keeping Jim alive really expressed her essence: was it truly who she was? After a while she admitted that, when she probed into this story, she could see it was not true. I asked her to let herself feel what this story created in her. After reflecting for a moment, she said, "It keeps me from living my own life. I feel like I'll never really stand on my own two feet." I pointed out that both these statements were themselves other stories — about Jim's illness (*you* story) and about herself (*me* story) — and neither named her immediate feeling, the actual sensation created in her by the idea "I have to keep Jim alive." I suggested that she let her mind come down out of her head, where she was a spectator looking at herself, and instead sink into her body. Immediately, she said, "I feel tired and weak. I'm sad and angry. I feel hopeless."[1]

There will always be suffering in our lives. The word *suffering* literally means "to bear up, or to carry." With conscious suffering, we are in the Now looking straight into our feelings without letting the mind flee into stories. With that gaze, we carry the real weight of our situations; we are not victims. How we understand our situations, as well as how we feel in ourselves, is transformed by the presence we bring. But this cannot happen until we doubt the truth of our stories, until we recognize that, because we are aware of the story, we must be more than it.

Sarah had to bear seeing Jim weaken; she had to carry the sense of impending loss. But the stories she was telling herself, and the way each one engendered a new one, generated so much additional and unnecessary misery. When she could clearly feel the dependency, worry, fatigue, hopelessness, and even despair that her stories were creating beyond the real hardship of the situation, she looked at me and spontaneously declared, "It's crazy. It's crazy to do this to myself. I've been so self-involved. I haven't been able to really be with Jim and enjoy our time together. No wonder he keeps telling me that the way I am with him makes him feel worse." She began to cry, but it was not self-pity. And then she began to laugh. She kept shaking her head like it was all a revelation. She was waking up.

This kind of shift — returning to the beginning of the self — as the result of skillful self-inquiry must be experienced and practiced continually until we begin to live from a new center. In this new center, our true story begins Now, and we no longer read from old scripts and obey old conditioning.

Accepting the Vulnerability of Unknowing

The quality of doubt implicit in the inquiry "Who am I?" leads us to unknowing. Unknowing is not our deepest state, but it is what we temporarily experience when we recognize that we have been depending on our serial identities to affirm the illusion of our existence as special and discrete. We experience a phase of unknowing because initially our sense of self no longer rests in a specific identity and the stories that sustain that identity. To become unknowing is to be exquisitely vulnerable, at least temporarily. But once we learn not to react to the vulnerability — not to let it throw us into *me, you, past,* or *future* stories — we begin to live more and more freely as our spontaneous and authentic essence. Mature psychological health cannot exist unless we are capable of doubting any form of conceptual certitude about ourselves or anything else.

Absolute conviction, whether about ourselves, about others, or about any belief, is at the root of all human evil. We must remember that beliefs of any kind are our own creations. If we cannot doubt and question them, our thinking closes in upon itself. Closed systems inevitably defend themselves, sometimes to the point where violence against another becomes enjoyable.

The Emergence of Compassion, Self-Forgiveness, and Gratitude

Understanding how we have created our own unnecessary pain is an essential step in stopping the re-creation of that pain. When we consciously suffer, we are not victims. We are choosing to be fully present. To understand what we are feeling, to empathize with how our own untrained minds have made us victims of so much unhappiness and stress, is to have compassion for our own ignorance. As we stop fighting against whatever we are feeling, this compassion for ourselves grows. It grows incrementally, but the more we feel it, the safer it is to be ourselves.

There is something about learning who we are, about waking up in the moment and recognizing that there is a choice — whether to follow our mental constructions, which lead us away from ourselves, or to rest in the now-ness of ourselves — that spontaneously begins to awaken a sense of inner tenderness. The world takes on a wholly different glow, and we begin to naturally experience gratitude — for life in the fullest sense, and for the simplest things, even for our own suffering. Life in the present is always more meaningful than the life we create by Self-avoidance. Living more in the present, we stand nearer to the Source. And as we understand why we have suffered, we also gain empathy for the suffering that other people generate in themselves through what they think and believe.

This new emotional environment that is characterized by self-forgiveness, a gentle inner gaze, and compassion for, instead of shame for, our feelings is the radiance of our essential beings. Our sense of ourselves and our worlds grow healthier. We feel grateful and carry ourselves with quiet authority and dignity. This relationship to life becomes so immediate that we readily recognize any thought that takes us away from the fullness of our beings. I have found that, as I live deeper and deeper in this space, I often lose the sense that it is my life. I am simply being lived.

True Insight and Choosing New Behaviors

Although we have been looking at the predominantly false nature of the stories we tell ourselves, and their emotional consequences, certainly not all the things we tell ourselves are false. Each of us has the capacity for conscience and self-reflection that brings us to genuine insight. How then, in the context of the Mandala work, do we know when a story is true? The answer is in our felt sense of self, and what happens to our minds. Authentic insight gives us back to ourselves, gives us a sense of place and connection. It stops our frantic thinking — the reactive mind's stories-chasing-ever-new-stories — and makes things clearer. It allows us to be penetrated by new feelings: a sense of immediate relief and unburdening, or sometimes a painfully clear understanding. But painful or not, there is an undeniable sense of integrity, of rightness; and with it comes the recognition of at least the seeds of new, more appropriate behaviors that we want to adopt.

Being able to choose new behaviors is central to a conscious life. There is no meaningful insight without action, no consciousness that isn't ultimately some form of behavior. To be able to recognize an old pattern of contraction, feel it, and know that we are more than it, and then to choose to let our story begin anew in the Now, *is* the awakening process. If we see that we are in a familiar pattern of anger and withdrawal in the midst of a marital quarrel, instead of believing the *you* stories about what the other has done, or moving into a *future* story about divorce, we could choose to embrace our own feelings, soften around them, and touch that contractedness with respect and gentleness. As we do this, a new feeling — a deep vulnerability or receptivity — might emerge, and from this new space we may realize that our partner too is suffering, and we might risk expressing empathy. We might ask our partner what is really bothering him or her, or even be willing to let our partner tell us what we do that is so disturbing.

What makes our stories new — why I say that our true stories begin Now — is the ever-generative nature of attention: when we change the quality of our attention, we change our perception of self and other. With a more sensitive, empathic relationship of self to Self within us, something emerges that could not emerge through our old patterns of self-identification. And by learning to create a new inner relationship, by starting from a new place in ourselves, we invite a whole new potential of relationship to everyone and everything else.

We are conditioned to believe that tamed emotions are real, and that to be authentic is to be true to them. But tamed emotions are always derivative. The only thing that is real is the quality of attention that we bring to ourselves in the Now, which determines our experience of ourselves and everything else. Our loyalty, therefore, should be not to our emotions but to the relationship we create to them, moment by moment. This relationship is the most fundamental act of creation that we can ever undertake in our lives.

To begin our stories anew does not necessarily make us feel good; it is not an escape or a clever reframing of our experience to avoid feeling. On the contrary, it is a movement closer to authenticity, and it can cause us to experience profound suffering, such as the excruciating remorse that may come when we suddenly awaken to just how poorly we have been treating ourselves or someone else. Yet such a revelation also brings with it a tremendous sense of clarity and empowerment, provided we let the feeling live in us without creating further stories.

To be penetrated by a difficult insight hurts, but it also restores us to a deeper connection to ourselves and gives us the clarity to recognize which direction is a better one to take. Indeed, only when the truth penetrates the defenses of our *me* world, and we begin to choose new behaviors, do we begin to really heal. When our defenses have been penetrated, our egos feel the wound. But if we allow this wound instead of rallying to a new defensive posture, the very act of being penetrated in this way starts, and is, the healing process.

We don't have to keep recreating our third holding environment. If we make our stories conscious and allow the energy of doubt to return us to the beginning of ourselves, then we are automatically restored to the fourth holding environment: the Now moment. Even if what we then have to face is a difficult feeling, being able to hold that feeling without being thrown once again into story — *me, you, past, future* — restores our faith in ourselves. This is the basis of true and abiding Self-realization.

Undressing

I call the process of making *me* stories conscious — that is, less likely to interfere with and limit any relationship — "undressing." The metaphor comes from the image of two lovers removing their clothes to become available for greater intimacy. The intention of undressing ourselves psychologically is much the same. We can undress the *me* stories about needing to be understood, wanting approval, and requiring security.

I try to live this unhindered availability in every relationship, but especially when I am about to formally assume the mantle of teacher, such as right before I give a public talk or counsel anyone. My intention is to move toward the unknown potential of such moments in a way that allows the greatest possibility to emerge. I let myself become quiet and sink down into my being in order to try to recognize the holding environment I might be subconsciously creating. If I have a *me* story about needing to be eloquent, having to be helpful, or wanting to be admired and loved, I know that these stories are inevitably creating anxiety and distrust, and that this will cause me to try too hard. In this environment I will not be as transparent and authentic as possible. I do not tell myself that these stories aren't true; I simply let them rise to my awareness, with the faith that just by making them conscious I am already operating from a larger potential.

When we can undress our own *me* stories, we pierce through the veil of the *me* world. We become our own teachers; we learn how to learn who we really are. This capacity for self-awareness distinguishes us as *awakened into* rather than *captured by* the world.

Doubt and Religious Beliefs

The doubt implicit in the deep inquiry "Who am I?" is not generally welcome in religious circles that rely extensively on dogmatic beliefs. Dogma is an assertion that is implicitly accepted to be true or necessary but that cannot be proved. The assertion "Jesus is the only Son of God" is a basic Christian dogma. Unquestioning belief in church dogma and especially in dogmatic assertions about "God" is considered a virtue and essential to religious faith. To transcend such belief as a result of deep contemplation has, in the past, been called heresy. The German Christian mystic Meister Eckhart wrote, "When I am, there are gods. But when I am not, there is only God, and I am God." For this assertion he was declared a heretic, and he died in prison before his planned execution.

If we look at Eckhart's statement from the perspective of the Mandala of Being, it is likely that what he was saying was not so much a new dogma but an attempt to express his direct experience. When he was in the Me position — with the various stories about himself that constituted his *me* world — then simultaneously God (for him) was an object-of-consciousness in the You position. As long as his awareness emanated from his *me* world, he could tell himself many stories about "God." I assume it was in this sense that he realized there are many gods. But as deep self-inquiry and contemplation led him to the Now position and his consciousness unified, then "he" was "not" — his *me* world had utterly dissolved into the fullness of being

— and this state for him was "only God." When there is only God and no *me*, then self and God become identical. This is the same assertion that Jesus made: "I and the Father are One." But in Catholic dogma, for anyone but Jesus to assert this is heresy, and the price in Eckhart's time was death.

In differentiating between dogma and direct realization, I am pointing out that, for most of us, all we actually know is un-challenged dogma or our own stories about God. Even if we have a realization such as Eckhart's that makes God more alive for us, as soon as we try to speak about it we are automatically in a mental construction, and therefore God once again be-comes an object-of-consciousness, a category of "other."

I heard a rabbi in a radio interview make the claim that "God is only good, but nature can be cruel and do bad things." This was his way, or so it seemed, to not hold God responsible for his son's death from congenital illness at age fourteen. For him, God could not have done this "cruel" thing, therefore something else had to be responsible: nature. But to hold the dogma that God exists as something transcendent of and not, as well, immanent in nature certainly limits God's omnipo-tence. I guess in his grief the rabbi needed to divide reality into "God" and "Not-God" (nature) in order to make his "God" loving. Of course, if we can each choose our own dogma about God, then we are right back with Eckhart and the notion of "gods." Whether they have been consciously chosen or uncon-sciously assumed, we all have many stories about God.

If this is so, then it becomes meaningful to ask: what are the consequences, energetically and psychologically, of our be-liefs about God? To attempt to find an answer to this beyond my own experience, I conducted an experiment with a group of Europeans, mostly of Catholic and Protestant backgrounds, in which I asked them to move to the You position and begin inquiry into their various beliefs about God. Some of them looked at the belief that "God loves us" or, on the contrary, that "God doesn't care about us." What I wanted to discover in my experiment was the relative effect of these stories. If we inquire into them in terms of their emotional and energetic consequences, can we discover for ourselves whether we are actually empowered by our God stories or weakened and in some cases infantilized?

Initially, standing in the You position and feeling what their God stories created, most people felt safe. There was a God story that made them feel loved and protected, or a God story they could blame for things they couldn't let themselves feel without profound despair, such as the apparent cruelty of natural disasters and human violence. Several people linked their beliefs in God to their beliefs in life after death, and these beliefs consoled them. But as they rested in these various stories, I asked them to sink deeper into themselves and try to gauge how "old" they were emotionally and to sense their life forces.

Almost universally the answer was that they were younger, still children, often between six and ten years old. Some characterized the sensation generated by their God stories as being gentle and soothing, yet they also said that they did not feel as if they were really in touch with their own energies. But it was not supernatural energy or some other kind of exceptional energy that they felt; on the contrary, many thought that it came from their parents or what they had been told in religious school. They generally felt *comforted* by what their God stories created in them, but as they really felt into the space of their beings, few of them felt *empowered*.

In this experiment, it was not important what the beliefs were. Instead, what was really important was to compare how individuals felt while standing in the You position and listening in their bodies to what each of these beliefs created. Then I asked them to move to the Now position and experience how they felt in themselves without their God stories. It was not a question of refuting their God beliefs or having to deny them. Instead, they had only to imagine just being present in the here and now and resting in their essential beings, independent of any God stories. Many found this initially difficult to do. They felt discomforted and some became angry, while others admitted they were frightened. To move away even slightly from these beliefs made them feel endangered. The individuals willing to stay with this discomfort said these stories felt so embedded that at first they could not trust the feeling of just relaxing into the present, as if somehow, without their God stories they would be abandoned and even damned.

Although most of us throughout our lives do not keep these stories in the foreground of our minds, few of us appreciate how deeply embedded they are in our worldview and how closely they are tied to fear. To consciously move into the present and relax their identification with their God stories was hard for these individuals. They resisted at first because they discovered they couldn't hold their God beliefs *and* at the same time let their attention rest in the present. But after taking enough time to gradually let themselves rest in the Now, they described a very different quality. Most admitted that the energy they then began to feel actually seemed more sacred than the energy they had felt while holding onto their God stories. When they compared how they felt energetically and emotionally when deeply resting in the Now to how they had felt when resonating with their God stories, they noted that they somehow felt older, more mature, more independent, and more self-reliant in the Now. I observed that many of them stood in a noticeably more erect and grounded posture, and that there was a change in their voice quality, as though they were speaking from their core. In effect, what many came to realize was that they had greater faith without their God stories than with them.

Do we have greater faith in life — a deeper maturity and strength to face all that life presents — because we believe, for example, in life after death? Or do we have greater presence without that belief? What set of God stories has us bowing unwittingly to the forces of fear? And do our God stories allow us to be vulnerable in a way that opens our hearts to life and reality as it is? Is this a God that helps me or rescues me, or a God that lets me struggle with my own questions and fears and lets me answer them as I am able to?

To imagine a God that ultimately intervenes and saves us from fear is to be weakened by that God. Fear is then made even more powerful, for if we need God to help us face fear, then fear must be very powerful indeed. For myself, without having the least idea about God, I choose a God that lets me face fear on my own; and I do not know and perhaps will never know whether fear or love will prevail. I join with Walt Whitman, who wrote, "Ah, more than any priest O soul we too believe in God. / But with the mystery of God we dare not dally."[2]

I have no dispute with our freedom and right to conceptualize God and express our opinions about God as we choose. But it can only be opinion, and when identification with any idea about God sets our hearts and actions against other human beings whose conceptualizations are different from our own, at that moment doubt, not belief, is the greater virtue.

The immediacy of the present moment — our felt sense of ourselves — and how we are able to face it and relate to it, defines reality far more truly than any thought. When religion or any belief system becomes the impetus that supports us in injuring other human beings, then that belief has pulled our minds out of the present, allowing us to lose sight of ourselves in our essential humanity and blinding us to other human beings in their essence. In this way our minds darken our souls. Self-inquiry that engages our capacity to doubt any of our beliefs, and listening to the immediacy of our felt sense of being without letting our minds reactively move into thinking, are two prerequisites for true intelligence.

Doubting Fear

In a culture dominated by and addicted to fear, the one thing we seem incapable of doubting is fear itself. We are more likely to distrust happiness or well-being. We are willing to doubt the latter feelings because we believe that, sooner or later, something bad could take them away. We might even distrust kindness because we are afraid of being manipulated. But fear itself, we do not doubt. We do not see fear as simply a sensation that also goes away the moment we meet it in the Now, differentiated from the events or stories we believe substantiate it. We allow ourselves to perpetually remain the victims of fear.

Whether our fears concern global warming, trade policies, health care, or religious fanaticism, our ability to make wise choices and take intelligent action is impoverished when we start from fear. Isn't the capacity to build our society on something other than fear and survival the real issue?

Yet when it comes to fear, as with God, we don't want to doubt; we want to believe. Whatever the fear, we tend to generalize toward the gravest possible consequences on the largest possible scale, based usually on partial evidence or isolated specific incidences. The real concern is how readily we believe frightening things, even when we have only limited evidence that they are true. This is especially true with our stories about ourselves. We seem eager to believe anything that makes us fearful, as if we thrive on the familiar sense of self we get from simply being afraid.

This is why to be able to doubt every single one of our own stories that creates sensations of distress within us, and to have compassion for the suffering our beliefs have brought about for ourselves and others, represents a profound enrichment of our human intelligence. But to do these things, we have to choose a starting point for developing a relationship to our fears and for challenging the validity of our beliefs, and this starting point can exist only in the Now. To orient our attention always toward the Now — to realize that "my true story always begins Now" — lets us see that we have the capacity to hold the sensations that, left unmet, scare us into aggressive selfishness. This is the path that leads to compassion for all the suffering we see in the world. And each breath in which we are no longer the victims of the sensations within us underscores the miracle of this world and of our lives.

When we can see in this way, when we are standing in a sense of the fullness of our beings, rather than in fearful inadequacy, aren't we far more likely to make life-affirming choices? Each instant of consciousness is a relationship between our awareness and our *me*, *you*, *past*, and *future* stories, between our awareness and everything else. We can ask ourselves, "What is the quality of my attention? Where am I starting from in myself? What is being created in me right now?" When we are grateful, everything is a little more sacred.

Essence Qualities and the You Position

Once we have exercised the power of awareness and have become capable of facing our fears, particularly the untamed emotions, we know, firsthand, just how difficult this is to do. For this reason it is natural to feel compassion when we see others who, in any given moment, may be acting as the victims of their own survival psychologies.

We know from our own experience that when a person is caught in *me, you, past,* or *future* stories, they are living in an inherently distorted reality and unconsciously creating suffering for themselves. As difficult as it is to awaken from this delusional reality ourselves, it is also painful when we witness others still living in it. Whereas previously we might have become judgmental, now our natural response is empathy and compassion.

Compassion implies that we understand, with genuine empathy, the feelings of another. For any of us to be really seen by another, whether in our pain, our fear, or our giftedness, is one of life's greatest blessings. To be seen with deep compassion and not judged, even when we are ruthlessly judging ourselves, can break us open to self-forgiveness and inner acceptance. It is one of the surest ways we can help one another to grow.

Compassion doesn't have to be expressed as anything more than the fullness of our attention and as something we feel in our hearts for others. It is not intentionally an intervention to alleviate the suffering of another. Even when there is a request for help, compassion, in itself, does not come from a consciousness that has an agenda to fix, save, or help anyone. Just the presence of our attention engaging the other with a deep respect and witnessing how they feel in that moment conveys an unconditional quality of relationship. Often, people do not want to be exposed in their unhappiness or vulnerability, but everyone, whether they are aware of it or not, wants to be seen just as they are. When someone whose attention is emanating from the timeless present sees us, we know it, even if we do not realize what is happening. A gaze that begins from the infinite, and yet has the warmth of the heart so palpably present, is profoundly comforting.

The great spiritual tradition that places major emphasis on compassion is Buddhism. If we have — and I don't believe this happens just once — "crossed the ocean of despair" as the Buddha is described as having done, we know how much this journey was not only about courage and hard work but also about grace. Knowing that we have been the recipients of grace — that something has happened beyond our efforts, our understanding, or our insights — creates humility. This humility is what protects us from becoming egotistically involved in grandiosity and self-importance about whatever level of liberation we may have achieved.

Seeing that our own deepest changes often emerged through suffering gives us greater trust in the transformative potential of the suffering in another. This frees us from the egotistic obligation to be rescuers. Compassion is a reflection of our emotional and energetic resonance with the other. Separateness from the other is diluted because, in the now-ness of ourselves, we resonate in a universal consciousness.

No one who has authentically made the journey to the beginning of himself or herself creates a special identity from having done so, an identity that makes one feel superior to others. The sense of gratitude and the feeling of "there but for the grace of God go I" leaves us without a position in which to be self-righteous. Once our hearts have been cracked open, the other becomes a part of us, but since we are no longer running from our own fears, we do not have to help others run from theirs. We know that, while each life is unique, the journey of the soul presents each of us with similar challenges. But we have no authority or right to expect others to meet any challenge for their own sake or ours, or to deny them our trust that in their own souls' timing they will be called to the transformational fire. Compassion creates an environment that helps to transmit faith, but it is never in a hurry.

Empathic Attention: Leaving Our Me *World to Experience the World of Another*

When we move the locus of our attention to the Now position, we leave our *me* world. Pure awareness does not have a *me*. We gain an open and unbiased quality of attention that is present for another without our usual strategic agendas. Instead of seeing other people as extensions of our own psychologies and, therefore, in terms of how they can help or hurt us, we see them in their uniqueness.

Then, it is not a question of admiration or pity, of liking or disliking them, of analyzing or interpreting them, or of condoning them or forgiving their behavior. People become interesting, even fascinating, in their own right; they might be neurotic or complex, maybe even dangerous or destructive, but also ultimately mysterious, unfathomable. We feel a spontaneous affinity with their humanity if not with their characters and personalities. As we extend our attention from the now-ness of ourselves, we see that all beings have something we can respect. When we see others suffering because they are captured in false identities, it naturally evokes a compassionate response in us.

As with anything that we conceptualize, we learn of compassion long before most of us are capable of consciously living it. As noted earlier, young children have an innate capacity for compassion and fairness, and if they have been raised with consistently loving attention they are more likely to continue to feel and express compassion as adults. But even with such a childhood, by the time most of us go through the full ordeal of contemporary enculturation, too often the light of compassion is nearly extinguished in the prevalent atmosphere of survival fear and distrust. Then, if we are introduced to the idea of compassion at all, it is likely because we are being judged for behaving in a way that someone else deems as lacking compassion. It is a form of training in which shame is the weapon and compassion is noticeably absent.

The most respectful and effective way that we can learn compassion is by being guided by a teacher to bring our minds into the present. As we learn to do so, a compassionate teacher will oblige us to face our own suffering until we can grow more transparent to it. Compassion then spontaneously emerges in us as an essential characteristic of our being rooted in the present, having held the feelings that ordinarily drive the mind to take refuge in stories.

If, as part of our moral training, we emphasize compassionate behavior, this is just as likely to result in suppression of authenticity, spontaneity, and aliveness as it is in the creation of an authentically compassionate heart. This is always a potential pitfall of wanting to teach or embody spiritual values. If we attempt to adopt behaviors we deem admirable because they fit with our notions of being good people, the acts become only more masks of the survival project and self-involvement. The subconscious motivation is self-protection. Any effort to impart, or train ourselves in, ethical principles that do not evolve organically out of a deep insight into our own natures inevitably becomes a repressive strategy. A cultivated identity, regardless of its spiritualness, can never be truly authentic, nor can it carry the spontaneous compassion innate to our true selves.

The sure road to compassion is the journey that brings us to the beginning of ourselves, and in making this journey we will experience times of despair. How could we be spontaneously compassionate if we ourselves had not sat long nights with our untamed emotions or had not witnessed the pernicious nature of our own self-involvement and recognized how readily we were captured by our survival personalities and acted manipulatively and judgmentally? To see the strategic nature of how, in our own *me* world, our love is dependent on what others do or don't do, and is not a spontaneous outflow from our essential selves, is to realize that we may have never really loved, but have always waited to be loved, or have acted to get love or approval or to feel safe. It is a recognition that pierces our self-involvement and can make us cringe in despair. Can we ever trust that we are being authentically loving? To act in a loving way and not know whether it is love at all, this is true humility; there is no pretense of goodness.

One does not take a spiritual path to become a good person or for any other idea about what we should be like. The higher potential of our essential selves can come to light — to whatever degree it does — only through the power of awareness and by grace, because we have had the courage to make a ceaseless inquiry into the now-ness of ourselves.

Penetrating the Shell of Self-Involvement

For compassion to be truly enduring, our *me* world must be pierced by the depth of insight that lets us finally see and feel the consequences of our self-involved attitudes and behaviors. We must not shield ourselves from the painful revelation that much of what we have lived has been "all about me." In our relationships and our work environment, if we really look at how we behave and what we want, we see that much of it is about ourselves alone. This is often the case when we want others to change or even to grow. We flatter ourselves by believing that we are doing what is best for other people, but much of the time we want to "help" them be different so that we can feel better.

As we raise our own children, we are sometimes so emotionally invested in having them turn out the way we want them to, or are so embedded in our own *me* world, that we hardly ever accept and appreciate them as they are. We may so want them to live our unfulfilled dreams that we fail to listen to their needs, support their passions, and nurture their unique talents. We may so want them to make choices that reduce our fears for their future that we undermine their spirits of adventure and trust in themselves.

Even when we believe we are responding with genuine compassion, we may discover that we can still listen more deeply to another. I was told about a four-year-old Argentinean girl who began to cry when her mother left to do some errands. Even though the child was with her grandmother, aunts, and siblings, and her mother assured her that she wouldn't be gone long, the little girl cried inconsolably. Her grandmother picked her up, held her, and asked her why she was crying. The child said, "I am all alone." Her grandmother responded, "No darling, you are with me and with your aunts and your brothers; you are not alone." With this the little girl cried even more. And then a few moments later, she said to her grandmother, "Abuela, we *are* all alone."

If we are willing to look carefully, we will see our self-involvement nearly everywhere in our lives. The grandmother automatically assumed that the child's perception was wrong, as any of us might in a similar situation. Rather than acknowledging that, yes, in fact her granddaughter did feel all alone, she responded from her own *me* world, seeing reality only through her own eyes and understandably wanting to consol her. It is startling to realize that sometimes a grandmother's spontaneous consolation of a grandchild can be more about the grandmother than about the child.

People cannot learn to care more about others than they care about themselves unless such behavior is modeled for them or they have done the work to see beyond their stories and have learned to leave their *me* world. There is an anecdote about Meher Baba, a great spiritual teacher of the early twentieth century, who was asked why he always tried to give everyone who came to him what they wanted. He responded, "If I give them what they want, then maybe one day they will ask me what I want." What, I wonder, did he want? Did he want perhaps to be seen just as a man and not as an avatar? Did he hope that one day someone would come to him who could look at him with compassion and respect and see first and foremost a fellow human being, not a great soul with the power to offer blessings and to heal? Did he, from out of the depths of his recognition of what a human being can be, want for someone at last to see him with the same selfless witnessing he offered to everyone who came to him? None of this would be because he needed to be seen, but rather because any person who could see him in this way would have transcended their *me* world, just as Meher Baba had done. He would know that such a person had experienced the greatest grace — the revelation of their own truest humanity — the very thing he no doubt desired for everyone who came to him.

When I think about the spiritual giants like Gandhi, Mother Teresa, and Sai Baba, I wonder how much they suffered because, in response to the exceptional nature of their love, they were no longer perceived in their humanity? Wouldn't it be ironic if we were actually diminishing ourselves and our own spiritual models by treating them as great souls instead of as fellow human beings? And how unconscious is our self-involvement — how deeply lost are we in our *me* world — in the way we adulate certain people? In the Now of ourselves, is there really any difference between the so-called saint and any one of us? How paradoxical that some souls are so present that, in their company, many people, rather than finding themselves, lose themselves (actually, give themselves away) because they cannot bear the energy of that presence. It can be disconcerting when mind meets no-mind and there is only love.

Forgiveness and the Past Position

Imagine that you have landed, by whatever grace, in the fullness of yourself. It is one of those rare moments when, without knowing why, you feel the rightness of all things. You feel so complete that, if your life were to end in this moment, it would be fine with you. Now consider what would happen if you turned toward your past, all the many memories, and still remained in that graced state of wholeness. How would you regard the mistakes you have made and may deeply regret?

Any time we truly come home to ourselves, we no longer regard the past as responsible for the present. We appreciate that, for better or worse, what we have lived has given us the depth of experience that permits us to understand the lives we have. Of course we have made mistakes, things which, in retrospect, we wish we had done differently. But in the fullness of the present, there are no mistakes. It is simply the path we took. We regard what has been with acceptance and humility. We acknowledge that all of it made us who we are right now. In revisiting our memories, we find so many people and so many situations to be grateful for, especially if we realize that, when we lived those relationships and experiences, we were too self-involved to be grateful.

When we experience the fullness that has always awaited us, but which we could not embody while our minds were lost in *past, future, me,* and *you* stories, the most profound feelings we can have for our pasts, even the painful memories, is forgiveness. While forgiveness is a part of all the wisdom traditions, it is emphasized particularly in Christianity. Forgiveness is Jesus's central message in the New Testament parable of the prodigal son, who, despite his sins, is unconditionally welcomed home by his father, and in the injunction "Let he who has never sinned cast the first stone." There is significant controversy among scholars as to what Jesus's actual teachings might have been, but his plea for forgiveness for those who "know not what they do" suggests to me that when we fully surrender our hearts to the Living Presence, even in the midst of terrible suffering, forgiveness is always near at hand.

There is a prevalent misunderstanding that forgiveness — as a behavior — can be taught, or that at the very least it can and should be self-willed. For instance, we may be feeling resentful and envious because we believe someone intentionally outmaneuvered us to get a promotion we deserved. But we swallow our feelings, rationalize that forgiveness is the more generous attitude, and go to him and offer our congratulations. The intention is good, the gesture appears to be magnanimous, and we may feel better for a while. But if we ultimately remain bitter, little has been accomplished. When we try to coerce our feelings in any way in order to take the higher road, the result is never genuine forgiveness.

What many people call forgiveness is simply a form of repression accomplished by telling themselves a different story. So much of the "forgiveness" branch of the self-help industry is about advocating a kind of counterfeit emotionality: we are encouraged to make up a better story in order to bring about a better feeling. We are not guided to meet, in the now-ness of ourselves, whatever pain we may be actually feeling and to deconstruct the false stories that underlie all this.

There is also an element of grace in experiencing true forgiveness. Wanting to forgive may predispose us to it, but wanting is not enough. Forgiveness is not a function of ordinary thinking that arises from our *me* world, such as we are using when we tell ourselves, "He has his problems, so I forgive him." Who is this "I" that is doing this "forgiving"? As long as we are identified with an "I" that we imagine has the power to "forgive," we are just using the idea of forgiveness to create a more satisfactory identity. This kind of forgiveness is a mental sleight-of-hand, a form of self-involvement that only temporarily distracts us from feelings we are not fully recognizing or facing. It is part of the counterfeit goodness that we like to cultivate as a facade for our *me* world, and not the natural emergence of our essential wholeness.

Some of what has been written about forgiveness describes psychological rescue more than true wisdom. If we try to invite positive emotions such as forgiveness, or create more acceptable interpretations of past events so that we can "forgive" them and thereby diminish or eliminate our pain, we are just protecting our basic survival structures. It may afford us some temporary peace of mind, but it does not lead us to the now-ness of ourselves. We are still caught in our *me* world, living from the primacy of our egos. Sooner or later, because this forgiveness does not arise from our deeper essence, we will demand something in return, some contrition or some recognition to reward us for the "generosity" of our false forgiveness. The payback does not necessarily have to come from the person we purportedly forgave. We may have forgiven John last week, but we won't forgive Judy this week. Forgiveness becomes a kind of commodity rather than the natural expression of our essence.

When there is true forgiveness, the significance of the past — as a cause for one's present state — is fundamentally transformed, since the *me* who was injured or betrayed is no longer the center of one's identity. Instead, our true selves, the ineffable quality of being at the beginning of ourselves, arise fresh in the Now, breath by breath. The old pain simply does not create a sense of identity. We are not thrown into stories, and the memory has no hooks that can pull us into reactive or protective psychic maneuvering. In this sense the psychological force of a memory has been given up, or fore-given. This is not because a negative emotion has been released, or a positive one created, but because the identity that accompanied that emotion is no longer dominant.

We can say we have become transparent to the past and to the pain associated with it. If a movie screen were suddenly transparent, there would be no movie to see. Such is the case with forgiveness: the old movie about our wounds no longer appears on the screen of our being because the identity to which it corresponds is no longer present to project upon. I am not suggesting that what we have lived through be forgotten. If we were to do so, there would be no depth to our souls. To deny the past or to pretend it is over and done with is a form of self-protection, and it indicates that we are running away from feelings. When we become transparent, the past is forgiven because the self it relates to is no longer the meaningful core of whom we know ourselves to be. The true core is the ever-renewing sense of presence and fullness. We accept and encompass our histories, but we are not defined by them.

Trust and the Future Position

Mohandas Gandhi, the great spiritual and political genius who led India to freedom from British rule, was a devoted student of the Hindu sacred text the Bhagavad Gita. Determined to find nonviolent ways to liberate India, Gandhi said that, amid all the spiritual wealth of the Gita, the teaching most important for him personally was the wisdom of nonattachment to the fruit of one's actions.

To release our attachment to results means to trust that life will unfold as it will. This quality of trust is far more than Pollyannaish optimism or hopefulness. It is a dynamic relationship to the present. The future has to be taken into account, but its possibilities are never more important or more life-giving than the current of presence and fullness that flows through us every moment.

Just to be aware that we can choose to act without attachment to the outcome helps us immediately return closer to our center. It frees us from the lure of hope, which only drains our appreciation of the present and masks our feelings of vulnerability. And when we know that we are living the fullness of the moment and have no power to control the future, our non-attachment to the results lets us break the cycle of anxiety and hope. The moment we feel anxiety or hope, we can stop and see that we have just had a thought linked more to an unconscious identification with the future than to the immediacy of what we are living right now.

To live with this kind of trust is to be fully present in an action instead of anticipating the result of that action. It means that our actions are not tentative, not bargaining chips to be used on the way to somewhere else. Each action is its own truth, and therefore moment by moment, no matter what we are doing or how far we have progressed toward some long-term goal, nothing is truly left undone or incomplete.

In Taoism this way of acting is known as *wu wei*, sometimes expressed as "doing by nondoing." But, as with practicing forgiveness or compassion through intent, reminding ourselves to release our attachments to outcome and to consciously experience the fullness of whatever we are doing must eventually evolve into acting with true faith. Deep faith in ourselves as we are, not as who we might become, causes us to trust in life, moment by moment. We do what is needed and, at the same time, are so present in what we are doing that thoughts of success or failure are not what motivate us.

In the fullness of ourselves, there is nothing more that we need. This does not mean ignoring the future, saying, "What will be, will be." Every moment creates possibility and dances with uncertainty. Why not risk our dreams? We would be foolish not to take into account our future needs, and we would deny the invitation of our souls if we did not want to better ourselves. We would be the person who, in the parable of the talents, buries the coin given to him by his master because he fears losing it, and fears being unable to return it when the time comes (Matthew 25:13–30). But as the parable says, the master rewards the ones who take risks to increase what they have received — that is, to grow themselves — and scorns the ones who live without growing.

But in risking our dreams and developing our talents, we do not have to identify with our goals. To live for the future, always reaching for the next goal, hungering for the next experience, is like rushing past your life instead of striding *into* your life and tasting the sweetness of being alive. We must unequivocally decide whether fear is driving us to become what we are unable to see ourselves as already being, or whether we are responding to the adventure of life with excitement and genuine enthusiasm. And we must do so over and over again.

I write this having gradually understood over many years that this is how I am choosing to live my life. More than anything else that I might aspire to achieve or experience, to live each moment with trust, no matter what happens, gives me the deepest meaning and opportunity of my life. If I open the door to anxiety for the future, personal or collective, I immediately become aware that I have returned myself to a fearful, distrusting holding environment, and that my heart is closing. In that instant, having placed myself, with a single *future* story, into the awareness field in which fear begets fear, I know that I have left the beginning of myself and become a transmitter of fear. I do not believe this state serves me or anyone else, no matter what feeling, story, issue, or purported facts may insist on my apprehension and distrust. I choose to place my trust in trust.

We can unconsciously transmit fear even when we appear to be positive, because appearing positive can be one of our survival adaptations to fear. But this does not mean we cannot transmit faith and love even when feeling fear. On the contrary, the more differentiated we become, the more we can be present with many different feelings and aware of many streams of possibility, and fearfulness is just one of them. This is the essence of vulnerability: to hold fear but not to make choices from fear. And this too is the essence of trust: to feel pain or fear or despair and still choose the self that is more than those. Trust is not trust in a specific outcome but a relationship to freedom within ourselves. This is not about the future or the past, and it is not about *me* or *you* stories; it is about a relationship to the Now in ourselves and our expression of it.

Our most inspired ideas and noble intentions do not help us change fundamentally unless we live from a sense that we are already the outcome that we seek. It may sound like a cliché, but peace does begin in each of us, even when we do not feel peace within. If we cannot make peace in ourselves, we cannot sow peace in the world.

Years ago I had a dream that guided me then and has guided me ever since. In the dream, I am sailing out of a harbor toward storm-tossed seas aboard a three-masted schooner. From a lighthouse on my left, I hear a voice that says, "Many are lost in these waters; if you do not know how to sail in these seas, turn back now." I next find myself walking up a pier toward a small grocery store. I go inside and ask the clerk how I can get back to the mainland. He is a chubby, bald man wearing work clothes covered by a dirty apron. He says to me, "If you wait until I finish my chores, I will take you." I look at him incredulously and say, "You?" In the next scene, I am again sailing out of the harbor, but this time aboard a large modern ship far bigger than the schooner. The seas ahead are rough but not too rough for this larger ship. As we leave the harbor, a voice from deep within me says, "Steer for the light on the waters."

There are many important points in this dream, but what stands out the most is my astonishment that such an unimpressive-looking man would have the ability to guide me. At that point in my life, I was always striving to appear more knowledgeable and more powerful than I felt. Moreover, I was always holding my energy field at the maximum level I could sustain in order to be as inductive as possible with other people, even when not in my role as a teacher. But this man was ordinary, and he did ordinary work. I took this as a signal to deal with my own grandiosity and the underlying feeling of inadequacy that was its source.

The second key element of the dream was the words that came from within me, not from outside as the first instruction had. When I recall those inner words, "Steer for the light on the waters," I am not certain whether the voice said "light" or "bright." But I know from years of working at the ocean when I was a teenager that wherever the sunlight's reflection is brightest, the ocean's surface is calmest. The message told me that the surest way to enter the oceanic depths of the Self was to trust the energies that were most peaceful, rather than focusing on what was frightening or powerful. From that point on, I consciously paid more attention to whatever brought me a sense of ordinariness and stillness. I started to relax the intent to be exceptional and decided to trust that, whatever "my" presence might be, I would just be myself without this grandiose and stressful focus. And with each taste of deep calm, I became more mindful of the thoughts that disturbed this stillness and caused the seas of emotional life to become turbulent.

Synchronicity

As we learn to live with our minds present in the Now so that we trust what *is* and are less caught in our *future* stories, we begin to observe an increase in the phenomenon of synchronicity. Carl Jung popularized this term, using it to refer to phenomena that occur without any known causal explanation yet are always important and meaningful to us.

Every one of us has experienced synchronistic events: We're thinking about a friend, and at precisely that moment we meet her in the market or she telephones. We go to a bookstore, and a book we weren't looking for falls off the shelf at our feet and turns out to be exactly what we needed. During a speech, I heard the author and teacher Deepak Chopra describe meeting a new acquaintance at a dinner party who happened to know a woman Deepak had long wanted to meet. The next day this acquaintance called him with the phone number of the woman. Deepak immediately dialed the number on his cell phone, and when the woman (who lived on the East Coast) answered, she was at that moment in Los Angeles, sitting in a restaurant at the corner where he was stopped at a traffic light. Five minutes later they were sitting together.

Examples of synchronicity are legion, and they go way beyond what we might think of as coincidence. When we are living more from the beginning of ourselves, our consciousness is not confined to local time and space in the way our *me*-world levels of awareness are. Therefore everything, everywhere, and "everywhen" is already in relationship to us. Our consciousness, at this level, resonates with the consciousness of everyone else. This is the domain in which one inexplicably synchronistic event after another takes place.

This interweaving of our lives and destinies with the lives and destinies of others goes on all the time. Many of us have such experiences without realizing what they show us about the interconnected nature of reality and, specifically, the states of consciousness we inhabit at the moment these events occur. To use the example of the Mandala of Being, the incidence of synchronicity increases as we move closer to the Now position. We move into a more universal consciousness, so we automatically reside in a far more interconnected sphere of relationships.

When we trust, so much of what we might otherwise fear will not happen without our insistence and anxious supervision seems to occur spontaneously, almost miraculously. We become attractors (in the sense in which this term is used in chaos theory) vibrating in sympathetic resonance with others whose lives and destinies are in alignment with our own consciousness and intentions. Our lives become far easier and often take new directions. So much of what we want to accomplish, but that we might never have imagined in our *me* world, flows toward us in unexpected ways that no amount of thinking and worrying could ever bring about.

Even when the present is filled with challenges, and we are confronted by a difficult feeling, by meeting that feeling in its pureness we live something original. This authenticity makes us far more available to a deeper intelligence. So many times, therapists and other helping professionals have told me that when they have felt undone, because they were struggling with dark feelings of their own, their work was often clearer and more effective than ever. This is how the intelligence of staying present with untamed feelings is reflected back to us by life. We may feel further from ourselves while facing these feelings, but we are really very close to our essential beings. The untamed emotions are like guardians at the threshold between the *me* world and our true selves. We can be filled with difficult sensations, but even then if we set aside our self-involvement to be present with another, and we do not allow our own suffering to throw us into *past*, *future*, *me*, and *you* stories, we transmit faith in the wholeness of our own lives as well as in life itself. Others become beneficiaries of our inner relationships, for they find themselves called closer to their own essence.

Moment by moment, whether we are feeling wonderful or frighteningly vulnerable, we can learn to remain present and to expand our capacity for trust. Distrust and fear about the future do not make us safer. They only ensure that we will continue to feel unsafe no matter how successful we are. If we release our attachments to results, whatever comes forward will not necessarily be what we expected or wanted. But if our choices emerge from the fullness of our beings in the Now, whatever our futures turn out to be, they will continue to support that fullness.

LOVE

In discussing the emergence of higher-self functioning, I have spoken very little about being loving, which no doubt most of us consider to be among the essential elements of our higher natures. Certainly I do too, but I also feel that we tend to be glib about love. There is love in our *me* worlds: romantic love, love for our families, and love for our causes. Yet as precious as this kind of love is, this very love becomes the basis of so much attachment. And often when personal love is threatened, we respond with some degree of violence.

So while I have not emphasized the capacity to love as a key element of higher functioning, but see it more as something that graces us as we live closer to the Now of ourselves, I actually have a vision of love as the very soul of life. To again use the example of the Mandala of Being: When love regards the future, it is unattached to what happens and it is accompanied by a sense of trust. When love encompasses the past, it expresses itself as forgiveness. When it embraces others, it shines as empathy and compassion. When we stand at the beginning of ourselves and regard our own flawed characters, self-love is a deep sense of empathy and acceptance for our human weaknesses. And the deepest love seems to be a kind of humility in which our egos disappear, and what we then feel and know in the core of our beings is gratitude.

CHAPTER THIRTEEN

The Heart
of Genius

Personal growth, like Self-realization, is never really an end in itself. Just as we each rest upon the shoulders of our ancestors and what they discovered, dreamed, imagined, and built, we ourselves are the ancestors for descendants who may never know our names but will stand nonetheless upon our shoulders. I believe it is valuable for each of us to think of ourselves as ancestors and then to wonder what legacy we have left behind. What have we lived that our descendants might look upon with gratitude and build from?

For all the greatness of what we human beings have conceived and will continue to discover and manifest, the true genius of the human soul is and always has been that which leads to the greatest depth of intimacy and communion with ourselves. But the soul's journey is never for ourselves alone. To know ourselves is to simultaneously be called to a deeper caring and compassion for one another. Self-interest is greatest when we feel isolated and separate, and it diminishes as we understand more of our true selves. Then we create relationships that honor the interconnectedness and nobility of the human spirit. Awakened self-interest is always that which serves the highest good for all of us. Intimacy with ourselves, the path that leads to deep self-knowing, brings us to humility and opens us to love, compassion, forgiveness, and gratitude. With these, we build the best of human relationships and, thereby, a healthy, enlightened culture and society. Upon this foundation we can create untold possibility.

My dream is that at some point soon humanity will reach critical mass in the evolution of human consciousness, and after ages of being ruled by the god of fear we will at last claim our true place as free and conscious beings. Then our descendants will look back at us and recognize that our legacy was not just what we added to the progression of technological and scientific advancements but also our commitment to consciousness education, independent of religious belief systems. Such an education is grounded in understanding the alchemy of relationship.

Relationship is the warp and weave of all human existence. Each relationship creates its own consciousness, its own energetics. This amounts to far more than the interaction or combination of two individuals. It is a dynamic distinct from either and capable of transforming both. Relationship is a vessel for consciousness evolution. Through our relationships, we can become pioneers of spirit incarnating a new intelligence, a new emergence of human possibility. When we discover this potential and consecrate ourselves to becoming responsible for what we bring not merely to the other but also to the relationship for the relationship's sake, we enter the most fundamental level of creativity. We become transmitters of a new faith in life's infinite intelligence. We are freed, at least in moments, from the grasp of our old narcissism. Relationship is not merely for our own needs but also for the needs of spirit, the needs of a consciousness that is awaiting us when we move beyond the dominion of fear into real service to life.

Relationships have the potential to create a spiritual synergy that opens us to the kind of love that we want to bow down before and give thanks to. This is far more than sentimental love based on need. It is a love in which we are deeply grateful to the other for helping us to discover more of our true selves and thereby allowing us to receive such a love. It is a love that makes us lovers of love itself, and as Saint Bernard wrote: "He who loves, loves love, and loving love forms a circle so complete, there is no end to love." This is the real possibility and flowering of human genius. It is what Teilhard de Chardin meant when he wrote that one day we would rediscover fire in the form of love. This love is a blessing that awakens our minds and hearts to a much more integral intelligence, one in which we become obliged not merely to our own needs but also to the needs of love itself. When we start close to the roots of our own being, in the Now, together we open to an even greater beingness. This love can heal us profoundly, but it can challenge us as well, for it is part of a much greater aliveness that requires spiritual maturity and wisdom if it is to flourish within us.

A MORE ESSENTIAL MAN AND WOMAN

We have explored the effect on our relationships of the many stories we all tell ourselves. But it is also important to be aware of what we might call "meta-stories," stories that live in the collective consciousness. These overarching cultural stories direct our perceptions and attitudes every day, but because these stories are embedded, most individuals are unable to recognize them as actively operating within themselves.

Today, one of the greatest obstacles to inviting new wisdom and love into our worlds is the entitlement within our gender roles, which takes many forms, both obvious and subtle. To put it simply, in the millennia in which patriarchal consciousness has dominated, we men have evolved a sense of self that expects and even requires the advantages that we take for granted as due us solely because we are men. We have had the privilege of a fast track for our intellectual and artistic self-expression and the privilege of social power that has been, and still is, far more accessible than that permitted (or even imagined) for women. We unconsciously expect to be seen and accepted as though our ideas, values, and needs are automatically correct, essential, and appropriate. We tacitly expect this in our relationships with women and in society as a whole. This basic sense of entitlement, this psychology in which the male consciously and subconsciously presumes that he is more important and therefore must be fostered and even pampered in educational institutions, in the work environment, in the home environment, and by women in general blinds men to so much of life, to themselves, and especially to women.

Despite their advantages, and perhaps because of them, most men remain emotionally unborn. They require women to carry their emotional life, especially their fundamental sense of security, just as early in life their mothers carried this for them. Many men cannot accept much of a woman's challenge to their will or point of view without reverting to a power position, aggressiveness, or self-pity. Alternatively, many men abdicate emotional vitality, surrendering the domain of deep feeling to the women in their lives and becoming emotionally passive. One way or another, women are unconsciously expected to be the extension of this male entitlement, as a symbol of the man's power or as his muse, his comforter, his caretaker, or foe.

This unconscious entitlement makes real intimacy between men and women difficult. Yet at the same time, men dare not get too far from any woman who provides their emotional anchor, for to do so is to risk feelings of annihilation. For some men, power and wealth become a surrogate mother, providing solace and filling the void within. But it is a masculine conception of power, and its view of life is more or less devoid of genuine feminine intelligence. Until men are able to carry the feelings they unconsciously expect women to protect them from, such men will remain emotionally and spiritually crippled despite their power in the world. And as we have too often witnessed in the present and in history, this is disastrous for everyone.

It is essential at this time in the evolution of consciousness that men begin to examine themselves and learn to make space for each woman to express her authentic sense of self. Of course, it is not the task of men to make this happen for women. Women have to undergo the same kind of journey. They have to inquire deeply into themselves and engage their relationships with men from the fullness of themselves, not merely as counterparts to them. Many highly capable women are still at the mercy of childish fears of abandonment, or they tend to orbit men and to be more attuned to a man's psychology than their own. But the two halves of a whole humanity (male and female) are not obliged to each other as much as they are obliged to the whole. And none of us truly know the extent of that whole or what it can be; we just know what it has been. The increasing turmoil in relationships, and specifically the high rate of divorce, shows us that our paradigm for relationship is simply inadequate to the real potential of the ceaselessly emerging true self in both sexes.

But when women attempt to make the journey to their true selves and then express themselves in the world, they face obstacles very different from those that men face, perhaps more difficult ones. In my work (and it is true of most consciousness work), women usually outnumber men two to one. I believe this is because women feel a far greater inner imperative to create themselves anew, since what is proscribed for them within cultures so long dominated by patriarchal consciousness (and which they themselves until recently tended to recognize and accept as a woman's "self") diminishes and undermines their essence. Women are struggling to become more conscious of their own deep feminine qualities, values, and wisdom. They are developing a sense of self that goes beyond the circumscribed roles of wife, lover, mother, and homemaker sanctioned by patriarchy. Women have entered into the worlds of business, science, and politics to express their intelligence and power in ways formerly reserved for men. But with so few models, the self that most women initially seek, or are expected to have, is still a self that is unconsciously influenced by masculine psychology and values. Now women are attempting to identify the values and wisdom of the deeper feminine and how to live by these in the world.

Only in very recent history have women begun to demand that the patriarchal mentality that has imprisoned them be dismantled so they can discover for themselves an authentically female (and feminine) expression of Self. They have done this first by fighting for and gaining the right to their own property, the right to vote, and — hardest of all to gain — the right to determine what happens to their own bodies. Still, we are just beginning to recognize how unconscious we have been in our lack of respect for, indeed our contempt for, feminine values. We are beginning to appreciate how this not only has been devastating to women but has compromised men as well.

Male entitlement means an inferior maleness that stands beside a diminished femaleness. This inferior masculine and diminished feminine cocreate each other. We do not yet even know what human consciousness is with an empowered feminine and an empowered (versus entitled) masculine. If we dedicate ourselves to uncovering and actualizing this potential, then we will have begun to create a truly profound legacy for future generations. But for this to happen, both men and women must risk a great deal of discomfort in the depths of their relationships. We will have to move to our now-ness and make an enormous space for trust that the new relationship we are being called to is more intelligent than we are yet capable of perceiving and accepting. We have begun to invite the potential for male-female relationships in which the self of women is not derivative of the male self, and where men are likewise able to start from something more truly of their essence. However, as we lose the familiarity and security of traditional gender roles, great confusion and pain will inevitably continue, as will power struggles. But if we persevere, we may also find profoundly beautiful and deeply transformative love.

In our essential consciousness, we are neither male nor female. As Jesus said, "When you make the male and the female into a single one, so that the male will not be male and the female not be female...then shall you enter the Kingdom."[1] He is referring to consciousness prior to body identification, pure consciousness without subject or object. It is a consciousness perhaps few of us will realize directly. But even in the absence of full Self-realization, we can certainly begin to stand in our own now-ness, closer to our true selves. And as we do, we will gradually deconstruct our age-old beliefs about man and woman that deny to both their true potential as conscious beings. This is some of the most difficult work of all, because we don't know who we are outside the profound conditioning of patriarchy. Pioneering the unknown self as man or woman without clear models is threatening. In doing so, we explore unknown territory, reinvent male and female in the world, and together invite the unknown marriage of two parts of a single wholeness that is the human being. It is a relationship for which our romantic ideals and biblical edicts are a far too limited and constrictive foundation. Freeing ourselves from these is not possible without profound and sincere self-inquiry. But neither gender is served by male entitlement or its constraints on women, which make women invisible to men and even to themselves. To make our way to a new potential for relationship, we will have to make space for feelings such as rage, desperation, invisibility, suffocation, and abandonment in both men and women without each blaming the other and without trying to restore harmony by forcing women back into an old role.

I believe we are ready. Working with the Mandala, I have seen how, without stories, we can remain present with far more intense feelings than we might imagine we could bear. We can move beyond our stories, learn to hold the deep fears that our relationships challenge us to meet, and from our openness, invite each other to a new level of intimacy. A man who lives more from his true self offers inspiration and energy that a woman can use to realize her true self. And just as essential, a woman who risks claiming herself from the depths of her inner search enables all men to see their entitlement and helps them to fall back upon something more essential in themselves. As we choose our now-ness over our stories, we will, together, invite that deeper love to find a place within us. In so doing, we are creating a firm foundation not only for ourselves personally but also for the collective consciousness that we can hardly begin to imagine now.

THE TWO ARCS OF CONSCIOUS EVOLUTION

The full circle of conscious living has two arcs. As we move into the present and stop resisting what *is*, we become expanded, clear, and secure in our own being. When we meet one another from this place of innate strength and joy, we can potentially ignite the evolutionary fires for our society. I refer to this as the ascending arc. *Ascending*, in this sense, means drawing closer to the Source, experiencing unity, connectedness, love, and clarity. In the language of the Mandala of Being, to ascend means to stand in the Now position and learn to speak and act in closer alignment with our true selves. When we ascend, the sense of expansion affirms the deep yearning for something more that is inherent in all of us. We feel free and much less reactive. We can more readily accept our circumstances because a presence is arising from within us that brings a sense of completeness and security not dependent on anything outside us.

But the circle is not complete until we thoroughly understand how we lose our energy, weaken our wisdom potential, and become self-involved and defensive, even when we have touched more expansive states. We need to make this *descending* process conscious. Our energy body is like a sieve that leaks presence away faster and faster, the further our minds move from the Now. When we remain lost in *past*, *future*, *me*, and *you* stories, we cannot adequately replenish ourselves. We default to our much more practiced and collectively reinforced survival psychology, where subconsciously fear becomes our god and security and happiness our goals.

The Mandala of Being models how to integrate spiritual practice and psychological self-inquiry into a concrete and fundamental transformation of our daily lives. The dance of conscious living is a ceaseless movement between the true self, which is ineffable consciousness, and the false selves of our *me* world. We are always breathing between what we can call the dark and the light of ourselves. This is not a "dark" that is evil and a "light" that is Divine but a continuum of the soul's potential expression in life. Which of these two poles dominates depends on how consistently we live in the present.

WHAT ABOUT AGGRESSION?

When we live with our minds far from the present, embedded in a sense of separation, and thoroughly identified with our various stories, then aggression, whether with words or guns, becomes a way of extending and protecting our self-interest. However, as we move our attention closer to the present moment, our psychology begins to reflect wholeness rather than fearful self-interest and we become much less defensive. Then we stop viewing the world through the prism of survival and security and instead gain both a sense of inner fullness that unites us with life, and a sense of inherent compassion for ourselves and others.

Aggression is not innate; it is derivative. It is a response to the fear that grows in us as our minds are pulled away from their source in ineffable consciousness. We cannot build healthy marriages or any relationships that create a generative energy when we start from fearfulness in any form. When we are not in our bodies, not in the now-ness of ourselves, we inevitably start (in ourselves) from unmet feelings or unchallenged beliefs. The relationships we then create tend to be combative attempts to maintain a sense of separate identity built on identification with our ideas and fear of our feelings, not relationships built from our essence and capable of enlightening our hearts and minds.

Aggression will inevitably appear in individuals and cultures that are based on survival, insufficiency, and fear, because aggression is so easy. It is the path that takes the least attention, the least energy, and the least intelligence and soulfulness. Staying in the present with our wounds until we find our way back to an open heart — so that there can be forgiveness, reconciliation and healing — takes so much more energy and requires so much more honesty and courage. It is too facile, too cynical, too lazy to declare that aggression is a primary drive. What is more helpful is to see that not being able to rest in the true self means living without a foundation. Then it is no wonder that terrorists can turn us into terrorists. We give them the power to create fear and hatred in us by the very stories we tell ourselves in reaction to their threats or attacks, and this makes us victims of our own minds, not of their actions.

OUR GENIUS ARISES FROM EMPTINESS

Who we are in our essence is ineffable consciousness, not reducible to any thing. The more our attention rests in the present moment, the more we realize this unlimited consciousness. Belief in an objective *me* that must be saved or fixed or improved before we can consider ourselves whole amounts to a subtle psychic cruelty. In this circumstance, we don't begin our relationship to ourselves from *whom* we are in the Now, but instead judge *how* we are by comparing ourselves to someone else or to some hypothetical preferred state that we want to achieve. And once we are cruel to ourselves, we believe in a cruel world in which we also can conclude, as Sigmund Freud did, that aggression is innate to human nature.[2] Only if we presume that we human beings are concrete "somethings," rather than aware beings exercising relationship to all experience, moment by moment, is it understandable that Freud and others would have such a cynical point of view.[3] Intellect can carry us a great distance, but it cannot carry us into the Now, where by its very nature the mind is silent and we know ourselves as at-one with existence in a universe whose binding spirit is love.

EMERGING FROM THE DARK PASSAGEWAY

Following the power of awareness into the present, beyond the *me* world's self-involvement and survival, involves repeatedly passing through a profound process of unlearning and unknowing. We unlearn the habit of relying on our stories to build the reality of ourselves or others in our minds. It is an unknowing relative to our familiar sense of identity within our *me* world, without knowing what lies beyond. We struggle in the dark, and at times we feel utterly lost and in despair. Initially, no one knows how to trust this process of emerging into a new and unknown self. In the intensity of our disorientation, we cannot understand that what we are experiencing is part of the soul's quest for greater embodiment. It is an inevitable evolutionary process, but it can become a trap of despair if we continue to let our minds throw us into *me*, *you*, *past*, and *future* stories. Further distancing ourselves from the Now in our efforts to understand what is happening and to find some way out will never lead to resolution of this kind of suffering. Understanding comes after we have rested deeply in ourselves, not before. Sooner or later we just have to trust, and the starting point of that trust is to surrender ourselves with consistent and very gentle attention into the now-ness of the dark times: "My true story starts now."

But learning to hold the untamed feelings in the Now is

only half the journey of awakening to a new self. To emerge from the dark passageway also requires risking ourselves in new ways in our relationships. New wine needs new wineskins. The new "wine" is a new depth of consciousness, and the "wineskins" are the relationships in which that consciousness manifests in the world. We have to create opportunities to see the new consciousness emerging in us and bring it forth in our lives, and this takes courage. Most of us, when we feel raw and unraveled, do not feel entitled to express ourselves. We don't trust that we could contribute anything meaningful when we feel so undone. We orbit our own stories about our suffering over and over again. We make ourselves victims trapped in a cycle of (old) self-involvement that can short-circuit the emergence of the new consciousness.

We all need wise guidance at these times. A teacher or counselor who has lived deep in the dark passageway can be immensely helpful. When we need to talk of how unraveled we feel, then it is wise to speak to someone who can show us the transformational potential of what we are experiencing and act as an awakener whose energy can help to stabilize and deepen the process.

So how do we begin to express the new consciousness? There is no one path, but the essence of any path will begin with the quality of our listening. We cannot understand our own changes until we bring ourselves into the vessel of relationship. And as we listen to our friends, family, clients, and associates, we discover that we have a wholly new capacity for listening, a deeper connection to our intuition, a natural empathy. As we grow in consciousness, it is not a matter of needing to be heard or understood by others. That is the old relationship dynamic, the old wineskin. More important is our willingness to be truly present, to offer our full attention even in our vulnerability. Then we may begin to get feedback about our presence, about how it helps others listen more deeply in themselves.

Once we have committed ourselves to really listening, the next discovery is the most marvelous of all. Out of that listening, we begin to find a new voice. We understand things we have never even thought of before. We say things that are emerging from our emptiness, not from anything we have been taught. And in the aliveness of discovering this new voice, we begin to understand that all our own struggling was part of the dissolving of the "sugar cube" of our old identity so that we could become part of a greater consciousness. When we listen deeply, the space that is invited supports our awakening intelligence. When we feel this intelligence spontaneously emerging from us as we speak to another, it can be a most marvelous experience of aliveness. Then the terror of the "dark night" begins to recede. We will still have times of feeling undone and scared, but once we experience what this is opening us to, we begin to trust. The dark passageways are never easy, but they are, when faced and accepted, essential to our awakening.

EXTERNALIZING OUR FEARS TO AVOID THE DARK PASSAGEWAY

One way we tend to short-circuit the transformative potential of our own despair and avoid the dark passageway is by projecting our pain outward onto others, or the world in general, rather than fully engaging it within ourselves. And to be sure, painful relationships, human cruelty and violence, dehumanizing institutions, environmental degradation, terrorism, and every manner of injustice and repression certainly provide us with ample reasons to point the finger of blame "out there."

But we believe we know what the world — or our relationships — should be like, because we know what we do not want to feel. We want to create an environment in which we will not be forced to feel whatever we believe we should not have to feel, or fear we would be unable to bear. It is an egocentric and grandiose paradigm, because we are in effect requiring other people, and even the whole world, to change in order to make us feel comfortable and safe. At the same time, we make ourselves victims, with our happiness dependent on what others do or don't do. We stay fearful about the future and angry in our rejection of all that is wrong.

Of course, we also believe that we know what we *do* want: freedom, justice, happiness, and so on. Surely these are valid desires in their own right; it is true that not everything has to be explained by our motivation to escape threatening feelings. But the crucial question is "Can we achieve freedom, justice, and happiness when we have not yet truly faced our own deepest fears?" When we defend our *me* world by externalizing our own unmet feelings, blaming others, and judging the world, we become determined by our own stories. We abandon our own beginning and therefore can never really be self-determined. As much as we may want the outer world to change and become the carrier of our wholeness and security, if there is no real wholeness or security within us, this can never happen.

I believe that what we want and what we don't want create each other. We become trapped in a cycle of dissatisfaction that causes us to forever seek satisfaction. But enduring satisfaction never arrives at this level. The whole process of creating opposites that continues to polarize our hearts is unavoidable at the level of thinking, but it is less a compelling "fact" of reality as our consciousness becomes more adapted to being fully present and less in conflict with what *is*. Dualistic thinking, and the polarization it can lead to within us and between us and others, is created by and intensifies with the distance of our minds from the Now of ourselves. As our minds return to our now-ness, an atmosphere strong in tolerance, trust, and compassion emerges spontaneously. This healthier and happier state is not the antithesis of a negative or lesser reality. It is not a question of opposites where if there is "good," there must also be "bad," but it is simply that the distance between our minds and our true selves has diminished.

TRUE SECURITY

The gulf between fear and love is not a gradient, not a matter of degree. It is a discontinuity, a complete shift of the organizing center of our lives. When fear is our god, we value security and happiness more than truth and real freedom. When love is our god, we know that everything is love; and when there is fear, we look to see what relationship we are creating within ourselves that brings fear so convincingly into our hearts. In the Mandala teaching, we have seen that fear tends to rule us as we move further into the four positions. Love becomes our deeper understanding as we return to the center.

After the 9/11 attacks, President George W. Bush, with the support of most of Congress and many world leaders, declared a "war on terror." Instead of making me feel safer, this declaration saddened me. I knew we were once again following the fear god, once again taking the age-old path of reaction, in which all we really do is make ourselves the victims of the stories we create about our enemy. We were attacked and it was terrible. Shock and grief in such a situation is natural, as is taking action to defend ourselves. But going to war in anger and self-righteousness is imagining that we can have physical security without having spiritual security. It is the way power has always maintained power, but it is not about true security.

I read that the Dalai Lama was asked why he continued to express forgiveness and compassion for the Chinese, who had invaded his country and oppressed and murdered his countrymen. His answer was both simple and profound: "It makes me feel better." This response is the essence of what I mean by spiritual security: We do not let the actions of others determine our internal states. Spiritual security begins with understanding that "my true story starts Now" and taking full responsibility for what we create in our hearts through our own stories. I doubt that we can ever really achieve complete protection from the violence and hatred of others. If this is so, what do we create in our hearts by continuing to imagine that we can, and by hating our assailants — real or imagined — in return?

Why should any conscious person be made a victim of terrorism? We need not let hatred and fear contaminate our hearts. What if, instead of moving into grandiose patriotism and knee-jerk warfare, we could let ourselves feel how much in ourselves we give away through fear, how deeply we poison our own hearts with our own stories? What if we had examined our own rhetoric and heard within it our grandiose national *me* stories and all the angry, distorted *you* stories about Islam, Arabs, and the so-called Axis of Evil? What if we could have realized that our own reactions were infecting our hearts with fear, anger, and hate, and that in externalizing these feelings we were creating more of the same in the world? Terrorists do not do this to us; we do it to ourselves. I believe recognizing that our own minds are our worst terrorists would have helped to heal us and bring us closer to true security, if we could have let ourselves really feel that insight.

In the years since I began to write this book, a crescendo of fearfulness and polarized opinions and judgments has been reported and promulgated in the popular media. Blame is ceaselessly thrown back and forth. We are inundated night and day with stories that in their repetitive, hyperbolic reporting are designed to heighten our reactions of fear, outrage, and judgment. Whether the focus is on terrorism, rogue states, earthquakes, hurricanes, floods, global warming, the next pandemic, other health concerns, pollution, government and corporate corruption, economic catastrophe, human rights abuses, pornography, or immorality, everywhere we look it seems that we thrive on telling ourselves the stories that keep us anxious, afraid, outraged, and discouraged.

Are we morbidly fascinated with fear, aggression, loss, and suffering? Are we addicted to angst and adrenaline? Or are we perhaps unconsciously inundating ourselves with fear because we are actually reaching the threshold of the collective understanding that fear is the god we can never defeat at its own level, and beginning to wake from our fearful dreaming? To begin a relationship with life in which fear is not our god, we must start from the place in ourselves that may well *feel* fear, but is not itself afraid. If we want to reach greater wholeness, we must start from the place in ourselves in which we are, and have always been, whole.

We have a choice about what we let determine our states of being, always. As we live closer to our beginning, we gradually drink more deeply from the fullness of our souls, and the world and everyone in it changes before our eyes. Then we notice that we have less fear, less anxiety, and less urgency: life is good right now. There may always remain the unsettling taste of the unknown, and our lives will inevitably invite us to greater humility, but this begins to fill us with wonder instead of fear. A sense of how loving our universe is begins to grow until, eventually, we trust that we are flowing in harmony with life and are always supported, buoyed by a great and gracious current.

Acknowledgments

I am deeply grateful for the blessing of my wife, Ariel, for her inspiration, for her insightful feedback, and for her crucial support at all the right moments. So much of this book is a testimonial to what we have lived and learned together.

For her editorial help and collaboration in the writing of this book, I owe an immense debt of gratitude to Susan Jane Griffin. Her assistance has profoundly benefited this book, for which I am truly thankful.

A work of this nature grows from countless influences. I am thankful, first, for the grace that has filled my life, beginning in childhood with what I received from my parents, Simon and Alice, and later through the call of Spirit, which knocked on the door of my soul and awakened it from slumber. And then for the inestimable richness that my three stepchildren, Tassos, Maria, and Andreas, have brought to my life these past twenty years.

I am grateful for history's great thinkers, mystics, and poets, as well as for contemporary teachers whose lives or writings have helped me in my quest to comprehend the mysteries of awakening consciousness. I particularly honor Franklin Merrell-Wolff and Brugh Joy, my first consciousness teachers. And I honor Darshan Singh, who modeled gentleness, humility, love, and generosity.

I am especially grateful to Deborah Bacon, a dear friend who has been my gifted French translator for twenty years, who learned the Mandala work as I taught it and helped me refine it along the way. And to Francis Lery and Bernadette Blin for supporting my work in France and sponsoring trainings with psychotherapists in which the Mandala model further evolved. Svend Trier I thank as well, for his long friendship and for sponsoring my work in Denmark for so many years.

My deep gratitude goes to my friends Roberto Solari and Agueda Marshall for organizing my work in Argentina, for providing a wonderful space in which to write, and for many hours of discussion, which enriched this book.

I acknowledge my deep appreciation for friends Richard and Marigold Farmer and for Richard's invaluable help with leading the summer seminars in France for so many years. I am thankful to Pierre-Henri Cuendet, who, with enormous efficiency and grace, runs my office and organizes my seminars in Europe, and to Sylvaine Cuendet, also a longtime friend and supporter of my work. Their home became my Swiss resting place and writing base.

I am deeply thankful to the Three Mountain Foundation for providing funds for a writing sabbatical that helped get this book into its initial draft, and specifically to board members Walter Dilts, Dent Goodyear, Susan Jane Griffin, and Scott Sherman, for their many years of support.

I give my heartfelt thanks to Robbie Armstrong-Dunham, my assistant and office manager, for years of dedicated and efficient and caring assistance. She has helped me and this work in innumerable ways and held the fort when I frequently disappeared to write. I am grateful to Gordon Dunham for technical support and for giving me the impetus and format for developing the original *Mandala of Being* workbook that became the basic outline of this book.

I acknowledge Graham Cock, Jim Dunne, Lorraine Edwards, Eric Gordon, Rebecca Hathaway, Janne Helle, Christiane Henningsen, Valerie Love, Barbara Russell, and Hildegard Sieve for reading an earlier draft and offering valuable feedback.

Finally, I extend my deep gratitude to the many individuals who have attended my seminars. It is your lives, struggles, and questions, not unlike my own, that I have sought to address in this book. In your presence this work evolved, and you were never far from my heart as I wrote.

The Autonomous Nature
of Awareness Fields

The notion of an autonomous field of awareness that operates upon us subconsciously, influencing our behaviors and values, is far more than what is meant by "corporate culture" or an organization's vision or mission statement. It is an actual self-organizing field of consciousness specific to that arena of activity.

The author and physicist Rupert Sheldrake has postulated the existence of what he calls "morphogenic fields." *Morphogenic* means, literally, "form-creating."[1] An example of the genesis of a morphogenic field is the so-called hundredth-monkey story first popularized by author Lyall Watson.[2] The story is based on the work of Japanese researchers who studied a tribe of monkeys on Koshimo Island. The researchers supplemented the diet of these monkeys by dumping sweet potatoes on the beach. As the monkeys squabbled and grabbed for the potatoes, the tubers got mixed into the sand and, invariably, most monkeys ended up getting a mouthful of sand along with their portion of potato. One day an eighteen-month-old female learned to wash the potatoes in a nearby stream. She taught this behavior to her mother; very quickly other females imitated her and, in turn, taught it to their young. Gradually the behavior spread throughout the group, except to the older males, who continued to eat sandy potatoes. Eventually, when all the older males who had not learned the behavior had died, all the members of the group employed this means of washing.

At about this time, a mysterious phenomenon, poetically called "The Hundredth Monkey," took place. It seems that some kind of threshold was reached, because the new behavior spontaneously began to appear in other groups of monkeys living on islands too far away to have had direct communication. Sheldrake's hypothesis is that, once a behavior is sufficiently propagated, some kind of morphic resonance occurs, and this awareness field then engenders similar behavior in the other groups. For Sheldrake, the existence of morphogenic fields explains such phenomena as The Hundredth Monkey as well as the simultaneous appearance throughout history of nearly identical technologies in highly disparate human societies.

There is evidence to support the notion that these fields of awareness, once created, exist autonomously. Certain individuals known as idiot savants have the ability to determine, for example, what day of the week it will be on October 22 in the year 4031. They do this without any obvious means of calculation, simply because someone has posed the question to them. This suggests that some field of mathematical possibility exists that these rare individuals seem to be able to tap into, in ways that most of us cannot, though they themselves do not know how they do it. In another example, a young boy was able to recognize the year, make, and model of every car that drove past his apartment window, even though he could not read and had never seen any auto magazines.[3]

Further Thoughts *on the* First Holding Environment

Babies begin learning very early in life. For example, they more readily learn to speak the language heard in the womb than a different language they might be exposed to in the case of adoption. Also, if its mother is a deaf-mute, a baby has a more difficult time learning to speak. In a different example of influences in the womb, twins tend to be more coordinated at birth and initially continue to develop coordination more rapidly after birth than single babies. They also have a more highly developed sense of interpersonal relatedness, probably because they have been exchanging contact throughout gestation.

Of great concern to all of us is the fact that, although nature has excellently designed the first holding environment to protect the developing fetus, the womb is vulnerable to many known and unknown factors reaching in from the extended environment in which the mothers live. Good maternal nutrition, especially adequate folic acid, reduces the risk of several common birth defects, while exposure to ionizing radiation and the consumption of popular drugs such as alcohol, cigarettes, and marijuana increases that risk. Many prescription medications, if used during pregnancy, can result in birth defects or predispose the child to cancer later in life.

But even if mothers-to-be stop using known teratogenic substances, eat only wholesome foods, and are blessed with a loving, secure situation during pregnancy, they cannot escape the effects of thousands of synthetic chemicals that permeate our air, food, and water. Modern health care, though it has made enormous progress in decreasing maternal and infant mortality and disease, has no remedy for what our bodies were never designed to adapt to: mercury, lead, pesticides, herbicides, PCBs, and innumerable other toxic by-products of our modern lifestyle. Living near a garbage dump is a known risk factor for increased birth defects, but the sad truth for modern humankind is that just about everywhere is a garbage dump.

Mercury, for instance, which has highly negative effects on brain development, is pouring from the skies, contaminating crops and fish due to our decision to burn coal for energy in the most economical, but also the most polluting, way. Thus while improved nutrition has decreased the more common causes of birth defects, the incidence of new and formerly very rare birth defects, such as gastroschisis, where the intestines are born outside the body, has increased 250 percent, according to the North Carolina birth defect registry, and nobody knows why.[4] Even the most secure, loving, and conscientious mothers cannot protect their children from the by-products of our unexamined rush for security, abundance, and wealth. The womb, like every human being, is a holistic system, and each of us is embedded within and inseparable from other larger systems.

Further Thoughts *on the* Second Holding Environment

A baby is not ready to be independent from its mother at birth. For many months after birth, a baby requires close proximity with the electromagnetic pulse of its mother's heartbeat (or the heartbeat of another adult), as well as hearing the sound of her breathing, to stabilize its own heart rhythm. This is why hospital wards for premature infants have devices such as "breathing bears" to create the rhythmic sound of breathing. This also may be why, in cultures where babies are nearly continuously carried and co-sleeping is the norm, there is a much lower incidence of sudden infant death syndrome (SIDS).[5]

An infant's immune system continues to require specific proteins made in the mother's body that are received through breast milk. These model proteins stimulate the infant's immature immune system to begin to manufacture its own immune proteins. But breast-feeding is not only a means of transmitting food and essential nutrients; it is also an emotional transmission. As with healthy seeing, a baby's ongoing immunological maturity requires that the baby be held, stroked, and caressed frequently. The actual correlation between touch and immunity was first noted by Ashley Montague. He reported that in Russia after World War II, babies who were raised in large understaffed wards were found to be suppressed immunologically. Yet here again, biological immunity — the capacity to recognize "self" versus "not-self" at the molecular level — is more than just a genetic and nutritional process. The differentiation of "self" and "not-self," whether psychologically or immunologically, progresses best when a baby is held and lovingly caressed, and it is weakened by the baby's isolation. Where there is positive emotional connectedness, differentiation occurs without the "other" being perceived as foreign in the sense of representing a threat.

Throughout our lives, our immune systems always function best when we feel emotionally secure. This is one of the great paradoxes of our human species: We are healthiest — in terms of the immune system's ability to perceive the "otherness" of a foreign microbe, virus, or chemical and develop an appropriate and effective response to it — when we feel the most connected to ourselves, one another, and the world. Similarly, the more connected we feel, the less likely we are to overreact and create excess inflammation — the problem in autoimmune disease — whereas the more separate we feel, the poorer our ability to differentiate self from other at the immune level, and the more likely we are to generate unnecessary inflammation and sickness.

Notes

CHAPTER 1.
OUR EARLIEST RELATIONSHIP TO OURSELVES

1. Thomas Lewis, Fari Amini, and Richard Lannon, *A General Theory of Love* (New York: Vintage Press, 2001).

2. Not all women stay at home as full-time mothers now, and not all men leave home for their work. As more and more women hold down full-time jobs and can spend only short periods of time in the crucial early nurturing role, surrogates for mothers, such as day-care attendants, are assuming more responsibility for the early process of cultivating children's sense of self. No doubt some of these surrogates are inferior, and some superior, to the mothers themselves. In a small minority of families, men become stay-at-home dads and assume the role of nurturer. More rarely — given the dispersal of families — it falls to grand-parents. Thus the early mirroring process that helps cultivate

children's sense of self is less and less a function of mothers. It is a real question whether this circumstance adequately, or even close to adequately, serves our children's potential.

3. In ancient Greece, there lived a bandit known as Procrustes, or "the Stretcher." He had an iron bed on which travelers who fell into his hands were compelled to spend the night. Those who were too short to fill the bed, he stretched until they died. Those who were too tall, he cut short enough to fit in the bed. No one could resist him, and the surrounding countryside became barren. He was eventually slain by the great hero Theseus, an act considered to be Theseus's greatest challenge.

4. Joseph Chilton Pearce, *Evolution's End* (San Francisco: Harper-SanFrancisco, 1992), 195.

CHAPTER 2.
WHO ARE WE REALLY?

1. Stephen Mitchell, *Tao Te Ching* (New York: Harper and Row, 1988), chapter 1.

2. A. Guillaumont et al., trans., *The Gospel According to Thomas* (New York: Harper and Row, 1959), logia 2.

CHAPTER 3.
THE POWER OF AWARENESS

1. For an excellent discussion of self-idealization, see Karen Horney, *Neurosis and Human Growth* (New York: Norton, 1950).

2. Walt Whitman, "Song of Myself," *Leaves of Grass* (1855; New York: Signet Classics, 2000), 27.

3. A. Guillaumont et al., trans., *The Gospel According to Thomas* (New York: Harper and Row, 1959), logia 67.

CHAPTER 5.
TAMED AND UNTAMED EMOTIONS

1. For an excellent discussion of many historical and more contemporary exemplars of this emerging higher consciousness, I recommend the classic *Cosmic Consciousness*, by Richard Maurice Bucke (rev. ed.; New York: Penguin Books, 1991).

CHAPTER 6.
THE FOUR HOLDING ENVIRONMENTS

1. D. W. Winnicott, *The Maturation Process and the Facilitating Environment* (New York: International University Press, 1980).
2. Joseph Chilton Pearce, *The Biology of Transcendence* (Rochester, VT: Park Street Press, 2002).
3. J. N. Wood and J. Grafman, "Human Prefrontal Cortex Processing and Representational Perspectives," *Nature Reviews Neuroscience* 4, no. 2 (2003): 139–47.
4. Pearce, *The Biology of Transcendence*.
5. Ibid.
6. I have written about this experience in greater detail in two previous books, *The I That Is We* (Berkeley: Celestial Arts, 1981) and *The Black Butterfly* (Berkeley: Celestial Arts, 1987).

CHAPTER 7.
THE BEGINNING OF OURSELVES

1. Walt Whitman, "As I Lay with My Head in Your Lap, Camerado," *The Complete Poems* (New York: Penguin Books, 1977).
2. D. H. Lawrence, *New Poems* (New York: B. H. Huebsch, 1920).
3. Walt Whitman, "Passage to India," *Leaves of Grass* (1855; New York: Signet Classics, 2000), 350.

4. *A Course in Miracles* (Wisconsin Dells, WI: A Course in Miracles International, 2005), 17.

5. T. S. Eliot, "East Coker," *Four Quartets* (Fort Washington, PA: Harvest Books, 1968), 23.

CHAPTER 8.
THE MANDALA OF BEING

1. Stephen Mitchell, *Tao Te Ching* (New York: Harper and Row, 1988), chapter 36.

2. I am indebted to Faye Mindell and her book *Centering: The Book*, for the original diagram of past-future intersecting me-you. Faye presented her book to me after hearing my talk at a conference in which she too was speaking. She told me there was a great deal of similarity in what we were teaching. As soon as I saw her diagram, many things fell into place for me, which over several years evolved into my teaching of the Mandala of Being. Our approaches are complementary, and I heartily recommend any of Faye's books on centering.

3. Mitchell, *Tao Te Ching*, chapter 15.

4. T. S. Eliot, "East Coker," *Four Quartets* (Fort Washington, PA: Harvest Books, 1968), 23.

5. It is inherently difficult to translate mystical realization into subject-object consciousness, even for the person having the experience. It would be like trying to explain the nature of three-dimensional reality to a two-dimensional being. This is why mystical experience is typically communicated poetically, in parables, and especially through skillful practices supported by the presence of teachers who have had direct experience.

When the teachings of the great Self-realized beings become mainstream religions, the fundamental transformation that the founder underwent is replaced with ritual and dogma. We will continue to be misled by spiritual guides who do not have direct experience and cannot transmit the founder's original experience and intent. In fact, generally speaking, the greater the intellect and zealousness of the interpreter, the greater the distortion.

6. I borrow the terms *lower-* and *higher-self functioning* from George Jaidar, *The Soul: An Owner's Manual* (New York: Paragon House, 1995).

CHAPTER 9.
EXPERIENCING THE MANDALA OF BEING

1. Perhaps this is because speech and other forms of vocalization are an ancient capacity of our species and involve more complex neural pathways than does thinking alone. In the act of vocalizing, we are using the whole body, particularly the breathing musculature of the mouth, throat, chest, and abdomen. When we are trying to listen inwardly to recognize what our stories actually cause us to feel, this physiological component does seem to help us better identify what we are feeling.

2. Writing is a relatively recent development in human evolution. There is some suggestion that literacy tends to exaggerate left-brain functioning and creates disconnection between thinking, images, and feeling. See Leonard Shlain, *The Alphabet versus the Goddess* (New York: Penguin Group, 1998).

3. This step from the central Now position specifically to the Me position next, and indeed the whole progression proposed in this chapter, is an arbitrary choice on my part for the purpose of teaching.

4. In the midst of writing this book, I encountered Byron Katie's

exceptional work. Her questions "Is it true?" and "Who would you be without this story?" are wonderful tools for disengaging the mind from story and enhancing the potential to remain in the present. Her book *Loving What Is* (New York: Three Rivers Press, 2002) offers excellent support for appreciating the inquiry work described here, and vice versa.

5. Stephen Mitchell, *Tao Te Ching* (New York: Harper and Row, 1988), chapter 15.

6. Carlos Castaneda, *Journey to Ixtlan* (New York: Washington Square Press, 1972).

CHAPTER 10.
THE NATURE OF EMOTIONAL REALITY

1. Alice Miller, *The Drama of the Gifted Child* (New York: Basic Books, 1996).

2. Daniel Goleman, "A Set Point for Happiness," *New York Times*, July 21, 1996.

CHAPTER 11.
THE NATURE OF PSYCHOLOGICAL TIME

1. Thomas Lewis, Fari Amini, and Richard Lannon, *A General Theory of Love* (New York: Vintage Press, 2001).

2. Bruce Bower, "Words Get in the Way," *Science News* 163, no. 16 (2003), 250.

3. Elizabeth Loftus, "Creating False Memories," *Scientific American* 277, no. 3 (September 1997), 70.

4. George Jaidar, *The Soul: An Owner's Manual* (New York: Paragon House, 1995).

5. T. S. Eliot, "East Coker," *Four Quartets* (Fort Washington, PA: Harvest Books, 1968), 23.

6. A. Guillaumont et al., trans., *The Gospel According to Thomas* (New York: Harper and Row, 1959), logia 84.

CHAPTER 12.
THE NATURAL EMERGENCE OF ESSENCE

1. Sarah's movement into more stories about the feeling is typical of what we do when we are thinking *at* ourselves instead of being fully present *with* ourselves. It is a way of avoiding actually coming into the Now and feeling the sensation created by a story. Instead of moving attention into the now-ness of ourselves, where we can directly feel the sensations created by any story, we continue to abstract about ourselves.
2. Walt Whitman, "Passage to India," *Leaves of Grass* (1855; New York: Signet Classics, 2000), 349.

CHAPTER 13.
THE HEART OF GENIUS

1. A. Guillaumont et al., trans., *The Gospel According to Thomas* (New York: Harper and Row, 1959), logia 22.
2. In his *Civilization and Its Discontents* (1961; New York: Norton, 2005), a scathingly cynical examination of human nature, Freud argues that human beings are capable of limiting violence within their own defined groups only as long as their group then sanctions them to express their sublimated aggression against other groups.
3. Freud looked at human nature at the level of its fragmented, neurotic, and psychotic manifestations, but not at the nature of awareness itself. He did not have a concept of the Self based on fundamental realization or states of deep meditation,

so he could not grasp the potential for the conscious self and the unconscious to integrate in healthy ways as the mind merged with the Now. Therefore, he diagnosed elements of disease, not the potential for wholeness. He believed that various psychical phenomena have an autonomous origin in the id, ego, and superego, from which originates an almost ceaseless level of psychical conflict independent of our conscious relationship to them. And while aspects of the unconscious no doubt do operate autonomously relative to our personalities, the more we become adapted to the present, the more these dynamics become integrated into a growing wholeness of being. A psychology based on disease begins with identification with the body as a separate self-existence. Without penetration beyond this level of identification, there can never be any awareness of the continuum of conscious relationship that is the real essence of Self.

APPENDIXES

1. Rupert Sheldrake, *A New Science of Life* (Rochester, VT: Park Street Press, 1995). I recommend visiting Rupert Sheldrake's website, http://www.sheldrake.org.
2. Lyall Watson, *Lifetide* (New York: Simon and Schuster, 1979). Readers who want to investigate this controversial story in greater depth can search the Web under "Lyall Watson."
3. See Joseph Chilton Pearce, *The Biology of Transcendence* (Rochester, VT: Park Street Press, 2002).
4. Readers who want to learn more can search the Web under "Birth Defect Incidence United States."
5. Thomas Lewis, Fari Amini, and Richard Lannon, *A General Theory of Love* (New York: Vintage Press, 2001), 195.

Index

forgiveness, xvii, 127, 207–8, 242, 300–302
    See also self-forgiveness
freedom, 54, 325
Freud, Sigmund, 321, 345–46nn.2–3
friendship, 83
future
    anxiety about, 220, 220–21, 263–64,
        268, 305
    and expectancy, 254
    and false enthusiasm, 260–61
    and fear, 255–57, 261–62, 268, 305
    fleeing to, 126–30, 131
    and God, 266–70
    and hope, xvii, 220, 220–21, 257–60,
        261–62
    living for, 304
    in Mandala of Being, 159, 159–60,
        162, 162–63, 170
    and money, 264–66
    and possibility, 257–60
    stories, 208–12, 219–20, 220 (*see also*
        stories, that sustain false identi-
        ties)
    and trust, 303–7
    and uncertainty, 255–57
    and worry, xvii

G

Gandhi, Mohandas, 298, 303
gastroschisis, 336
gender prejudices, 110
gender roles, 12–13, 314, 317–18, 339–40n.2
genetic engineering, 263
genetic expression, 108
genius, heart of, 311–28
    and aggression, 320–21
    arcs of conscious evolution, 319–20
    emerging from the dark passageway,
        322–24
    externalizing fears to avoid the dark
        passageway, 324–26
    genius arises from emptiness, 321–22
    more essential man/women, 313–18
    overview, 311–13
    and true security, 326–28
God
    as a creation of our minds, 37, 62
    dogma regarding, 285–86
    doubt about, 286–89
    earning his love, 18
    and faith, 48, 61, 288–89
    and fears, 289

and the future, 266–70
gratitude toward/speaking to, 266–67
as judging/punishing, 18
knowing will of, 78
omnipotence of, 286
as powerful other, 231–32
problem with, 62
realization of, 124–25
gods/goddesses
    as dominant unconscious force, 59
    of fear vs. love, 59–61, 97, 326
    within, 76
Golden Rule, 4–5
grace, 293, 301
grandiosity, *220*, 220–24, 227–30, 265, 293
    See also self-glorification
gratitude
    and essence, 281, 310
    as innate, 157
    and neediness, 202
    toward God, 266–67
Groundhog Day, 241
group mind. *See* awareness fields
Guest, 43
guilt, xvii, 220, *220*, 241–42, 244, 246–47,
    252–53

H

Hafiz, 43
happiness, 325
hatred, 94–95, 233, 235, 327
healing, 147, 267, 283
heresy, 285
heroism, 133
higher-self functioning, 167–68, 275, 275,
    310
    See also essence
Hitler, Adolf, 90
holding environments, 103–22
    conscious, creating, 135–37, 144–45,
        149
    emotional environment during nur-
        turing (second environment),
        106–12, 236, 337–38
    internalized emotional/psychological
        reality (third environment),
        112–18, 171, 216, 262, 334–36
    overview, 103–4
    present moment (fourth environ-
        ment), 118–22 (*see also* the Now)
    womb (first environment), 104–6,
        335–36

About *the* Author

Richard Moss, MD, is an internationally respected teacher, visionary thinker, and author of five seminal books on transformation, self-healing, and the importance of living consciously. For thirty years he has guided people from diverse backgrounds and disciplines in the use of the power of awareness to realize their intrinsic wholeness and reclaim the wisdom of their true selves. He teaches a practical philosophy of consciousness that models how to integrate spiritual practice and psychological self-inquiry into a concrete and fundamental transformation of people's lives. Richard lives in Ojai, California, with his wife, Ariel.

For a calendar of future seminars and talks by the author, and for further information on CDs and other available material, please visit www.richardmoss.com.

Or contact Richard Moss Seminars:

Office: 805-640-0632

Fax: 805-640-0849

Email: 2miracle@sbcglobal.net

NEW WORLD LIBRARY is dedicated to publishing books and other media that inspire and challenge us to improve the quality of our lives and the world.

We are a socially and environmentally aware company, and we make every attempt to embody the ideals presented in our publications. We recognize that we have an ethical responsibility to our customers, our employees, and our planet.

We serve our customers by creating the finest publications possible on personal growth, creativity, spirituality, wellness, and other areas of emerging importance. We serve our employees with generous benefits, significant profit sharing, and constant encouragement to pursue the most expansive dreams. As a member of the Green Press Initiative, we print an increasing number of books with soy-based ink on 100 percent postconsumer waste recycled paper. Also, we power our offices with solar energy and contribute to nonprofit organizations working to make the world a better place for us all.

Our products are available
in bookstores everywhere.
For our catalog, please contact:

New World Library
14 Pamaron Way
Novato, California 94949

Phone: 415-884-2100 or 800-972-6657
Catalog requests: Ext. 50
Orders: Ext. 52
Fax: 415-884-2199

Email: escort@newworldlibrary.com
Website: www.newworldlibrary.com